"A NATION IS DYING"

"A NATION IS DYING"

AFGHANISTAN
UNDER THE SOVIETS
1979–87

Jeri Laber

and

Barnett R. Rubin

Northwestern University Press
Evanston, IL

Northwestern University Press
Evanston, IL 60201

Printed in the United States of America

Photography Credits: 159, 160, 161 bottom left, 162, 163, 164, 169 top, 170 top, 172, 174 bottom, Jeri Laber; 161 top, 165 top left and bottom, 166 top right and bottom, 167 top right and bottom, 168, 169 bottom, 170 bottom, 171, 173, 174 top left and top right, Bentley Kassal; 161 bottom right, Salvatore Vitale, Philadelphia Inquirer; 165 top right, 166 top left, Barnett Rubin; 167 top left, Saira Shah.

Library of Congress Cataloging-in-Publication Data

Laber, Jeri.
  "A nation is dying."

  Bibliography: p.
  Includes index.
  1. Afghanistan—History—Soviet occupation, 1979-
2. Human rights—Afghanistan. I. Rubin, Barnett R.
II. Title.
Ds 371.2.L33   1988   958'.1044   88-1681
ISBN 0-8101-0771-6
ISBN 0-8101-0772-4 (pbk.)

To the memory of Professor Sayd Bahauddin Majrooh (1928–88), colleague and friend, Director of the Afghan Information Centre, Peshawar, assassinated in his exile home, 11 February 1988.

He documented the violence and fell victim to it.

CONTENTS

ACKNOWLEDGMENTS

Many of the interviews included in this book are the result of several fact-finding missions and reports that were carried out under the auspices of Helsinki Watch and Asia Watch, human rights organizations based in the United States. We are grateful to Helsinki Watch and Asia Watch for their continuing commitment to monitor human rights problems in Afghanistan and to the J. Roderick MacArthur Foundation for its sustained support of the Afghanistan projects undertaken by these organizations. A portion of the introduction to this book originally appeared as an article in *The New York Review of Books*.

We also wish to thank all the people we met—in the United States, France, Sweden, Austria, India, and Pakistan—who were willing, indeed eager, to help us and to share with us their knowledge and information about Afghanistan. We are especially indebted to the French medical groups Médécins sans Frontières, Aide Médicale Internationale, and Médécins du Monde, and to the Swedish Committee for Afghanistan.

We received special assistance and encouragement from Professor Sayd B. Majrooh, Director of the Afghan Information Centre in Peshawar and editor of the Centre's invaluable *Monthly Bulletin*; from John Dixon, former Public Affairs Officer of the U.S. Consulate in Peshawar; and from Abdul Karim Muheb of the Central Asian Studies Center of Peshawar University. We also thank Syed Fazl Akbar, Director of the Afghan Information and Documentation Centre in Peshawar and editor of the biweekly *Afghan Realities*; Rosanne Klass, Director of the Afghanistan Center at Freedom House in New York; Dr. Mohammad Azam Dadfar, Director of the Psychiatry Center for Afghans; Gay Le Clerc Brenner of Freedom Medicine; Steven Segal of the International Rescue Committee; and the staff of the Afghan Obstetrics and Gynecology Clinic, especially Farhat Saeed and Dr. Mohammad Mohmand, the clinic's director. The cooperation of Ahmed Zeb Khan, Protocol Officer of the Afghan Refugee Commissionerate in Peshawar, was indispensable in conducting interviews in the refugee camps of the North-West Frontier Province and we gratefully acknowledge it. We also owe a special debt of gratitude to our interpreters, some of whom must remain nameless, but who include Sher Mohammad Ettebari and Sayed Hasan.

We also owe thanks to Amnesty International, and to the members of AFRANE (Amitié Franco-Afghane), who shared with us the contents of their documentation center in Paris. Some interviews in the United States were done with the assistance of Patricia Gossman, Hans Wahl, and Catherine Fitzpatrick. We also thank Betsy Fee and Karen Sorensen for their good-natured cooperation in the preparation of this manuscript.

We could not have done without the painstaking help of Louis Dupree and Nancy Hatch Dupree in guiding us through the complexities of Afghanistan. Whatever errors remain are our responsibility.

A word must be said about the many Afghans—some of whom must go unnamed—who freely shared with us their nightmare experiences. They maintain unwavering dignity in adversity. Adrift in a foreign land, beset by recent traumas, they display remarkable openness, stoicism, warmth, and humor. Their words make up the body—and certainly the soul—of this account.

INTRODUCTION

"A whole nation is dying. People should know." This terse statement befitted the speaker, Engineer Mohammad Eshaq, a resistance leader from Afghanistan's Panjsher Valley, a man of courage and conviction. Yet his eyes clouded over with tears when he told us about the fate of two men from his ancestral village of Mata—brothers, aged ninety and ninety-five. Old and blind, they stayed behind when the rest of the villagers fled during the spring offensive. "The Russians came, tied dynamite to their backs, and blew them up." He paused to collect himself, then added simply, "They were very respected people."

For eight years now, in their remote, mountainous land in the center of Asia, the people of Afghanistan have been defending their independence, their culture, and their very existence in a desperate battle with one of the world's great superpowers. Yet the inherent drama of such a confrontation does not appear to have captured the world's imagination. Afghanistan remains remote.

There are many reasons for this. The Afghan government officially closed its doors to most of the major world media and to international humanitarian organizations, and the information it has released has been dictated by the needs of official propaganda. The few outsiders who have been allowed to visit the capital city of Kabul are shown only what the government wants them to see, and their movements are carefully watched. The Pakistan-based Afghan resistance parties, on the other hand, are hardly objective sources of information and are often at odds with each other as well. Independent investigation has involved entering the country illegally from Pakistan, trekking for weeks over forbidding terrain, and braving the dangers of a war without fronts. The largest group of victims consists of uneducated people who seem almost from another century and have no idea of how to tell their story to the modern world.

What little news we receive comes from a handful of intrepid scholars, doctors, and journalists who have taken the risk of "going inside," usually under the aegis of one of the resistance groups. Their reports, covering a variety of aspects of the Afghan conflict, have included numerous accounts of atrocities and other human rights abuses since the Soviet invasion of December 1979.

In September 1984 we made the first of several trips to the Afghan border—to Peshawar in Pakistan's North-West Frontier Province; to Islamabad, that nation's capital; and to Quetta in Baluchistan—to collect information about human rights violations in Afghanistan by interviewing some of the Afghan people who have sought refuge there. We went as representatives of Helsinki Watch and Asia Watch, human rights organizations based in New York. We had already interviewed Afghan refugees in the United States and Paris and had read extensively in preparation for our trip. Nothing, however, prepared us for what we were to see and experience during that visit and others that we made over the next few years.

The vast scale of the exodus—an estimated five million or more refugees in Pakistan and Iran, representing one-third of Afghanistan's prewar population—is immediately apparent in Peshawar, where the largest concentration of the more than three million Afghan refugees in Pakistan has settled. It is hard to imagine what Peshawar, always a colorful frontier town at the entrance to the Khyber Pass into Afghanistan, was like before this transfiguring, heartbreaking influx.

Everywhere there were Afghans, most of them Pashtuns, who have the same language and appearance as the Pakistanis of the North-West Frontier Province but who are ill suited to the summer heat of the city and to the passive life of the refugee. On the whole, they have not been assimilated into Pakistani life. They are waiting, as close to the border as possible—the women and children seeking food and shelter, the men seeking arms and support as they commute back and forth to the war inside Afghanistan. Their goal is to resume their lives in Afghanistan, the only country they have known.

The refugees arrive in a steady procession. They come on foot over the mountains on journeys that often take a month or more. Their children and possessions are carried by horses, mules, or camels; their caravans are helpless targets for Soviet bombers and helicopter gunships. They come from every province in Afghanistan, every walk of life. Those who left at the beginning of the war have been settled in refugee camps around Peshawar. Others, wounded by bombs, mines, shellfire, or gunshots, are being treated in hospitals. Tens of thousands of recent arrivals huddle into makeshift tents just over the border, filthy, hungry, and diseased. The Pakistani authorities have begun refusing to register new arrivals or to provide them with regular rations unless they agree to be relocated to other parts of Pakistan.

There are some refugees who have found homes and a purpose in Peshawar, often working with one of the many Afghan political parties based there or with one of the relief organizations that are trying heroically to cope with the crisis. But most are just waiting, lost and unhappy, bewildered by the unexpected devastation of their lives and by what they have experienced.

During four visits that we made to the Afghan border since 1984, including refugee camps in the tribal areas of North Waziristan and Bajaur, we interviewed some four hundred Afghans representing a cross section of Afghan society, old and young, men, women, and children. We met with educated people from Kabul—professors, doctors, teachers, students, lawyers, former government officials—and with Afghanistan's leading poet in the Persian language, Khalilullah Khalili, and its leading graphic artist, Ghausuddin. We spoke with villagers—farmers, shepherds, nomads—driven from their land. We visited hospitals where we met paraplegics and amputees, victims of antipersonnel mines left behind by retreating Soviet and Afghan forces or of the camouflaged plastic "butterfly" mines that are dropped from helicopters and intended to maim, not kill, the shepherd children and their flocks. We met with political leaders and resistance commanders. We interviewed deserters, Soviet soldiers barely out of their teens, themselves victims of a vicious war. We even met a defector from the Afghan secret police (KHAD), who described to us its inner workings.

Just about every conceivable human rights violation is occurring in Afghanistan, and on an enormous scale. The crimes of indiscriminate warfare are combined with the worst excesses of unbridled state-sanctioned violence against civilians. The ruthless savagery in the countryside is matched by the subjection of a terrorized urban population to arbitrary arrest, torture, imprisonment, and execution. Totalitarian controls have been imposed on institutions and the press. The universities and all other aspects of Afghan cultural life are being systematically "Sovietized."

Soviet personnel have taken an increasingly active role in the Afghan government's oppression of its citizens. Soviet officers are not just "advisers" to Afghan KHAD agents who administer torture, routinely and savagely, in detention centers and prisons; according to reports we received there are Soviets who participate directly in interrogation and torture. Moreover, because of the uncertain loyalties of Afghans who have been recruited into the army, Soviet soldiers have been led to adopt an increasingly aggressive military role. The Soviets have taken the lead in air and ground attacks on Afghan villages, looting, terrorizing, and randomly killing Afghan civilians, including women and children.

Just about every Afghan has a story to tell. Our interpreters, our guides, people we met accidentally, had personally experienced atrocities as great as those of the "victims" we interviewed. An Afghan doctor who had impressed us with his gentle kindness as he interpreted for us in a hospital for war victims had a sudden outburst as we were leaving. "What's the point of all this? People should know by now. There are no human rights in Afghanistan. They burn people easier than wood!" He went on to tell us that he had lost forty-two members of his family under the present regime and had just learned that two had been burned alive a few weeks before.

We talked to a group of refugees camped by the side of the road, peasants who had just arrived that morning from Nangarhar and Kunduz provinces. The stories they told were the same we heard over and over again: "The Russians bombed our villages. Then the soldiers came. They killed women and children. They burned the wheat. They killed animals—cows, sheep, chickens. They took our food, put poison in the flour, stole our watches, jewelry, and money." Two young women, encountered at random, had each lost five children in a recent attack. One of them, who had also lost her parents and sister, displayed the burns from bombings on the limbs of her remaining children, the three youngest, whom she had managed to take with her as she fled from her house when the troops arrived. "I don't know how the days become nights and the nights become days," she lamented, her eyes flashing in anger and desperation. "I've lost my five children. Russian soldiers do these things to me."

The strategy of the Soviets and the Afghan government has been to spread terror in the countryside so that villagers will either be afraid to assist the resistance fighters who depend on them for food and shelter or be forced to leave. The hundreds of refugee families crossing the border daily are fleeing this terror—wanton slayings, reprisal killings, and the indiscriminate destruction of their homes, crops, and possessions. We were told of brutal acts of violence by Soviet and Afghan forces: civilians burned alive, dynamited, beheaded; bound men forced to lie down on the road to be crushed by Soviet tanks; grenades thrown into rooms where women and children have been told to wait.

Although the terror has desolated much of the countryside, it has failed to crush the resistance. None of the villagers with whom we spoke blamed the mujahedin for their troubles. How could they? The mujahedin are their husbands, sons, fathers, brothers. The resistance and the civilian population are inextricably entwined. "We need our people," a resistance commander told us. "But we are also responsible for them."

Refugees driven from their homes are also bombed and strafed on their way to Pakistan. "It's a ruthless policy," a Pakistani official told us. "They take away their lands. Then, when they leave, they bomb them. There's no logic, just cruelty." The Soviet and Afghan governments seem intent upon ending the exodus to Pakistan. Perhaps they are alarmed by the huge refugee population in Pakistan and the international attention it must inevitably attract. Certainly they are concerned by the support the resistance finds in Pakistan: a chance to rest, organize, rearm, and reenter—sometimes with foreign press, for the Afghan resistance has begun to grasp the importance of the press in enlisting outside support. We received reports that refugees on their way to Pakistan have been arrested by the Afghan militia or the KHAD, who turn them back, herding them toward their devastated villages or to the cities, already swollen with more than a million internal refugees. Those who persist in the trek to Pakistan risk attacks by bombers or the dreaded helicopter gunships. Along the arduous mountain trails used by refugee caravans are many tattered flags flying over hastily dug mass graves. The Afghan Air Force has made numerous incursions into Pakistani airspace, bombing public places and killing hundreds of Afghan refugees and Pakistani civilians. Pakistan is no longer a secure refuge.

At the same time, the Afghan government is now trying to lure refugees back to Afghanistan, promising monetary and other rewards as part of a new policy of "national reconciliation."

Most of the Afghan urban intelligentsia is either in prison or in exile. Professionals and academics have been killed, arrested, censored, or dismissed. University curricula require study of the Russian language, Russian history, and Marxist-Leninist philosophy. Book publishing and the press are under strict censorship. Tens of thousands of Afghan youths are being sent, sometimes against their will, to study in the U.S.S.R. Children of nine and ten are being trained in Pioneer groups to inform on their parents and infiltrate the resistance. State-controlled agents and informers watch every office and classroom. It is estimated that thousands of people are now in Afghan prisons, where they have been brutally tortured and subjected to vile conditions.

We interviewed a twenty-one-year-old student who had been released from Pol-e Charkhi Prison in Kabul just two weeks before. His eyes were bloodshot, his body tense, as he nervously fingered his "worry beads," telling us that if we mention his name in print his father and brothers in Kabul "will be finished." After his arrest for distributing "night letters" protesting the Soviet invasion, he was subjected to routine torture—he was hung by a belt until almost strangled, beaten until his face was twice its normal size, and his hands were crushed under the leg of a chair. He described an overcrowded prison cell with no windows, crawling with lice and with only one pot for a toilet. Others told us about prison cells with one toilet serving five hundred people. Still others described cells with no bathroom at all, in which prisoners were forced to defecate on the floor. Former prisoners told us about electric shocks, nail pulling, lengthy periods of sleep deprivation, standing in cold water, and other punishments. Many prisoners have been executed after summary trials.

Nor are women spared, a source of special torment to Afghan men as well, whose code of honor requires them to shelter and protect their women from the outside world. We heard of mothers forced to watch their infants being given electric shocks, and of men held in torture chambers where women were being sexually molested. A young woman described how she and others had been forced to stand in water that had been treated with chemicals that made the skin come off their feet.

One could feel his pain as an Afghan refugee, a former civil engineer from Kabul, described three women who were in the same prison as he: "In the night, many times, we could hear them crying. We did not know why— probably they were tortured. We could hear them crying many times."

Many of the crimes already discussed are violations of the Geneva Conventions. There are other violations as well, such as the deliberate bombing of hospitals and the summary execution of prisoners of war. The resistance forces are also guilty of violations, in particular in their treatment of prisoners of war and in their training of young children to fight, spy, and assassinate. Whenever possible, we have documented these crimes as well. The Soviets and the Afghan government have accused the resistance of numerous crimes, but we were unable to investigate these allegations because the Afghan government has refused our requests to visit Kabul.

In 1987, however, as part of a new policy of reconciliation by the Najibullah government, the International Committee of the Red Cross, which has been operating medical facilities from outside Afghanistan, taking wounded refugees from the border to Red Cross hospitals in Pakistan, was invited to inspect prisons in Kabul. In addition, the Afghan and Soviet governments, which had previously refused to cooperate with the Special Rapporteur on Afghanistan appointed by the U.N. Human Rights Commission, in 1987 invited him to Afghanistan. Some Western journalists have also been permitted to visit, although their visits have been limited and controlled by the Afghan government. These moves go hand in hand with overtures in the Geneva peace negotiations to bring the conflict to an end.

Perhaps the Soviets really want to extricate themselves from Afghanistan; perhaps their concessions are merely aimed at improving public relations. Whatever the case, the warfare against the population continues, with all its resultant suffering. Whether the war ends tomorrow or stretches on into the distant future, we have a duty to try to preserve each victim's memory, name, and voice. "They killed many people, and this is a story people should not forget," said one refugee. Another added, "They were able to silence the people for the time being, but history cannot remain silent."

1
HISTORICAL BACKGROUND

On 24 December 1979 the Soviet Union began a massive airlift of troops into Kabul, the capital of Afghanistan. On 27 December, after securing the main intersections and roads, those troops assaulted the Dar-ul-Aman Palace, killing President Hafizullah Amin of the People's Democratic Party of Afghanistan (PDPA). Babrak Karmal, leader of an opposing faction of the party, became president. As 50,000, then 85,000 Soviet troops took up positions around the country, a new stage opened in the centuries-long struggle for control of the strategically located territory of Afghanistan. Today about 112,000 Soviet troops are still engaged in the struggle with a variety of indigenous resistance groups.

A mountainous country of about 650,000 square kilometers (the size of Texas or France), Afghanistan sits at the crossroads of the great civilizations and empires of the Middle East, Central Asia, and the Indian subcontinent. A sparsely populated country, where an estimated 15.5 million people lived before the war, it is of interest to world powers mainly because of its location, rather than for its poor and undeveloped economy.

The major economic activities in Afghanistan continue to be agriculture and pastoralism, although smuggling has long been a major occupation of the border tribes. Agriculture produces mainly wheat and rice for consumption by the cultivators and sale on the domestic market. It also produces commercial products, some of which are exported, such as cotton and both dried and fresh fruit. Herds of sheep and goats, besides producing meat, dairy products, and fiber for local use, also produce the wool for the knotted carpets and karakul lamb skins that are major exports. There are also important fields of natural gas in Afghanistan, developed by Soviet experts. Virtually the entire production is piped directly to the Soviet Union in exchange for Soviet goods.[1]

The ethnic variety of the country's population reflects its geographic location. The largest group are the Pashtuns, or "Afghans," who made up roughly half, or slightly less, of the prewar population. They speak a language called Pashto, related to Persian but quite distinct. The Pashtuns are divided into various tribes and clans, which are the focus of strong loyalties. They view themselves as a warlike and independent people and boast of having never been conquered. The Pashtuns predominate in eastern and southern Afghanistan, although they have also established important colonies in the north and northwest in the past century. The Pashtuns have been the politically dominant ethnic group in the country. They are also the major ethnic group in the contiguous North-West Frontier Province (NWFP) of Pakistan, but they are a minority in Pakistan as a whole.[2]

The second largest linguistic group in Afghanistan is the Persian speakers.[3] Those native to the valleys and mountains north and northeast of Kabul are known as Tajiks, ethnically akin to the Tadzhiks of Soviet Central Asia. In the west are some Persian-speaking seminomadic herders known as Aimaqs and a settled Persian-speaking population, akin to the neighboring Iranians, known as Farsiwan. In the far north are about three million Turkic speakers, Turkomans and Uzbeks, who, like the Tajiks, are related to fellow ethnics across the Soviet border.

The remote massif of central Afghanistan is home to the Hazaras, an ethnic group with Mongol features. As Afghanistan's only predominantly Shia group, they have traditionally held the lowest status in the country. They speak a variant of Persian called Hazaragi. In a few high valleys of eastern Afghanistan live the fair-skinned Nuristanis, who practiced a form of Indo-European polytheism until their conversion to Sunni Islam in the 1890s. They are related to the "kafers" (unbelievers) of Chitral in Pakistan, who continue to practice the religion of their ancestors. In southwest Afghanistan live a few Baluch tribes, related to those of the contiguous areas of Pakistan and Iran. Scattered among all these groups are *sayyeds*, who claim descent from the Prophet Mohammad and who are considered descendants of Arabs, rather than members of the ethnic groups among whom they live.

Although there are a few thousand Hindus and Sikhs, and some Jews and Armenian Christians in the major cities, over ninety-nine percent of the people of Afghanistan are Muslims. About eighty-five percent are Sunnis. Unlike the Iranians, most Persian speakers in Afghanistan, including the Tajiks and most of the Farsiwan, are Sunni Muslims. The Hazaras and a few other groups are Shia.

Islam in Afghanistan embraces a wide range of beliefs and attitudes. Each village has its mullah to teach children the fundamentals of religion and lead prayer in the mosque on Friday, the Islamic Sabbath. The Islamic scholars, the *ulama*, often known as *mawlawis* in Afghanistan, preside over courts and have traditionally played an important role in the official legal system. Many Afghans are followers of one of the mystic orders of the Sufis. The most prominent orders in Afghanistan are the liberal Qaderiyya and the more orthodox Naqshbandiyya. Some devotees pursue personal spiritual development with Sufi teachers, or *pirs*; others venerate *pirs* as possessors of special grace.[4]

The territory of Afghanistan, lacking ethnic or geographic unity, became a single political unit as a result of its location in the border area between empires: the Iranian Safavid and the Indian Mogul empires in the eighteenth century, and the Russian and British empires in the nineteenth and twentieth. In 1747 the foundering of both the Safavids and the Moguls allowed the Abdali tribes of the Kandahar area to declare their independence and elect one of their own, Ahmad Shah, as "King of the Afghans." Ahmad Shah was also called "Durr-e Durran," meaning "pearl of pearls," as a result of which the Abdalis came to be known as "Durranis." The Durrani monarchy lasted until 1973.[5]

In the nineteenth century, as European empires replaced the Asian ones, Afghanistan became the focus of the "Great Game" played by Britain and Russia for control of the Central Asian approaches to India. Fearing that the continuing Czarist advance into Central Asia threatened to place the traditional invasion routes of the subcontinent under control of a hostile power, Britain attempted to bring Afghanistan into its sphere of influence. The British invaded Afghanistan twice. In the First Anglo-Afghan War (1839–1842), the Afghan resistance, led by Amir Dost Mohammad, drove out the invader. After the Second Anglo-Afghan War (1878–1880), the ruler who emerged, Amir Abd-ur-Rahman Khan, was obliged to concede control over foreign affairs. In 1893 England forced the weakened country to sign the Durand Treaty, which demarcated the area under the control of the British in India and the area subject to the administration of the Afghan monarchy. This demarcation left millions of Pashtuns outside Afghanistan, a situation that has caused tension with Britain's successor state, Pakistan.

Amir Abd-ur-Rahman Khan began to build the institutions of the territorial nation-state. With British subsidies of arms and cash he created a centralized army and state bureaucracy. The Amir thus left a consolidated state to his son, Habibullah, who succeeded him peacefully, an event with no precedent and, thus far, no sequel, in the history of Afghanistan.[6]

Abd-ur-Rahman Khan's grandson King Amanullah, who succeeded to the throne upon the mysterious assassination of Amir Habibullah in 1919, upset this stability by waging a brief jihad against the exhausted British and recovering Afghanistan's full independence. This victory earned him broad support, but when he tried to use the state structure inherited from his grandfather to impose Western-oriented social change on his subjects in the absence of a firm political or fiscal base, his army collapsed. In the face of several revolts, he fled the country in 1929.

The country was ruled briefly by Habibullah, a Tajik social bandit and former army officer popularly known as Bacha-e Saqao (Son of the Water Carrier), but the Pashtuns soon reasserted themselves. Another branch of the royal clan led tribal forces into Kabul, ousting the Bacha and setting Nader Khan on the throne.[7] Nader's nineteen-year-old son, Mohammad Zaher (Zaher Shah), succeeded his father after the latter's assassination in 1933 and reigned until 1973.

The long reign of Zaher Shah saw efforts to strengthen the state and develop the country economically. In the 1950s Afghanistan asked for economic and military assistance from the United States, but its irredentist policy toward the Pashtun lands across the Durand line led Pakistan to protest. Since Pakistan was a pillar of two U.S.-sponsored regional pacts, CENTO (Central Treaty Organization) and SEATO (Southeast Asia Treaty Organization), the United States refused Afghanistan's request for aid. Afghanistan then turned to the Soviet Union, from which, since 1955, it has purchased most of its military equipment and obtained training for most of its officers.[8]

This policy of cooperation with the Soviet Union was engineered by Zaher Shah's cousin Daoud Khan, a strong prime minister who in effect ruled Afghanistan from 1953 to 1963. Daoud's decade saw the acceleration of modernization based on building a strong army, investing in infrastructure such as dams and roads, and expanding modern secondary and higher education to train the personnel needed for modernization. These programs changed Afghan politics by creating a new urban class of high school and university graduates who had some knowledge of the modern world and expected to be employed by the state in the modernization of Afghanistan.[9]

From 1963 to 1973, in an attempt to accommodate new social forces, especially the newly educated, Zaher Shah, ruling without Daoud, who had resigned in 1963 over a crisis in relations with Pakistan, instituted a parliamentary system known as New Democracy. Although this system provided a useful expansion of public discussion and debate, it never developed into true representative government. The king refused to delegate authority to the government, and he never signed the legislation providing for the legalization of political parties. Nevertheless, the increased freedom of expression permitted the organization of various political groups. Three main tendencies emerged among the Kabul intelligentsia: Marxist, nationalist, and Islamist.[10]

The first group to organize formally, in 1965, was the PDPA, which united a small group of pro-Soviet Afghan leftists. The two most important leaders of the party were Nur Mohammad Taraki and Babrak Karmal. The PDPA's main base was among students and recent graduates in Kabul, but it soon began recruitment in the military. Three PDPA members were elected to parliament in 1965.

In 1967 Babrak and Taraki became the leaders of the two factions that split the PDPA and represented the two main social groups within it. Taraki, together with Hafizullah Amin, who had returned from his studies at Columbia University soon after the formation of the PDPA, became leaders of the Khalq (masses) group. Babrak formed the Parcham (banner) group. Each called itself the PDPA and accused the other of splitting the organization. Khalq, composed mainly of first-generation educated rural Pashtuns, called for a mass uprising, whereas Parcham, composed of long-time urbanites of mixed ethnic origin and higher social standing, called for alliances with other forces to push for accelerated modernization.[11]

The nationalists were probably the largest, and least organized, group among the intelligentsia. They favored continuation of the gradual reforms of the monarchy. This tendency dominated most of the cabinets under New Democracy.

The last group to organize was the Islamic radicals, whom Westerners often label "fundamentalists" but whom some scholars prefer to call "Islamists." They regarded the Afghan state as corrupt, based on the un-Islamic principle of tribalism and penetrated by anti-Islamic foreign powers, especially the Soviet Union. They organized at Kabul University as the Muslim Youth Organization. In exile in Pakistan after 1973, they organized the predominantly Tajik Jamiat-e Islami (Islamic Society), led by Burhanuddin Rabbani, and the predominantly Pashtun Hezb-e Islami (Islamic Party), which split into two groups, one led by Gulbuddin Hekmatyar and the other by Yunus Khales.[12]

Rising protest movements in Kabul, a decrease of foreign aid, and, finally, a famine with which the government could not cope, gave Daoud Khan an opportunity for a comeback. With the help of Parcham, some of whose members had key positions in the armed forces, he staged a bloodless coup against his cousin in 1973, abolished the monarchy, and proclaimed himself president of the Republic of Afghanistan. Alarmed by the influence of the Parchamis, many Islamists fled to Pakistan. There they received some military training and support from the government of Zulfiqar Ali Bhutto, who was concerned that Daoud would agitate the Pashtuns in Pakistan and wanted to have something with which to counter him. The Islamists' attempt at an uprising in 1975 failed.

Daoud, meanwhile, removed the Parchamis from his government and, with the encouragement of the Shah of Iran, began to distance himself somewhat from the Soviet Union. In 1976 the Soviet Union started pressuring Khalq and Parcham to reunite, which they did in March 1977. The mysterious assassination of a Parchami leader on 17 April 1978 led to massive demonstrations in Kabul, to which Daoud responded by ordering the arrest of the PDPA leaders. Hafizullah Amin, however, managed to send orders to PDPA military officers, who killed Daoud and his family in a coup on 27 April. A few days later the officers handed power over to the Revolutionary Council of the PDPA, which proclaimed the Democratic Republic of Afghanistan (D.R.A.). The PDPA calls this coup the "Sawr Revolution," after the Persian zodiacal month (Sawr = Taurus) in which it occurred.[13]

Nur Mohammad Taraki, general secretary of the reunited PDPA, became president of the Revolutionary Council and prime minister; Babrak Karmal and Hafizullah Amin became deputy prime ministers. Prominent political leaders of the New Democracy period were immediately arrested and executed. Large numbers of Soviet advisers arrived and moved into government offices and educational institutions.

Conflict soon broke out again between Parcham and Khalq. In July six leading Parchamis, including Babrak Karmal and his successor Najib, were sent abroad as ambassadors. In August a group of Parchami army officers was arrested for planning a coup, and Taraki and Amin purged Parcham from the administration.

Khalq proceeded with its program of radical social change and mass repression. It launched quickly formulated reforms in land tenure, rural debt, and marriage and started a literacy program, even as the newly formed political police, AGSA, arrested and killed thousands.[14]

Those arrested and killed included political leaders of the New Democracy period; Daoud's family and other members of the royal family; religious scholars and spiritual leaders; high school teachers and students; university professors and students, including leading scholars; lawyers and judges; government and diplomatic officials; military officers; Parchamis, Maoists, Social Democrats, and members of Islamic political organizations; Hazaras and Nuristanis (whose homelands were among the first to revolt); and local dignitaries in many parts of the countryside.[15] Testimonies collected by Michael Barry, an anthropologist with long experience in Afghanistan, suggest the atmosphere in the prisons at that time.

Testimony of a professor: "Torture began at ten o'clock at night, and lasted until four in the morning. It was electric shocks, and also a sort of electric chair. . . .

"There was a man there, the commander of Pol-e Charkhi [Prison], his name was Sayyed 'Abdollah. He could decide death for people, he could have them shot at once, he could bury them alive . . . in the earth.

"Especially at night they put people against the wall, and turned on them a sort of blue light. Then they shot them. Collectively. Ten persons. Twenty persons. Sometimes 45. One night 120 persons were killed under the wall.

"Someone's cell was searched, and they found a ballpoint pen. That was the most dangerous weapon there. The prisoner was brought before the line of inmates. The commander told them: 'He has done something very serious. He has had a pen reach him inside the prison. We are going to teach you a lesson. If any one of you does the same thing, he will be punished the same way.' The prisoner was thrown into the pool of filth [excrement—the professor had drawn a map showing the location of the cesspool]. He tried to get out, but it was soft, he sank, the soldiers around pushed him with sticks, and drowned him."[16]

As parts of the country passed into resistance, the regime responded with massive reprisals against civilians. In March 1979 the army collected twelve hundred men in the village of Kerala, Konarha Province, and asked them why they were helping the resistance. When they received no answer,

> "The Godless Commander Nezamuddin said, 'Prod!' [Pashto for Lie down!] There were perhaps twelve hundred people who lay down. Then he gave the order: 'Fire!' Twelve hundred people, all the Muslims, were killed in this firing. And then there was a tank, what you call a bulldozer. This tank drove over the Muslims and lifted them up in the air and threw them in the ground. Some were still alive, but they were buried in the earth. The others were dead. They were buried in the earth."[17]

In April–May 1979, soon after a group of Hazaras had overrun government posts near the northern provincial center of Samangan, Afghan troops with Soviet advisers rounded up all the males from one village and drowned them in the Amu Darya (Oxus River). Other Hazaras were thrown into a nearby ravine.[18] In August 1979 the police arrested about three hundred Hazaras living in Kabul, half of whom were burned with gasoline and half buried alive.[19]

There are various estimates of the number killed under the Khalqi regime, most concerning only those killed in prisons in Kabul.[20] As Olivier Roy, a careful scholar, summarized:

> In February 1980, the government of Babrak Karmal [describing the reign of terror under the previous government] admitted that 12,000 people were "officially" dead, but this number only involved those who had disappeared in the prison of Pul-i Charkhi. (The number of executed and missing persons in the countryside was also very great although these victims received less publicity than those at Kabul.) In all, between 50,000 and 100,000 people disappeared. . . . Partial inquiries have been made but the story of this wave of repression has yet to be written.[21]

The spread of arrest, torture, and mass executions, together with the sudden imposition of alien "reforms" on the traditional peasantry, soon led to outbreaks of revolt. Some were spontaneous, such as the Nuristani uprising of July 1978, which was apparently the first. Others were organized by military defectors or Islamist militants, such as the March 1979 revolt in Herat, where army officers belonging to Jamiat-e Islami coordinated a mutiny in the garrison with an uprising in the city organized by Jamiat militants who had returned from Iran.[22] The army, disintegrating because of mutinies and desertions, could not check the spreading insurgency.

These developments caused concern in the Soviet Union, which had become increasingly committed to the Sawr Revolution. Brezhnev and Taraki signed a treaty of "friendship and cooperation" in Moscow in December 1978,[23] but control over events eluded the Soviets. The Afghan regime's extreme radicalism and repression and its elimination of Parcham contributed to the growth of the resistance and alarmed the Soviets. Yet the D.R.A.'s strongman, Hafizullah Amin, resisted Soviet attempts to make him change his policies.

It appears that the Soviets plotted with Taraki to remove Amin in September 1979, but the plot failed, resulting instead in Amin's assassination of Taraki and the further embitterment of his relations with the Soviets. Amin asked Pakistan to relay to the United States a request to help him maintain his independence from Soviet pressure. Meanwhile, the taking of American hostages in Teheran had increased Soviet expectation of American intervention in the region. Fearful of the collapse or defection of their Afghan clients, and of the ability of the United States to exploit either outcome, the Politburo decided to intervene militarily and replace Hafizullah Amin's government with one dominated by Babrak Karmal's Parcham.[24]

Soviet troops in Afghanistan, which have had to take over most of the fighting from the demoralized and desertion-ridden Afghan Army, increased from 50,000 to 85,000 and then to around 115,000; they may have decreased to 112,000 following the announced withdrawal of six regiments in October 1987.[25] The Soviets also reorganized internal security and intelligence in urban areas, placing it under a new organization, KHAD (State Information Services), headed by Dr. Najib (or Najibullah), a young Parchami former student leader who was later to replace Babrak. KHAD, which operates under KGB supervision, became the core of the new regime. It became the Ministry of State Security in January 1986. Najib became general secretary of the PDPA, replacing Babrak Karmal, in May 1986.

The invasion expanded the resistance and accelerated the flow of refugees, who now number over five million, the largest refugee population in the world, equal to approximately one-third of the country's population. It also led to an expansion of foreign support to the Afghan resistance, or mujahedin, coming from the United States, China, Iran, and some Arab countries, as well as Pakistan.

The conflict between the Soviets and, on the one hand, their Afghan clients and, on the other, large sectors of the population of Afghanistan, led by resistance organizations based in Pakistan and receiving arms from abroad, has given rise to the violations of human rights that we document in this report.[26]

2
CRIMES AGAINST THE RURAL POPULATION

"We went along the asphalt road from Iran to Herat. The desert on the Iranian side was absolutely covered in track marks, the hooves of horses, of donkeys, of camels, footmarks, bicycle marks, you name it. By the time it was about nine o'clock in the morning, there were people in droves; a man with a camel: he'd lost all his family, and all his possessions were on top of the camel. There were some young boys who'd been orphaned. Then there were numerous donkeys with women riding on them with their husbands next to them. All of these people were on their way to Iran. I stayed in a village where they claimed there had been five thousand inhabitants. There remained one build-ing intact in the whole village. I didn't see more than ten inhab-itants there. To destroy this place the bombers came from Rus-sia. And there were craters everywhere, even where there were no buildings, so there was no pretense about 'we're trying to hit the mujahedin.' It was a complete blitz. All the way from there on into Herat there was no one living there, absolutely no one. The town that I stayed in, Hauz-e Karbas, looks like Hiroshima. And there had been tremendous amounts of vineyards there, and they were just reduced to gray dust."

Nicholas Danziger

Nicholas Danziger, a British lecturer in art history, is only one of many who have described such scenes of devastation in the Afghan countryside. People coming from almost every area of Afghanistan—Western scholars, journalists, doctors and nurses, as well as the Afghan refugees and resis-tance fighters themselves—tell of vast destruction: carefully constructed homes reduced to rubble, deserted towns, the charred remains of wheat fields, trees cut down by immense firepower or dropping their ripe fruit in silence, with no one to gather the harvest. From throughout the country come tales of death on every scale, from thousands of civilians buried in the rubble left by fleets of bombers to a young boy's throat being dispassionately slit by a Soviet soldier.[1]

This mass destruction is dictated by the political and military strategy of the Soviet Union and its Afghan allies. Unable to win the support or neutrality of most of the rural population that shelters and feeds the elusive guerrillas, Soviet and Afghan soldiers have turned their firepower on civilians. When the resistance attacks a military convoy, Soviet and Afghan forces attack the nearest village. If a region is a base area for the resistance, they bomb the villages repeatedly. If a region becomes too much of a threat, they bomb it intensively and then sweep through with ground troops, terrorizing the people and systematically destroying all the delicate, interrelated elements of the agricultural system. The aim is to force the people to abandon the resistance or, failing that, to drive them into exile.

> "When the people gather the harvest, the Russians completely burn the harvest with tanks, rockets. When they come to the village they kill children, ladies, [unmarried] girls, old people, and they say, 'We don't need the people, we need the land.' When they captured some old people they told them, 'We don't need the people, we need the land.' "
>
> "They announced something, 'We don't need the people, we need the land.' That's why they're killing the people. They said, 'If there are any Afghan children, we will not be able to rule Afghanistan, so we have to finish this nation.' "
>
> "They announced it by loudspeaker when the troops came. I heard this from the Russian soldiers, 'We don't need the people, we want the land.' My name is Ataullah; I am here. What I have told you is all the truth. You may ask me again and again." (Testimony of refugees from Kunduz and Laghman provinces; interviewed in Munda refugee camp, NWFP, Pakistan, 21 August 1985)

Indiscriminate Bombing

Regardless of fluctuations in the conduct of the war, the bombardment of the rural villages has been almost constant. The MiG-25 jet fighter bomber, the Mi-24 Hind armored helicopter, and the Grad BM-13 mortar have become as familiar to the Afghan villager as the bullocks that pull his plow. The Tu-16 Badger high-altitude bomber, flying directly from bases in the Soviet Union, is well known in the Panjsher Valley.

Every time we asked an Afghan villager why he or she came to Pakistan, the answer began with the words *shurawi bombard* (Soviets bomb). Most of these bombings, reported by Western observers as well as Afghan refugees, show a blatant disregard for the laws of war that require military action to be directed against military targets. In Afghanistan the most common target is the peasant village: the homes, fields, orchards, and frequently the mosque. In provincial towns the marketplace and residential areas often become targets. These attacks are responsible for the vast majority of the estimated hundreds of thousands of civilian deaths.

The following account is typical.

"It was nine o'clock on the morning of January 11, 1985, when a squadron of gunship helicopters became visible above the village of Wonkhi located in Wardak Province seventy-five kilometers southwest of Kabul city. They flew extremely high over the village. The common people who have turned expert in guessing the intention of the aircraft from their height were confident that their village would not be bombarded on that day. Moreover, the planes passed over the village very fast, which was a further reassuring sight for them. So they started their routine occupations. But not much time had passed when the planes returned, this time at a low height over the village. They came from the east. The villagers guessed this time that the planes were passing over the village to go to Kabul town, as they usually kept that height on return journeys. But suddenly the planes started indiscriminate bombing of the villages of Wonkhi and Hassan Bake, belonging to Sayed Abad District of Wardak Province. The MiG planes preceded the gunships. When the planes left the area the helicopters took their place and started shooting guns and missiles against the houses of the villages and against their occupants. The task of the helicopters was different than the task of the MiG jets. The MiGs had already destroyed the mosques, shops, and houses. They had also completely destroyed a mosque where thirty children of the village were busy studying. They were not the only ones present in the mosque. Most of the villagers had also rushed there to take shelter but met the destinies of death and destruction. The gunship helicopters circled those miserable villages, flying very low over them, hunting any living being visible to them. The livestock, the cattle, and the beasts of burden were also main targets. In short the gunships fulfilled the task of not having anyone escape death. When the planes completed their operations and left the scene, the people of the neighboring villages, who witnessed the bombardments from distant places, rushed to the scene but found no living beings. They started to dig out bodies from the ruined houses, shops, and buildings. The work of removing the piles continued for three days, and the dead bodies of thirty-six men and three ladies were unearthed. They also found thirty seriously wounded people. In this tragic bombardment eighty houses and two mosques were totally destroyed in the two villages of Wonkhi and Hassan Bake." (Testimony of Najibullah, resident of Sayed Abad District; furnished by Abdul Karim Muheb, Central Asian Studies Center, Peshawar University)

Jan Goodwin, executive editor of *Ladies Home Journal*, witnessed a Soviet-Afghan offensive in Paktia Province in late August 1985. She described Su-25s and MiGs dropping 500-pound and incendiary bombs all day long, dozens at a time, on mud houses in the valley of Jaji. Many people and cattle were killed by shrapnel.

Rudy Seynaeve, a Belgian nurse working for Médécins sans Frontières (MSF), kept a detailed record of the victims he treated while working at a clinic in the southern part of Balkh Province during the first six months of 1985. The area where he worked was largely under the control of the Jamiat-e Islami resistance party. Soviet and Afghan government forces staged an offensive there in January, forcing the medical team and the villagers to escape for several weeks to nearby mountains.

"There has been a lot of bombing in December and January, also in February. This was the same time as the Soviet troops were in the valley of Zari. It was more to protect the troops and the tanks, you can say it was a military action, it was war, fighting against the army.

"Something else is the kind of bombing that we had in April. Marie [Basuyan, another nurse] and me, we arrived the ninth of April in Zari to install the hospital, because it was already one month and a half approximately that the valley of Zari was free, reorganized, the mines were detected and so on, so it was the eleventh of April at midday—we just wanted to eat—that jets and helicopters arrived above the valley, and they bombed a village named Mirzai that is in the valley of Zari.

"There were four bombs that fell in the proximity of a mill, where they mill the wheat, and four people were wounded by stones. It seems almost every time the bombs are fragmentation bombs, bombs that fall down, and they are razing the whole area with little or even big pieces, big as a hand or big as half of a tongue, pieces of iron. I have one with me that I extracted from a wounded man. There were two of them that had almost all the back and the legs full of pieces of wheat that had crossed the tissue [pierced the cloth]. The wounds were not too deep in general, but they were very dirty, because on the bottom of the wound you had the fabric of the clothes they were wearing, and then the wheat. They infected very quickly. In this area there was no military target. There is a *qarargah*, a barracks for mujahedin, on the border of the village of Mirzai, but it was far away, a center of thirty mujahedin residing there, but this was totally on the other side. The mill was on the other side. But four bombs fell down there. The four people wounded were not people from the valley of Zari itself, but people that came from high, the mountains, I think they had to come down to mill their wheat. It was the eleventh of April.

"The twentieth of April, jets and helicopters have bombarded the village of Amrakh. It's a valley in the south of Zari. There are mujahedin there, but there they have bombed I think blind, just blind. Fragmentation bombs also. Bombs and also rockets. One rocket pierced a house, and the house collapsed. One child who was in the house died, six years old, his mother got a big piece of iron, it destroyed the whole elbow, two bones were broken. It has been cured now, she has a little bit stiff arm. It was a very bad wound. And a child, a daughter, about two years, had the buttocks ripped open. It was all meat, it was nicely ripped open, it was *ugly* ripped open with shrapnel in a bad place for a child like this. There were two men that had slight wounds. Also a piece of bomb, a piece of metal, little pieces somewhere on the back and on the shoulder, flesh wounds, but it was also civilians, no mujahedin wounded, civilians also.

"Then, the third one, the twenty-third [April], again in Zari, near the bazaar, and it's there that Alphonse, the Belgian reporter, said he had seen one bomb—a lot of white smoke came out. And indeed later on we have seen a piece of a wheat field burned. I think something of twenty meters along. It was not all the wheat field that was burned. A piece. There there were two wounded, one was badly wounded. It was a farmer that was on his farm and pieces of bombshells came, were flying on his farm, crossed, broke his leg, pierced one leg, and got stuck in the other leg, and he was dying when he arrived, but now he is all right. He lost a lot of blood. And the other one was also slightly wounded, a flesh wound. But also fragmentation. Again we have found a lot of fragmentation. And we have seen. This is nice to see it, I mean a place where a bomb falls, it makes a hole, and then all the trees are cutted from down to up, like stairs all around the hole.

"A fourth bombardment, the twenty-fourth of April, also in Zari, very near the hospital and the bazaar. No one was wounded. Again, fragmentation bombs. Just blind. All these four bombardments gave the idea that it was rather blind, but to prove that they *can* bombard very accurate, let me look [in his diary] somewhere in May. There are three big *qarargah* [resistance bases] in the valley of Zari, where the commanders are sitting with their mujahedin when they are retiring from war. And one day, the thirtieth of May, in the afternoon at two o'clock—they said it is rather exceptional, normally all the other ones were in the morning from nine o'clock until eleven o'clock generally—then the afternoon at two o'clock, jets were coming, helicopters were coming. It seems it goes like this: helicopters are staying very high, above the target. The jets take off, and it seems the helicopters are giving the order to let the bombs fall. And then two bombs are falling, and precisely on the target they want to hit. Really precisely. It is not a matter of five meters. And they bombed the three places where mujahedin reside, the three *qarargah* precisely, with burning bombs and fragmentation bombs, and the three are destroyed. One mujahed was dead. So it means they have air pictures of the region; it means there are spies that know exactly where the mujahedin are, that have exact information about where are the mujahedin staying, and it means they have the technical means to do very precise bombing. It was the thirtieth of May.

"But also there have been bombardments the twenty-ninth of May with burning bombs, and this was in the neighborhood of one *qarargah*, but actually, it was a house where two families were residing, and eight persons were killed immediately, and six were heavily burned, some really all over the body, from the hair until the toes. Later on in the hospital, five days later, I think, one boy of eleven died. He was too heavily burned. We couldn't, we couldn't, but the other ones are still alive. And these are burning bombs. They have told me it's a kind of bomb that makes, that gives free a kind of liquid that is burning."

In some regions—those controlled by the resistance but not of major strategic importance—the bombing is random and desultory. Dr. Ghazi Alam, an orthopedic surgeon trained in Afghanistan, India, and the United States, was interviewed in New York City on 30 March 1984. He described such a pattern in Logar Province during the winter of 1983–1984:

"First of all the Russians terrorize civilians by bombarding the villages indiscriminately. They are killing civilians, especially the children and the women who cannot run away from their houses. There was not any firing, but they have bombarded regularly, each day or three times a week or twice a week, this region of Baraki Barak District in Logar [south of Kabul]. They have sent helicopters and MiGs. I have seen one case in Baraki Barak District that nine members of one family were killed by bombing. Only one was left alive. And this operation was just for psychological effect on people, that they should not feel security in their homes."

Refugees interviewed in Peshawar and Quetta in September and October 1984 had similar stories to tell.

"One and a half months ago [mid-August 1984] there were nine people in my village having breakfast, and a jet fighter bombed and killed them in their house. They were Nur Mohammad, five people from Musa Jan's family—his wife and children, aged from six months or a year to eight—a woman and two children. They are flying and doing this all the time without reason!" (Testimony of Abdullah Jan, twenty-two, a farmer from Delawar Khan village, Arghandab District, Kandahar Province)

Another refugee from Kandahar Province described how his two cousins, Shah Mohammad and Sardar Mohammad, sons of Mohammad Ismail of Qader Khel village, Arghistan District, were killed the previous August by rockets from a helicopter while airing out beds in the courtyard of their home.

Hafizullah, twenty-four, a farmer from Harioki Ulya in Kapisa Province, north of Kabul, reported in the fall of 1984:

> "I left because of the condition of my region. Not only days, but even at nights they attack from three or four directions with rockets and artillery. They are bombing since last autumn so often, continuously, ten to fifteen planes at a time. One type of airplane, the MiG-25, is coming every day with five to ten bombs. They drop them on the residences, on the mosques, just to get rid of the people. Some of my relatives were killed, including some women."

Mohammad Amin Salim, forty-three, former state prosecuting attorney, told us in 1984:

> "The reason that I am here now is that in the region where I was there is great pressure from the Soviets. As an example, I had no place to put my family, because most of the region was destroyed. There were no more houses in Qarabagh-e Shomali. Ninety-nine percent of the houses are destroyed."

A woman from Chardara District, Kunduz Province, on the Soviet border, told us:

> "Six months ago the Russians surrounded our village. The airplanes bombed us, and four of my children died."

The three boys were Najmuddin, Farwar, and Rahim, and the girl was Anisa.

Sayed Azim, a former government official and graduate of the Faculty of Agriculture of Kabul University, told us that his home region in Wardak Province, southwest of Kabul, has been bombed for years, even in the time of Taraki. Not long before our interview, twelve helicopters bombed the town of Maidan on 9 September 1984. They destroyed eight houses, killed nine people, and injured twenty-three others.

Nicholas Danziger, quoted at the beginning of this chapter, described days of relentless bombing in the Herat area in June 1984:

> "Every day they came to bomb. I was there at least two weeks, and I would say there were only five days that the planes didn't come. Sometimes they came once, sometimes twice; the helicopters often came three times. And not only that, there's also the shelling, which can last anything up to half an hour. It seems much longer at the time. And the people don't know how to build shelters. Every day mujahedin die, but if a mujahed has died you know that the people have died. And every day you heard the list, and it was one, two, four, three, six, this was mujahedin, but then the count of the people dying was always equivalent or greater. There were few occasions when there were fewer civilians dying than mujahedin. The people come down to work on their fields at

night, women wash their clothes at night, bake the bread at night, and as there are no shelters, they hide under trees, just waiting, waiting."

Another pattern described by many refugees is a sudden offensive combining intense airpower with a sweep by ground troops. A shepherd from a district in Kunduz, who asked us not to give his name or district, said that he had arrived in Pakistan five days before with twenty-four families from his village. In an interview in Peshawar in September 1984, he told us:

"The Russians bombed us. Then the soldiers came, took all the women and old men, and killed them."

Villagers who had just arrived in Peshawar from Batikot District of Nangarhar Province, east of Kabul, crowded around us as they told their story in overlapping voices: "Twenty days ago the Russians bombed our villages— Bela, Mushwani, and Lachapur—and 120 people died." They showed us a six-year-old boy with shrapnel in his leg from the bombing: "On August 27 the Russians came at 4 A.M. When they reached the village they started killing people. After they finished in Lachapur and Mushwani, they went to Bela. There were 130 killed. They killed them with Kalashnikovs and with bombs from airplanes." These interviews took place in September 1984.

Patrick David and François Frey, French doctors working with Aide Médicale Internationale, witnessed a Soviet-Afghan offensive in Baraki Barak District of Logar Province, just south of Kabul, in September 1984. "They were bombing the houses and the people doing the harvest in the fields. They shot rockets at them and killed them." They reported that two boys, the five- and seven-year-old sons of Gul Jan, who were playing in a melon field in Chalozai were wounded by rockets from a helicopter. Russian soldiers had come into the area and killed and looted. On 15 September the doctors saw a helicopter fly low over the village of Chehltan:

"Our translator said, 'Watch, this helicopter is dangerous.' It dropped something that left some smoke. A few minutes later four jets came and bombed where the helicopter showed. The targets were the people's houses. We saw the people running into the fields. The next day there were ten boys from Baraki Barak in the river, and a big shell exploded, a shell that had fallen in the river before. One boy died, and four were wounded."

Abdul Wahid, a Hazara student whom we met in Quetta, told us in an interview on 3 October 1984 of recent bombings and killings in Hazarajat.

"I came from Jalrez about ten days ago. When I was there, many air attacks were taking place. Every day the airplanes were flying in the area. When they failed to hit the military points, they bombed the bazaars and homes and the places where there was agricultural production. There were two bombardments in our village. They wanted to bomb the mujahedin, but couldn't, so they bombed the populated areas like houses and the bazaar, which caused some casualties. This was in Rasana and Jaghori, and also the valley of Tangi, about twenty days ago. Also in the center of Jaghori—every day there are helicopters flying in the area. In Behsud there was a recent offensive which caused about five hundred casualties, mostly women and children, about one and a half months ago. Ground forces came too, but most were killed by cannons."

Arielle Calemjane, a nurse working for Aide Médicale Internationale, returned in July 1984 from four months in the area around the Panjsher Valley. In a written account of her journey, she explained that it had been impossible to carry out a medical mission because of constant bombardments.

At four o'clock, the day breaks, and at five come the helicopters and airplanes in the sky. There seems to be some traffic today. . . . On the road, entire families are climbing the sides of the valley. The children in the women's arms have such big, black eyes; they do not cry. The women covered in the chadri hide their faces; impossible to know what they think. The men go on foot, staring into the distance, searching for cover. . . . There were two dead this morning. Near the village where we found our bags . . . the grass is tempting in the cool shadows of the trees. To sit is to fall asleep. But there is a rumbling nearby, too near, that wrenches me out of sleep, suddenly: the helicopters! . . . There are bombs exploding around us—what are they aiming at? There are a few houses nearby; the people are fleeing. I am seized by an uncontrollable trembling, prey to a feeling of total powerlessness against these black birds, these horrible black spots in the sky, these huge insects whose sound is the sound of hell and who sow destruction and death. . . . We are invited into the house where our bags are. . . . They tell us of a wounded man, . . . who is there, on the floor, his hand wrapped in a bandage from which blood is dripping. . . . The helicopter fired while he was on horseback, holding a child in front of him. The bullet went through his left hand, and the child died. . . . We have to amputate three fingers down to the knuckle.

Reprisal Killings

Pvt. Dzhamalbekov, a Soviet Tadzhik from Dushanbe who voluntarily deserted his unit, told us in Peshawar on 21 September 1984 about a massacre he had witnessed on the road between Tashqorghan (formerly Kholm) and Mazar-e Sharif in April 1982 while stationed in Balkh Province with the 122nd Brigade:

> "Besides our brigade's garrison, there was a special commando unit. The brother of the commander of the unit was a captain in the same unit. It was the birthday of the commander. They drank too much vodka. The captain took three soldiers and went to the town of Tashqorghan to get grapes and apples. When they went to the town, they were captured by the mujahedin. They were killed and then cut up and dropped in the water. When the drunk commander found out that his brother and three soldiers were killed by mujahedin, he took the whole commando unit at night. He went to the village and butchered, slaughtered all the village. They cut off the heads and killed perhaps two thousand people. The sun came out, and the mujahedin and others buried the people. I drove my APC [armored personnel carrier] there and saw the demolished houses. In the part destroyed by the commandos there was nobody living there. That's why I say it's a bad war, a dirty war."

This incident was also reported at the time by the BBC. The actual number of deaths was probably closer to two hundred.

On 1 November 1985 *The New York Times* correspondent Arthur Bonner quoted from an interview with a Soviet soldier who had defected to the Afghan resistance and adopted the Moslem name of Ahmed:

> "The Soviet troops can't find the mujahedeen so they kill civilians," he said, adding: "Our officers said we must go into a village and kill all the people and animals, sheep, horses, even dogs and cats. But I thought it was the mujahedeen who were fighting against us, not elderly people and dogs and cats."

Testimony in August 1985 from a former officer of the Interior Ministry in Kabul who was responsible for radio communications of some military units confirms that the killing of civilians in reprisal is intentional.

> "When the mujahedin ambushed a convoy, we got certain orders. For example, one time when a convoy was coming through the Salang Pass [on the major highway from the Soviet Union to Kabul] in Parwan Province, the mujahedin took positions in villages above the convoy. So the mujahedin ambushed the convoy. When they shot at the helicopters over the convoy, they lost control, and the helicopters escaped. Then they send a message to the nearest air base to ask for help and also to the nearest brigade or military post. Then maybe ten to twenty helicopters and MiGs appear and troops move in about two hours and destroy completely all the villages in the area. [Afterward] in reports they mentioned, we killed twenty *ashrar* [bandits], thirty, even one hundred

ashrar. They mentioned the ladies and children also. They were not saying separately the mujahedin and civilians or ladies and children. They were including any village giving help to the mujahedin. They would say thirty, fifty *ashrar* killed, including women and children, and 'we cleaned the area [*manteqeh-ra pak kardim*] from all *ashrar*.'"

On 30 June 1983, in an incident widely reported in the French press and later raised with the Afghan government by Amnesty International, Soviet soldiers killed twenty-four people, including twenty-three unarmed civilians, in Rauza, a village on the outskirts of Ghazni. Patrice Franceschi, a freelance journalist working with Médécins du Monde, was nearby at the time, and he was able to interview villagers in detail a week after the event.

The Soviet sweeping operations that had begun several days before reached Rauza on June 30. About 2 A.M., APCs encircled the village. There was no unit of the Afghan army with them. At dawn, the Russian soldiers left their vehicles, protected by helicopters, and began to search the village, street by street.

An eighteen-year-old resistance fighter, Gholam Hazrat, was then at home with his weapon. The suddenness of the Russians' arrival had trapped him. Frightened, he hid himself at the bottom of the well in his family's courtyard. Around 10 A.M., a six-man patrol, including one officer, broke down the door and began to search.

The officer and one of his men soon leaned over the well. When he saw that he was discovered, the resistance fighter opened fire, killing the officer and wounding the soldier. He immediately died under the fire of the other Russian soldiers.

This became the occasion for blind reprisals. The four remaining soldiers shot all the men in the house, the father, a cousin, and two uncles of Gholam Hazrat. Then they went out and assembled all the men they could find in the neighborhood, passersby, shopkeepers, etc. They were first beaten and robbed of any valuables (watches, money) before being summarily executed in the street. Twenty-three people were killed in this way.[2]

Franceschi collected the name, age, and profession of each victim and photographed the graves.

A number of sources, including *The New York Times* and the *Chicago Tribune*, described a massacre of civilians by Soviet troops in October 1983 in three villages southwest of Kandahar on the branch road linking the city to the Soviet military base at Mandisar airport.[3] On 10 and 11 October a local unit of the Jamiat-e Islami resistance organization had ambushed and destroyed several Soviet military columns. In retribution, on the morning of 12 October, a largely Soviet force with a few Afghans acting as guides or interpreters arrived in the villages of Kolchabad, Moshkizai, and Balakarez. Sardar Mohammad, fifty-five, a farmer from Kolchabad, hid in a grain bin when he saw Russian soldiers shoot his neighbor, Issa Jan. That afternoon, when he emerged from hiding, he went to the house of a friend, Ahadar Mohammad.

> "Everyone was dead. Ahadar, his wife, and his baby were lying on the floor covered with blood. His nine-year-old daughter was hanging over the window, half in the house, half out. It looked like she was shot as she tried to run away. The young son of thirteen years lay crumpled in another corner with his head shot away. I threw up. Then I carried the males outside into the courtyard and covered the women with pieces of cloth where they lay. I did not want anyone to see the women exposed the way they were."

Tora, daughter of Haji Qader Jan of Kolchabad, an eleven-year-old girl who survived the massacre by hiding under bedcovers, described how Soviet soldiers accompanied by an Afghan officer herded women and children into a room and killed them by lobbing grenades through the window and bayoneting the survivors. Other witnesses described similar scenes in Moshkizai and Balakarez. The villagers who dug the mass graves for the victims estimated that there were 100 dead each in Moshkizai and Balakarez and 160 to 170 dead in Kolchabad.

Further suffering was in store for the survivors. In January 1984, after two tanks were destroyed in the same area, Soviet and Afghan military units reportedly returned to Kolchabad, executed some village elders, and shot many more civilians. Many of the villagers who had fled to refugee settlements around Kandahar had to flee again, to Pakistan, when the Soviet Air Force bombed their camps in June.

Tora's story of women and children being killed by grenades is consistent with testimony from two Soviet deserters, Pvt. Oleg Khlan and Sgt. Igor Rykov, who had served as mechanic/drivers with the First Infantry Carrying Armored Corps based in Kandahar. Khlan stated: "During punitive expeditions, we didn't kill women and children with bullets. We locked them in a room and threw grenades."[4] In another interview, Rykov described the same procedure.[5]

Pvt. Vladislav Naumov, who served in a battalion specializing in punitive expeditions near Jalalabad, Nangarhar Province, described his training in the use of the bayonet to attack villagers:

> "At Termez [Soviet Uzbekistan, just north of Mazar-e Sharif across the Amu Darya] we built models of Afghan villages. Before every combat exercise, Major Makarov would constantly repeat: 'Look in the direction of the village: there are the *dushmans*. [*Dushman*, the Persian word for

enemy, is used by the Soviet press to refer to the Afghan insurgents.] Forward! Kill them!' They kill completely innocent people. And then the truly punitive operations would start. . . . Under the cover of the infantry's combat vehicles we would raze the village to the ground. Then, working under the scorching sun, we would rebuild the model, all over again. . . . We had bayonets and silencers attached to our rifles, and we learned to use them pretty skillfully. The major often repeated Suvorov's words: 'The bullet is a fool, the bayonet—a stalwart. Hit with the bayonet and try to turn it around in the body.' "[6]

While in Quetta in October 1984 we learned of another reprisal killing near Kandahar. Habibullah Karzai, a former diplomat who was Afghanistan's U.N. representative in 1972, told us he had received several independent reports of the killing of members of his Popolzai tribe in Ghundaikan village, seven kilometers west of Kandahar, on 27 September.

"The village is near the Kandahar-Herat road. On either side of the highway there are grapes. After two or three vineyards, you reach the village. The mujahedin had mined the grape gardens with antipersonnel mines. When the Soviets started to cross the gardens, they hit the mines, and six or seven of them were killed. They rushed to the village and killed about fifty people, mostly children, old ladies, old people, and so on, because the young people ran away. They tried to escape. The Russians seized the area for three days. One lady was locked in a room with two children. The two children were killed—we don't know why—but the lady is still alive. I have the name of only one of the victims, Said Sikander. He was a poor man."

The French doctors Frey and David told us of a reprisal killing during the offensive in Logar in early September 1984. On 10 September the Soviet units that had occupied Baraki Barak District for four days were supposed to be reinforced by a convoy of the Afghan Army coming from Kabul. One of the Afghan Army officers, however, defected to the resistance with much of the convoy. The next day Soviet forces arrested forty civilians, according to Dr. David.

"They tied them up and piled them like wood. Then they poured gasoline over them and burned them alive. They were old and young, men, women, and children. Many, many people were telling this story. They all said forty people had been killed."

This story was confirmed on 23 September by an Afghan doctor in Peshawar, who had recently learned by letter that two of his relatives were among those burned to death in Logar. A gentle man who had patiently interpreted for us while we interviewed patients in a hospital for war victims, he suddenly burst out: "What's the point of all this? People should know by now! There are no human rights in Afghanistan. They burn people easier than wood!"

Massacres

Massacres in which large numbers of villagers, including women and children, have been brutally killed have been reported since the Afghan conflict began. Such killings are invariably the work of Soviet soldiers, sometimes accompanied by a few Afghan party members who serve as guides. The massacres documented in this section are only a few examples of the devastating events that have become almost commonplace in Afghanistan.

Massacre at Darra-e Nur

In March 1986 a massacre took place at Darra-e Nur in Konarha Province, some twenty-five kilometers north of the city of Jalalabad. The massacre was documented by the Afghan Information Centre in its *Monthly Bulletin*, number 61 (April 1986); in reports prepared by Abdul Karim Muheb, a former official of the Afghan Ministry of Justice; and in testimonies by refugees whom we interviewed in Yakhagundh refugee camp outside Peshawar in September 1986.

Darra-e Nur is a large and once densely populated valley that had been under the control of the mujahedin for most of the war. On 9 March 1986 Russian artillery began an attack on the villages of Barkot, Duderak, Kashmand Qala, Janshegal, and Waigal. According to the Afghan Information Centre, the mujahedin fought back and killed about twenty-eight Russians.

> Thirty villagers were also killed. To avenge the death of one of their high-ranking officers in the operation, the Russians launched an attack on Sotan and Char Qala villages on March 13. They killed four villagers and injured two.
>
> A new Russian attack on the areas of Bamba Kot, Sheram Qala and Omar Qala was carried out on March 19. There was no resistance by the people: the Russians shot dead 40 children, women and old people inside the houses.
>
> On the same date, brutal operations were carried out in the areas of Sotan Kali and Majgandol. The Russians occupied the heights in the night and started massacring the people at 6:00 A.M. without facing any resistance. Civilians, including infants, children, women and the aged, were killed and more than 200 houses burned. The bodies of 80 civilians were recovered from the debris while many bodies are still lying under the rubble.

The Afghan Information Centre lists the names of more than sixty victims of the massacres.

Abdul Karim Muheb interviewed Toryalai Rokyani, who provided the following report and the names of many of the victims.

"When the resistance did not stop and people in the territory were still carrying on operations against enemy positions, the brutal forces of the enemy entrenched against the villages of Bambakoot, Sharum Qala and Uwnar Qala and ruined one hundred and fifty houses out of which about seventy were set on fire and the rest were demolished by shelling.

"They carried on the shelling of those houses indiscriminately and set fire to the grand mosque of Bamba Koot. In this shelling forty-three persons, including aged men, women and children, were martyred.

"On March 25th 1986 in the late hours of the night the enemy forces surrounded the villages of Suthan, Mujgandool and Quthran and stormed the houses in the early dawn. They entered Suthan at five thirty A.M. On storming the village they initially set fire to the grand village mosque where thirteen persons were burned to death while performing their morning prayers.

"Then they started house-to-house looting, killing occupants as they wanted. In this massacre they killed a man who testified that he was a hundred and fifty years old. His name was Haikal Khan. Another aged victim was Mo'enuddin, aged seventy years. A one and half year old granddaughter of Mo'enuddin was also martyred when he was still swimming in his blood. An eye witness reporter asserts that more than one hundred persons were martyred on this day in those three villages.

"During these massacres an old lady whose name was Bakhtawara and her twelve-year-old granddaughter, both of them blind, were martyred by bayonets.

"The most tragic moment of the massacre occurred when the invaders were bayoneting to death a handsome youth of only fifteen years whose name was Malang. Seeing what the criminals intended against her son, his mother stretched herself over him but the savages martyred both of them with Kalashnikov fire. While the mother and son were still breathing, the Russian brutals sprinkled kerosene over them and set them on fire."

In September 1986 we interviewed Nur Beg, a village elder from the Darra-e Nur valley, now a refugee in Yakhagundh camp. He described how the same villages, Sheram Qala, Omar Qala, Bamba Kot, and Sotan, were destroyed by Soviet troops in March 1986:

"Darra-e Nur is a mountain pass. The Russians had dropped paratroopers in the mountains in the middle of the night, on both sides of the valley. They entered the village by foot. The mountains were full of paratroopers. The people didn't know because they came at night, silently. In the morning planes also came, jets and helicopters. Guns began firing at the villages. The villages were unprotected. The mujahedin were far away. It was only Russians that came, with a few Parchami guides. About 180 people were killed altogether in the four villages. I have a list of the victims.

"The people ran to the mountains where the mujahedin were. The villages were completely destroyed. Most of the bodies were under the debris. It took six days to dig them out. The burning continued for forty days from napalm bombs with delayed action.

"All the survivors left for Pakistan. It took fifteen days to get here. There were Russian planes overhead but they didn't bomb us. There were mujahedin everywhere. And land mines, set by hand, around the area."

We met two young women from Omar Qala, the widows of Sayed Jamal, who was killed in the massacre. In addition to his two wives, Sayed Jamal left five sons and two daughters. The senior wife described the massacre:

"In the night they occupied the mountains near the village. At dawn they came down and entered the village. They entered the houses. Some people escaped, some were in the mosque. Our husband was inside the house. He was taken out by them. His hands were tied behind his back. They took him to the dry river bed and shot him. He was alone. We heard that the other men were lined up and machine-gunned. The village was full of people and many did not escape. I didn't see any Afghans there, only Russians.

"After our husband was buried, we left with the children for Pakistan. The people all started moving. We joined the caravan on foot; the children were on donkeys.

"Our husband was a very nice man. He loved both of our children. He did not say bad things to anyone. He was always at home, playing with the children . . . a good father who had much affection for his children."

Dindar, a farmer from Omar Qala, lost three daughters during the March attack.

"Our house was outside the main village. The Russians came in the night and were hiding. We were in the house, in the early morning, in the dawn. There was firing and we couldn't go out. My daughters were killed by mortar that came into the house. My wife survived. My house was destroyed. The village was half-destroyed. We came here to escape the Russians."

Dindar's daughters killed in the attack were Zaw Jan (twelve years old), Basri Jan (eight years old), and Marjanbame (six years old).

Ghaffar Khan, about twelve years old, told us about the attack on Sotan village. When the attack began, he started running with his father and grandfather. As they ran, they were ambushed. His father was killed. "Many others were killed also."

Massacre in Kunduz Province

We received three detailed, independent reports of a large massacre in Kunduz Province in December 1984 or January 1985: from Dr. Juliette Fournot of MSF, who met the survivors in Paktia Province as she was returning from a medical mission inside Afghanistan and they were on the way to Pakistan; from Abdul Karim Muheb of Peshawar University, who had interviewed a witness; and from the survivors themselves, interviewed in a Pakistani refugee camp. The three accounts differ somewhat on the exact dates of the events. The following account is based primarily on direct testimony from survivors.

On 14 December 1984 Soviet forces entered the Issa Khel area of Chardara District, Kunduz, and began searches in several villages. The Soviets looted houses, destroyed foodstuffs, burned cotton crops, raped women, and killed a number of villagers.

> "They also threw on this day three hand grenades into the house of my uncle whose name was Janan. My uncle was sitting by the stove in his dining room when the first hand grenade was thrown. As a result my uncle was martyred and the other members of the family sustained injuries of different dimensions, most of them very serious. . . . The first grenade was followed by two more, which ruined almost all of the house. It was not only the fate of my uncle's house but of many houses and families in that village." (Testimony of Mohammad Jan, son of Lal Jan, provided by Abdul Karim Muheb)

Resistance fighters in the area reacted by ambushing the Soviet column on its way back to its base in Kunduz city, inflicting some light damage. On Sunday, 22 December, apparently in reprisal, Soviet troops accompanied by a few PDPA members encircled the nearby village of Haji Rahmatullah at 10:00 or 11:00 A.M.[7]

> They entered systematically in all the houses, executing all the inhabitants, including women and children, often by shooting them in the head. Three pregnant women were eviscerated [with bayonets]. Fire was set to the houses, and the flames continued to burn for 5 days. The troops also took with them all items of value and money, which the people offered them hoping to be spared, without managing to save a single life

in this manner. (Report of Dr. Juliette Fournot, written 3 June 1985, Peshawar)

"The Russian troops entrenched themselves on all sides of the village, and anyone coming out was shot. . . . We suddenly observed that a small girl was running out of the village while all of her clothes were stained with blood and barefooted she was aimlessly running. One of our mujahed brothers approached the girl in spite of the danger. He asked her the reason for her sobbing, and she could only say that we were destroyed. . . . When we reached the village [after the Soviets had left] we were shocked to find that not a single human being had survived. . . .

"It was winter time, damp and very chilly. Every family's members were shot along with their small children while sitting by the heaters inside the rooms. Most of them were killed while still in sitting positions around their fireplaces. We saw many of the ladies holding their babies tight in their bosoms, both being shot together. In most of the cases many people were brought into one house and then the place was hand grenaded and fired [burned]. Hundreds of those martyrs remained under great piles of clay [the principal building material] unseen and untouched. When we started to take them out of the dust and ashes no one was able to recognize his or her relatives. In most of the cases just burned bodies were coming out. Those with no survivor left behind remained under the piles. Green banners [of martyrdom] were erected on houses or rooms where the dead were lying under the razed walls." (Testimony of Mohammad Jan)

"It was 10:00 A.M. when some Russians and Parchamis entered the village. We were sitting—we didn't know—and suddenly they started killing our people. Some of our neighbors were killed at that time. Then they came to my house. My mother, my brother, my mother's brother, in all eight members of my family were killed, including girls, boys. They were firing with Kalashnikov and Kalakov and they used bayonets too. [Those killed were] my mother, Ayat Gul; my brother Abdul Sami; Abdul Ahad, my uncle; my uncle's wife, Bibi Gul; my uncle's daughters, Safia and Maria; and Mohammad Hakim, my uncle's one-year-old son. Safia was two years old and Maria was three. They killed all four members of my uncle's family at once with bullets. Our neighbors, Mohammad Akbar, his wife, his mother, and his one-year-old son were killed. My own family, I saw them when they were killing my family, I saw with my own eyes, because I was hiding myself in the house. The others I didn't see myself when they were killed, but I took them to the graveyard. In one house of our neighbors twenty-three people were killed. They were all living in the same house, uncles and nephews, all in one house. And thirteen members of another family were killed, the head of the family was named Jawlan." (Testimony of Mohammad Taher, forty, farmer and graduate of Kabul University engineering faculty; interviewed in Panyian refugee camp, Haripur, NWFP, 23 August 1985)

With the help of some village elders who were also present, Mohammad Taher then listed the other heads of households in the village and gave the number killed from each family:

Narmurad: sixteen	Abuddin: eight
Sultan Murad: fifteen	Anamurad: twenty-four
Hayat Murad: twelve	Abdul Aziz: three
Pacha Qol: one (his wife)	Khal Murad: five
Auraq: nine	Diwanaqol: eleven
Abdul Majid: seven	Abdul Rasul: six
Ali Mohammad: eight	Ishbay: seven
Amir Mohammad: thirteen	Qasem: four
Gholam Hazrat: eighteen	Mohammad Yusuf: four
Mohammadi: twenty-three	Gol Mohammad: eight
Khaliyar: fourteen	Panur: nine

This makes a total of 250 victims.

The survivors of the village and the resistance fighters loaded the bodies of murdered children (and, according to some, of women and elders as well) onto bullock carts and took them in protest to the provincial capital.

"After the Russians had finished their massacres, we loaded the dead bodies of children and old people and sent them to the capital, Kunduz, for the governor. And the governor didn't care about the dead bodies, and he said, take your dead bodies away, I can't do anything about it. The Afghan military officers, the other people working with the government, KHAD, government servants, they told us, 'It was not our work, it is the Russians who are committing all these cruelties, and we don't have any power or right to do anything. So you can take your dead bodies back and put them in the graveyard, and we will ask them afterwards.' When we brought the dead bodies back to the village to bury them in the graveyard, at four o'clock in the afternoon, they shelled the village again, and we couldn't put the bodies in the graveyard. We had to postpone and bury them at night. We had no time, so we put six people, ten people in each grave." (Testimony of Mohammad Taher)

"Seeing these great piles of dead bodies, we decided to carry some of them in a procession to the city of Kunduz. The dead bodies of those babies whose ages ranged from infancy to two years were chosen so that the people of Kunduz would realize what destiny we faced. It would also draw the attention of Afghan officials to the Russian barbarism in which they were employed. The babies whom we collected from a part of the village filled ten carts, each cart containing fifteen to sixteen bodies. [Dr. Fournot's account mentions nine carts, each with twenty bodies of women and children.] On the way to Kunduz the people received us in every village with eyes full of tears. When the procession approached Kunduz city, the governor of Kunduz received the procession outside the city. The aged men and women of the region who had accompanied the procession could not control their sentiments on seeing the governor and started cursing him and calling, 'Shame to you and your criminals.' The governor, seeing the scene which had caused common rage and irritation, started soothing the masses and softening their sentiments with consoling words. He pleaded with them that the crime had been carried on without his knowledge. He also wanted to oblige the elders and ordered the district administration to present us three thousand meters of white cloth for the martyrs' shroud, not knowing that those who receive martyrdom in Islam are buried with their clothes on and do not need shrouds. He also tried to soothe them with saying that when they completed the burial ceremonies their elders must meet him to tell the case in its full detail. But not the least official mention is uttered of the crime till this day. They were able to silence the people for the time being, but history cannot remain silent." (Testimony of Mohammad Jan)

The killing reportedly continued in this district later in the year. A farmer from Chardara District who arrived in Pakistan in July 1985 explained his reasons for leaving:

"It was because of bombardments and the cruelty of the Russian troops. Because when the mujahedin were resisting, the Russians would bomb the villages, and when the mujahedin had to retreat, the Russians would come in the village and kill women, children, everyone. It happened to our village and to our houses also. Just last month they killed three hundred people in our district, and they killed more later around Khanabad [another district of Kunduz]. They used heavy bombs to bomb the village. The bombs make a well—the hole is so deep it brings up water. When they came inside the village they killed many children by cutting their throats. When they found more, they put petrol on them and burned them. They killed twenty, twenty-five children this way. I don't know most of their names, but there was Masum Khan, Mohammad Ibrahim, Gul Mohammad. I saw the children, women, old ladies, too. Mostly they killed children, girls, married women, and old ladies. I had escaped with the mujahedin, but when I returned to the village, I saw the children and women." (Testimony of Saleh Mohammad, son of Mullah Jamal, thirty, farmer, Gulbagh village, Chardara District, Kunduz; interviewed in Munda refugee camp, NWFP, 21 August 1985)

Massacre in Laghman Province

Soviet soldiers killed over five hundred villagers during an April 1985 offensive in several districts of Laghman Province.[8] This massacre was noteworthy not only for the number of victims and the cruelty with which many were killed, but also for the use of a new weapon, which refugees described as an intense light that burns people to death at close range but loses its effectiveness with distance.

Around 8 April Soviet troops secured the strategic Kabul-Jalalabad highway where it passes through Kats subdistrict on the southern border of Laghman. A column of troops then went north and split, half occupying the region around the provincial capital and half occupying Qarghai District. The troops then attacked the villages. After subduing some scattered armed resistance, they entered villages throughout the area, destroyed crops and livestock, killed whole families at a time, including children reported to have been bayoneted or burned alive, looted houses of all valuable objects, and then withdrew.

The Afghan Information Centre presented the following details of casualties, giving 505 as a minimum estimate:

> In Kats 72 children, women and old people were killed—In Mindrawar 50. Also about 100 cattle exterminated—Qarghayee-Haiderkhany, 150—Pul-e Jogi, 15—Kalakot, 35—Safu-khel, 12—Dehmazang, 10—Tarakhel, 8— Aghrabad, 9—Qala-e-Sarfiraz, 14—Abdurrahimzay, 15—Laramora 14— Nissir 10—Charbagh 35, also houses and the bazaar set on fire.— Qalatak, 9 elders executed—Ahmadzay-kelay 6—Kamalpur 4—Qala-e-Rahim 7—Bela 25—Pacha Kelay 5.[9]

> "At nine o'clock [at night] the atheist [Soviet] forces came and surrounded the area. The doors of the houses were locked, and they opened the doors with grenades. And one of our commanders was martyred, and they blew up his house. They killed the horses and they killed the cows. And they were searching the houses for ammunition, weapons, and also for money and anything of value. They looted 1,100 houses. They killed six people somewhere else—they were watering their fields. They had a lamp and were watering their fields, so when they were surrounded, they shot them. At one o'clock they started to kill all the people, ladies, children, old people, religious people. They went into the houses to search them and they killed these people and put them with the cattle. They killed nine horses too. After two o'clock the mujahedin learned what was happening, and there was fighting for three hours until early morning, when the airplanes arrived. At eight o'clock the mujahedin escaped, and three Russian corpses were left there, and mujahedin burned their bodies. Mohammad Idris, son of Shinki, a commander of mujahedin, was killed while he was praying in the mosque. Haji Nurani, son of Mirajuddin, an *alem* [religious scholar], was killed. Mullah Buzurg, the mullah in the Friday mosque, was killed also, and his books were burned inside the mosque. They killed him with a bayonet in the mosque and then they carried his dead body and put it with the cattle. Then there was Qiamuddin—he was asleep in his house, and they stabbed him in the stomach. Tor, Qiamuddin's son, when his father was killed he tried to resist, so he was killed. [He was twenty to twenty-two years old.] One of the small children hid himself in his mother's arms and they stabbed him with a bayonet in his mother's arms. They shot the mother in the breast— now she is in Peshawar. [The woman, named Bibi Nisa, wife of Annar Gul, was a cousin of Tor, who had come to visit them. The son was named Abdul Sattar.] At two o'clock in the afternoon fourteen MiGs arrived, and

thirty-five horses were killed in the fields. They dropped thirty-nine napalm bombs and destroyed many houses and shops. They fired rockets to burn the fields and orchards. Mostly they hit the trees and burned the orchards. When we came back to the village, there were many calves, chickens all killed, and most of the houses were destroyed. In my village we found thirty corpses cut into pieces, and the people could not even tell which were women and which were men. Some of them were cut up by bombs, and some by bayonets." (Testimony of Said Mohammad, son of Jan Mohammad, forty-one, farmer, Fatehabad village, Surkhrud District, Nangarhar Province;[10] interviewed in Panyian refugee camp, Haripur, NWFP, 23 August 1985)

Five orphan boys about ten years old from Fatehabad described other details of the killings there:

"When they were shelling Fatehabad village, my father was sitting near the cow shed, and he was martyred there by the BM-13. Then the Russians entered the village, burned the houses of mujahedin, looted their property, and they killed some other people also in the village with machine guns, rifles, bayonets. [Names of victims were] Abdul Nabi, Mahmud, Ghaffar, Mullah Imam Gul. [He estimated their ages at forty, seventy, seventy, and ninety.] The daughter of my mother's brother, Chata Gul, was killed [aged sixteen], and Khan Lala, son of my mother's sister [fourteen]." (Testimony of Nurullah, son of Abdul Malik; his younger brother, Dil Lala, also present)

"At night my father was going to the flour mill with a donkey. The area was surrounded by the Russians, and they killed my father on the way. He was shot and they also used bayonets. He had seventeen bayonet wounds in his body. Abdullah, my mother's brother, about fifty, was killed. So was Zalmay [twenty-two], and Shal [eighteen]." (Testimony of Yusuf Khan, son of Juma Khan)

"My father had a shovel, and he was going to the bazaar. The Russians were there, and they hit him with a grenade." (Testimony of Hasan Khan, son of Akbar Khan; boys interviewed in Panyian refugee camp, 23 August 1985)

The fifth boy was Nurullah, son of the *alem*, Haji Nurani, whose death was mentioned above. He testified:

"The Russians came and they stabbed my father with a bayonet. The Russians came and landed the troops before nighttime. Then at nighttime they came to the house. My father was asleep, and we were asleep also, and they came and stabbed him with a bayonet. My uncle Qiamuddin was killed. [The same Qiamuddin mentioned above.] Also Abdul Halim, Idris [same as Mohammad Idris, mentioned above]; Qaisi, my uncle's son, Lal, son of my uncle; Qiamuddin's daughter. Qiamuddin's daughter was also injured. Abdul Malik's wife was also killed with bayonets."

Tila Bibi, the wife of Akbar Khan, recounted the events in Fatehabad as follows:

"When the Russians came we fled from the house, my children and I. My husband was running too. The Russians threw a grenade at him, and he died. Eight people from my family were martyred, my husband's brothers, their sons, cousins, and other people. They looted my house and then they burned it. When the Soviets came first they turned on a light, something they put up in the sky so it was just like daylight, something they shoot up in the sky. Then they took the people out of their houses and cut their throats or killed them with bayonets, Kalashnikovs, looted the houses, killed the animals. My husband's brain was coming out, he had lost his hand, lost his leg. When I was running away, I saw them cutting the people's throats." (Interviewed in Panyian refugee camp, 23 August 1985)

There are several consistent testimonies of mass killing of the inhabitants of Shalatak village near the provincial center of Laghman.

"At the small village in Shalatak all the inhabitants were executed; a small girl was the only survivor. The people were burned with petrol. It was impossible to identify their bodies."

"In our region 150 civilians lost their lives in this second attack. Women were raped and summarily executed. At Shalatak, about 20 women and children had shut themselves inside a house. The Russians first threw hand-grenades inside the house and then set it on fire; all the occupants were burned to death."

"According to the reports of other mujahed brothers who have accompanied the wounded men, women, and children to Pakistan who are now in hospitals of Peshawar, seventy-four persons were martyred at Shalatak. Twenty-seven of them had been martyred in a double-story house belonging to a person named Raees. This tragedy has been narrated by a mujahed of the area who had himself seen the scene as follows: The whole family of Raees's kinship had mustered to his house in terror to take shelter because of the strong walls of the house, not thinking much on the fact that walls cannot have any protection to escape the most cruel type of human beings. Seeing the horrified men, women, and children running towards that unfortunate house, the Russians stormed the gates of the house and knocked on the door to allow them to enter the house. The occupants, being horrified, pleaded emphatically not to open the door. The Russians, observing the refusal of the occupants, interpreted it as a sort of stubbornness. Therefore they locked the house and set fire to it and thus cremated all of the occupants. When the crime was over and the Russians left the scene, the people from Joogi Qalaand Neelawat rushed to the scene with shovels in their hands to save, if possible, the burning occupants. But with each digging they were obtaining some leg or hand of some cremated one. Seeing the situation, a religous leader who had accompanied the group to the scene, whose name is Mullah Buzurg, told the people not to dig and instead make it a piled and raised ground to signify the shrines of those twenty-seven martyrs. The same reporter meanwhile narrated that outside a house not very far from the burnt house a martyred lady had fallen on the ground with a live infant child clinging to her breast, sucking it."[11]

"At noon, the Russians started to move out, and we began collecting the bodies of the martyrs. Many people we could not recognize, because the heads had been cut off, faces crushed by beating. I found my cousin, who was a teacher, at first, I could not recognize him. In each house we found 2 or 3 bodies. They had killed almost everybody. We went up into the Sheikh Mahmud Farindar area of the mountains, and there we found 14 more martyrs—some without clothes, they had been killed naked, or burned alive, the clothes burned off them. As we carried the bodies down, the Russians saw us and began firing BM-13 rockets, we brought the bodies to the village. . . . The Russians said, 'You are Muslims, believing in God—call your God to come and save you from death. Where is your God, and how is he?' And the people said, 'We believe in God, and whatever happens in God's will.' And the Russians killed them too." (Testimony of refugees from Qarghai District; unpublished interview with Rob Schultheis)

Witnesses emphasized that it was an entirely Soviet operation.

"As the rest of the civil population had fled, there were not enough hands to collect the bodies and bury them; mujahedin groups did the job. After the Russians' departure, an Afghan army unit came and dug ditches for the remaining bodies. The Kabul officials tried to convince the people that only Russians were responsible for the massacre. They promised food, blankets and shelter; but there were not many people to listen to them. . . . The Russian commandos were groups of 20, 25 or 50 men with a leader. . . . Persons knowing how to read and write were brought by the Russians in front of their leaders who killed the prisoners with one shot of a pistol on the forehead. Local teachers who shouted their sympathies with the Kabul regime, even people producing membership cards in the Communist Party organisations, were not spared. All had it. A few Party activists and Afghan army officers tried to resist; the Russians killed some of them and sent the rest in armored cars to their military headquarters." (Testimony of Jamruz, son of Abdul Hafez)

The various sources recount many more such scenes in Laghman. Refugees also tried to describe a new type of weapon that they claimed to have seen from a distance. We cannot verify their claims but present their testimonies in the hope that further research will clarify whether such a weapon exists and what its nature is.

"They are using a new weapon. It's like a bulb. They gather the people and use it like a mirror to burn everyone. [Several people present from Laghman and Kunduz provinces raised their voices to testify that they knew of the weapon.] Some people escaped to the mountains and hid themselves in caves—either natural caves or caves made by the mujahedin. In Laghman Province I know of four caves with forty or fifty people inside, where first they shot with Kalashnikovs and then took the mirror and burned them. . . . They first used this mirror in Sawr [April–May 1985], then in Seratan [June–July], in Tabi and then in Amber. The first time I saw the mirror. The second time, I didn't see it, but I saw the result. The first time I was not so far away. The first troops who came to the village, we killed them. Actually the first time it was not in a cave. Then more troops came and they collected the people, they pointed their Kalashnikovs at them, and then they used this mirror. It was in Garuch and Badpakh villages. They took people from Garuch and used the mirror, then they took them from Badpakh and used the mirror. The people they killed were ladies, old people, children. [Asked what it looked like, he showed a shiny silver-colored snuff box.] It was shiny like this. Maybe like the bulb of a car. When they used it, it gave a light. It's not very big—a man can carry it in his hand. All the pro-Soviet and Communist countries are helping the Soviets in this war, but the Afghan Muslims have only one power, which is Islam." (Testimony of Said Mohammad, son of Gul Mohammad, farmer, thirty-six, of Omarzai village, central Laghman Province; interviewed in Munda refugee camp, NWFP, 21 August 1985)

"I saw the light once before sunrise, but I didn't see the instrument properly. I saw the same weapon about two months ago, when they surrounded Alishang and Kalacha. [Despite the date, he probably meant during the April offensive in Laghman.] The mujahedin had come at night to their houses. In the early morning when they were trying to return to their bases in the mountains, the first mujahedin informed them that they were surrounded. Then before sunrise they used the mirror, but it had no effect. The mujahedin had left the village. It burned some of the houses, and the children, old people, women tried to put out the fire." Those present agreed that the weapon seemed lethal only at very short distances. (Testimony of Ataullah, son of Mullah Abdullah, mullah, forty-eight to fifty, Kalacha village, central Laghman; interviewed in Munda refugee camp, 21 August 1985)

"They are using some new kind of weapon. They use a glass to shine a light on people and burn them. . . . I never saw it, but other mujahedin say

the same thing, that they are using a kind of mirror against the people."
(Testimony of Saleh Mohammad, son of Mullah Jamal, thirty, farmer,
Gulbagh village, Chardara District, Kunduz; interviewed in Munda refugee
camp, 21 August 1985)

Massacre in Logar Province

An earlier massacre that took place in Logar Province in 1982 was
thoroughly documented by some intrepid Western observers. A commission of the Permanent People's Tribunal on Afghanistan—composed of Michael Barry, an American Afghanistan expert; Ricardo Fraile, a specialist
in international law; Dr. Antoine Crouan; and Michel Baret, photographer—
documented a massacre of 105 persons in the village of Padkhwab-e
Shana in Logar Province through on-site inspection and interviews with
witnesses.

Soviet armored vehicles, hunting down modjahedin surrounded the
village at 8 A.M. on September 13, 1982. Some of the fighters and
villagers, including children, found refuge in a "karez" (covered irrigation
canal). The Soviet soldiers asked two old persons to enter the canal and
summon the people to come out. Faced with the latter's refusal, the old
people came back up claiming there was nobody inside.

According to an old person's eyewitness testimony, a tank truck was
brought to pour a liquid, apparently oil, into the three openings of the
karez. From another tank truck they poured a white-looking liquid to which
they added the contents of a 100-pound bag of white powder. It was set
on fire three times thanks to "Kalashnikovs," and each time there was a
violent explosion.

They protected their eyes and heads with helmets and shot their
Kalashnikovs into the products, which exploded. Then they did the same
thing at the other opening of the canal. When the fire and smoke had
cleared, they started again with another hole. They stayed until 3 P.M.
When they realized the operation had succeeded, they applauded and
laughed as they left.

"The first day the population pulled out four bodies; the second day 30;
the third, 68. Seven days later, the last three. When we touched the
bodies, pieces would stay in our hands. The first day, when we wanted to
pull out the victims, the unbearable stench made us feel sick. . . . It is only
with great difficulty that we were able to extract the maimed bodies:
people could not even recognize their children or relatives. Whenever
they were identified, it was thanks to watches, rings, and other objects
they might be wearing."[12]

Summary Executions and Random Killings

According to the reports we received, when Soviet forces enter a village, they routinely conduct house-to-house searches. People are interrogated, after which they may be arrested or simply executed on the spot, especially if they resist interrogation. If evidence is found or if people are denounced by informers, they may be pulled from their houses and killed in front of their families. We received reports about the execution of groups of people at a time. We also heard frequently about ground troops that entered an area en masse after air and artillery attacks and shot wildly at anything that moved. Cases have been described of Afghan civilians killed by soldiers almost at random, not in the context of a military operation, but in the course of a robbery or simply as an expression of anger and frustration.

Groups of civilians have been killed from the air, by Soviet helicopters and jets that have, on a number of occasions, attacked weddings and funerals. There have also been systematic attacks on refugee caravans moving toward the border.

> "So many things have happened in the past five years that we are confused. All of our innocent people have been killed in different ways. They took many people from their houses and killed them. They were bombed by jet fighters or thrown alive in wells and buried under the mud. They were thrown down from airplanes, and some were put under tanks alive, and the tanks crushed them. They were all unarmed people. Some of them were given electricity and killed that way. Some were cut into pieces alive. These are things we could not remember even from the reign of Genghis Khan." (Haji Mohammad Naim Ayubi, sixty, former merchant; interviewed in Quetta, 3 October 1984)

Pvt. Oleg Khlan, a deserter from the Soviet Army, told *The Christian Science Monitor* on 10 August 1984:

> "We were ordered by our officers that when we attack a village, not one person must be left alive to tell the tale. If we refuse to carry out these orders, we get it in the neck ourselves."

Sgt. Igor Rykov, a defector from the Soviet Army, described the searches conducted by his unit in Kandahar Province:

> "The officer would decide to have the village searched, and if it was found it contained a single bullet, the officer would say: 'This is a bandit village; it must be destroyed.' The men and young boys would be shot, and the women and children would be put in a separate room and killed with grenades."[13]

Summary executions were described by Mohammad Amin Salim, a former state's attorney, who had also taught Islamic law at Kabul University, and who had returned to his village in the Shamali area north of Kabul:

> "When the Russians come into villages or places where there are unarmed people, they kill them with bayonets, even women and children. There are so many examples, and they are so atrocious, that it is difficult to speak of them. For example, last year [1983] I was in a village when the Soviets came to search the houses. In this village there were seven elders, including me. When the Russians came into the village, they locked up all these elders. I was separated from the others. I was in another house, and I saw what happened. They asked the old men, 'Where are your sons?' The old men said they had no sons. Immediately, when they heard this, they fired on two of the men, killing them with automatic rifle blasts. The third person—it was a very sad event—they put him against a tree and with a big nail [apparently a detached bayonet] a soldier stabbed him in the chest and nailed him to the tree. What I am telling you is what I saw myself. The other Russian had a big nail in his hand, and he stabbed another old man in the mouth, unhinging his lower jaw. The next they put in a well, and then they threw an explosive in the well. Then, when they went into another house, I managed to escape. After my escape, I returned to the village about twelve or thirteen hours later. I also saw two little boys who had been killed. This was last year in the month of Seratan [June–July] in Karez village. That is one of thousands of examples. It would take hours and hours to tell you what I have seen with my own eyes." (Testimony of Mohammad Amin Salim; interviewed in Peshawar, 29 September 1984)

Sufi Akhtar Mohammad, a fifty-two-year-old farmer from Zamankhel village, Pol-e Khomri District, Baghlan Province, told us of an incident he witnessed in Wardak (Maidan) Province on his way to Peshawar, about twenty-five days before we interviewed him in Peshawar on 30 September 1984. The Soviets had come to Awalkhel village to search for guns.

> "I was with a group of fighters on the way to Peshawar. When we reached Awalkhel in Maidan, there was a hustle and bustle. Russian soldiers were searching the houses. We hid ourselves. As soon as the Russians left, we went to ask the people what happened, and we noticed eight dead bodies. They told us that after the Russians searched the houses, they killed people of all ages, men, women, and children. Of the eight bodies, two were slaughtered [had their throats cut], and all of them were burned.[14] The Russians had asked the relatives to watch while they killed the eight people. The first two were slaughtered, and then the remaining ones were brought and shot with Kalashnikovs. They poured kerosene on them and set them on fire. The people said that the Russians were not alone. A few Khalqis and Parchamis were guiding them to the houses.

> When they were searching the houses, they found two Russian-made machine guns, captured from the Afghan Army in fighting in Ab-e Chakan. This was how they took their revenge."

Farmers and villagers interviewed in Peshawar in September 1984 had similar stories to tell. Bibi Makhro, wife of Abdul Jalil, of Chardara District, Kunduz Province, had pieces of shrapnel in her left leg.

> "Nine months ago the Russian soldiers came to our village. The mujahedin escaped, but I was in the street with two other women. When the Russians saw us, they threw bombs [grenades]. The other two women were killed, but I survived."

Lala Dad of Dasht-e Guhar, Baghlan Province, told us that when ground troops arrived in his area, they would kill anyone suspected of being a resistance fighter.

Other refugees described their experiences:

> "The government forces came and killed the people and took those they didn't kill to Kabul in tanks." (Testimony of women nomads from Baghlan)

> "The Russians came to my village three times looking for mujahedin. They killed people and animals. They killed women, children, and men for no reason. My neighbors were killed. They were asleep when the soldiers came, and the men tried to escape." (Testimony of a woman from Kohistan, Kapisa Province)

> "After they bombed and shot from tanks, they came on foot. They killed people and took their money. I lost Af 2,500 to the Russians. In one family headed by Mohammad Omar fifteen people were killed outside their home at 4:00 A.M." (Testimony of Rahmatullah, a farmer from Bela village, Nangarhar Province)

> "I lost my mother, father, and five children. The Russians came to the village, and the mujahedin were there. The fighting was hard. After the fighting the Russians came into the village and killed the people. They came into my house and wanted money. They accused us of being from America. My husband and I ran to the mountains, but I could not take five of my children with me, only these three. We spent five days in the mountains without food and water. We went back to the village and saw the tents were burned. I found my five children dead in the house. There were 140 people killed, including my parents and sisters. I don't know how the days become nights and the nights become days. I've lost my five children. Russian soldiers do these things to me." (Testimony of wife of Mohammad Kabir of Bela village, Nangarhar Province; her five dead children were Mohammad Shams, seven; Shams-ul-Haq, eight; Najibullah, ten; Naqibullah, fourteen; and Al-Hamula, fifteen.)

We heard numerous reports of summary executions by Soviet troops that entered Baraki Barak District, Logar Province, on 6 September 1984. Dr. Ghazi Alam told us in an interview on 22 September about an old man, Mohammad Rafiq, who was killed there in the village of Akhundkhel. The French doctors Patrick David and François Frey, who were in Logar Province in early September, gave us this report:

> "Baraki Barak District is on the way to Pakistan for all of northern Afghanistan. There were thirty men on their way to Iran [via Pakistan] to find work. They were all killed by the Russians. There were forty-five innocent people killed. Some were 'slaughtered' [had their throats slit], two in Baraki Barak [village] and one in the mountains of Saijawand. Some were burned with petrol. Some had dynamite put on their backs and were blown up. The Russians cut people's lips and ears and gouged out their eyes. We saw a man the Russians had shot in the foot after stealing his watch and money. Two boys escaped and hid themselves in a well. The Russians put some kind of gas in the well that exploded when it hit the water. One died, and the other, whom we treated, had a severe lung problem. A boy about twelve years old in Chalozai was shot in the elbow when he ran away from the Russians." (Interview in Peshawar, 22 September 1984)

Patients in an amputee hospital in Peshawar that we visited on 27 September 1984 told us of summary executions by Russian soldiers in their villages:

> "When the Russians came [in June 1982], they burned homes and destroyed the food. Two elders came back to the village, because they heard the food was burned. They asked the soldiers about it. The soldiers first shot them, then burned their bodies." (Testimony of Mohammad Sherdil, twenty-three, from Khanez-e Bazarak village in the Panjsher Valley, Parwan Province)

> "After the Russians retreated from Bazarak [in autumn 1982], I found the bodies of nine old men in the village. I found their bones on the ground. The bodies were completely burned. The only way we could recognize them was from their worry beads. I remember the names of seven of them: Yar Mohammad, Haji Karim, Mirza Shah, Mohammad Yusuf, Zaheruddin, Mohammad Gul, Ghiasuddin." (Testimony of Mohammad Hashem, twenty-six, of Bazarak, Panjsher Valley, Parwan Province)

Dr. Sultan Satarzai, whom we interviewed at Al-Jehad Hospital in Quetta on 3 October 1984, told us of a report he had received from one of the graduates of his first aid course, who had recently returned from Kandahar Province:

"About one month ago [early September] during a battle in Panjwai District of Kandahar, some gardeners were working. The Russians went and strangled them. Those who buried the dead saw that they had no wounds, but they had blue necks."

A number of reported killings of Afghan civilians reflect the anger, frustration, and lack of discipline of the Soviet soldiers. They had been told during training that they were being sent to Afghanistan to help the Afghans fight American, Pakistani, and Chinese mercenaries but found instead that they were surrounded by a hostile population and were often mistreated by their own officers as well. The following incident was described to us by a former broadcaster for Radio Afghanistan:

"In 1981 I was hospitalized in Aliabad Hospital [in Kabul]. There I met a small boy, about eight years old. He was injured by bullets of Russians. I talked to him sympathetically, but he was afraid of being put in jail and so on. He was not ready to talk to me. But after one or two days he found that I was a reliable person, sympathetic. Then he talked to me, and he said that he was living in Ghazni Province, and one day while Russians were passing by the village, he and some other children were playing and gazing at the Russians, and suddenly a soldier turned to them and fired on them, and he was hit on his feet and injured and brought to the hospital in Kabul, and two other children were killed on the spot, and the others escaped." (Name withheld on request; interview in Alexandria, Virginia, 25 March 1984)

Another incident, reported by the Afghan Information Centre in its August 1984 *Monthly Bulletin*, is almost unbelievable. When we questioned the centre's director, Professor S. B. Majrooh, about it in Peshawar, he assured us that several witnesses had confirmed the truth of the report.

Outside the village [of Lalma in Nangarhar, on 2 August 1984] a 10- to 12-year-old boy was watching his cows graze. He was playing with a toy—a roughly made small, wooden gun, which with the help of a rubber device was making little "tok-tok" noises like a machine gun. When the Russians arrived, the boy pointed his "tok-toking" toy in the direction of the advancing tanks. The boy was encircled and brought to the village. He was interrogated in front of the terrified villagers. The eyewitnesses heard the following conversation:
A Russian asked: "What is that in your hand?"
The boy answered: "It's my gun."
"What do you want to do with the gun?"
"To kill the enemies."
"Who are the enemies?"
"The ones who are not leaving us in our homes."

It was evident that by "home" the boy did not mean Homeland, Country, or such things, and by "us" he was referring to himself and his parents. "Nothing serious," said the man from Lalma and added: "But still a Russian seized the boy and another one took a sickle from a villager and with a powerful and quick movement of the hand, he cut open the boy's throat and threw the sickle away. It all happened very fast. The parents were not present. Then one of the Russians did a strange thing: he dragged the dead boy to higher ground, covered him with a rug, and put a bed upside down on the body."[15]

Robbery is sometimes the motive for killings.

"When the Russian forces come to a village, the mujahedin leave. The Russians search the houses. In each house they look everywhere. If they find carpets, radios, cassettes, watches, they take them for themselves. If the family resists, they kill them. For example, Inayatullah was killed last year in the fall of 1983. He was an old man. He had Af 5,000 in his pocket. Some Russian soldiers wanted to take it, but he said no. They shot him. Another case: they were searching houses and came to the house of a teacher, Azizullah. They took a radio and other things. But his small daughter did not permit them to take the radio. So they beat the daughter and threw bombs [grenades] at the whole family." (Sayed Azim, former government official; interviewed in Peshawar, 25 September 1984)

Even the mosques are not safe. Mullah Feda Mohammad of Pashmul village, Panjwai District, Kandahar Province, described in a written interview how he and about fifteen other worshippers were captured by Soviet troops in the Pashmul mosque as they began the dawn prayer on 25 August 1984:[16]

"Before taking us out of the mosque they searched us and the mosque for fear of any possible weapons. Then they took us to Zidanian mosque, where a dozen other villagers arrested by the Soviet troops were also waiting with their Soviet guards. In that mosque, the Soviets lined us up against the long wall, and we thought that they would shoot us (you know this is very common with the Russian pigs), so we started saying our *kalima* (prayer). Then they ordered us to keep our hands up, and of course we did so. After that two Soviets started searching in our pockets and took away whatever cash we had together with our wristwatches. Stupid Obaidullah refused to hand over his cash, and immediately he was shot and died instantly; the rest of us knew what to do."

Question: "Who was Obaidullah?"

Answer: "He was the young son of Haji Nematullah, a poor farmer in our village."

Soviet forces have also killed large numbers of people at weddings and funerals. Dr. Jean Didier Bardy of Médécins sans Frontières has described how he and his colleagues in the dispensary of Behsud, Wardak Province, were called to the village of Jalrez in August 1981 to treat the victim of a two-hour attack by four helicopters on a wedding party. The attack left thirty dead and seventy-five wounded.[17] Soviet aircraft also reportedly attacked a wedding near Sorkhakan in Laghman Province on 14 April 1983 (seventy dead), and in Anbarkhana, Nangarhar Province, on 14 August 1984 (dozens dead by one report, 563 by another).[18]

We also heard of attacks on funerals:

> "Two days later, after the burial, when the people were coming to console the families, the Russians came again and killed one woman and five men. The people were escaping, and the Russians opened fire from tanks. This was in Jo-ye Nau village. The men killed were Haji Zafar Khan, Amir, Zondai, Kapa, and Said Rahman, who was fourteen years old. The woman was from another village, so I do not know her name." (Testimony of Sufi Akhtar Mohammad, fifty-two, a farmer from Baghlan; interviewed in Peshawar, 25 September 1984)

> "We have a custom, when someone is buried, to go to the grave for prayer. But while they were praying, the Russians came by helicopter. Two helicopters were flying overhead, and two landed Russian soldiers, who fired with Kalashnikovs. Those who were running away were shot by the flying helicopters, the rest by the Russians who landed. There were forty-one killed, including Abdul Rahman and Abdul Sattar, sons of Abdul Khair; Abdul Mohammad, son of Faizullah; and Lala Akhundzada, son of Bagram Akhundzada. My other brother was there, and he brought back the dead. Thirty-five of the men had arms, but six of them didn't. They were just by the grave, burying him, but they were killed too." (Testimony of Bakht Mohammad, forty-seven, a landlord from Kalacha village, Kandahar; interviewed in Quetta, 3 October 1984)

There are many reports of Soviet aircraft attacks on refugees fleeing to Pakistan. *Christian Science Monitor* reporter Edward Girardet witnessed one such attack:

> Having reached the [Pashal] valley floor by early evening the day before, the nomads had pitched a sprawling camp by the side of the river [on 18 August 1984]. Shortly after the first light, the Antonov [reconnaissance plane] appeared and made several passes over their distinctive black tents, smoking fires, and grazing animals before returning to base. . . . The MiGs took the refugees completely by surprise. Appearing at 10 in the morning, the swing-wing fighter first unloaded two bombs each, believed to be 500-pounders, and then made repeated runs firing rockets and strafing with their 23mm Gatling guns. Nine women and five children

were killed instantly and more than 60 injured, many of them severely. Overall, by the time the Soviets completed their attacks in the area, at least 40 refugees had died.[19]

A nomad woman from Baghlan who had arrived in Pakistan five days before we interviewed her on 25 September 1984 said that on the way to Pakistan Soviet bombers had killed almost all the animals, sheep and camels, and burned their tents and clothes. She pointed to burns from bombings on the limbs of her children.

Azizullah, seventeen, had just arrived in Pakistan from Madrasa District of Kunduz with twenty-three other families. In the mountains around Jalalabad, Nangarhar, their caravan was bombed. Eight people were killed, including his mother, Jamal. In an interview on 24 September 1984, he showed us the burns from this bombing, which had occurred about three weeks before.

Antipersonnel Mines

We received reports about a variety of antipersonnel mines used in Afghanistan by Soviet forces. Often they are used, not for conventional military purposes, but against the civilian population. Some of these mines are powerful enough to kill, while others have charges that only maim.

Soviet soldiers leave minefields around their bases when they leave an area. Their helicopters drop camouflaged "butterfly" mines around populated areas, on roads and in grazing areas. During sweeps through villages, soldiers leave antipersonnel mines in food bins and other parts of the houses of people who have fled. We even heard of mines left in mosques, of booby-trapped bodies that exploded when relatives attempted to move them, and of trip wires placed in fruit trees that injure the harvester. There are also persistent reports of mines disguised as toys, pens, and watches.

> The Russians know quite well that in this type of war, an injured person is much more trouble than a dead person. . . . In many cases, he will die several days or weeks later from gangrene or from staphylococcus or gram-negative septicemia, with atrocious suffering, which further depresses those who must watch him die. The MSF has also seen the damage caused by the explosion of booby-trapped toys, in most cases plastic pens or small red trucks, which are choice terror weapons. Their main targets are children whose hands and arms are blown off. It is impossible to imagine any objective that is more removed from conventional military strategy, which forswears civilian targets.[20]

Unmarked minefields around Soviet bases have caused many civilian deaths. Sgt. Nikolai Movchan, a Soviet soldier who was stationed at a post near Ghazni before his defection in 1983, described an incident that occurred while he was on guard duty:

> "The area around the post was all mined. I saw an Afghan man step on a mine. He was wounded, so I asked if we should send someone to help. They told me to forget it." (Interview in New York City, 3 May 1984)

After the Soviet Army has left an area, the local population tries to remove these unmarked minefields, but it is difficult and dangerous work: The Afghans do not have the proper equipment, and many of the mines are plastic, rather than metal, and thus much more difficult to detect. Sometimes mines are laid in pairs, so that a person removing the first mine is injured or killed by the second. Dad-e Khuda, a thirty-eight-year-old farmer from Abdara in the Panjsher Valley, told us in a 27 September 1984 interview in Peshawar that he had lost his leg this way in the winter of 1982.

In addition to mines around their bases, Soviet forces systematically leave antipersonnel mines in areas where they are likely to kill civilians. One type is oval or disk-shaped and is placed by hand. Another type, the so-called butterfly mine, has two plastic wings, enabling it to flutter to the ground when dropped by a helicopter; there is a detonator in one of the wings. Butterfly mines are dropped in canisters that explode in midair, scattering the mines over wide areas.[21] They apparently come in two camouflage colors, green for grazing areas and sand for roads and mountain paths.

The French doctors working in Afghanistan have frequently testified to the use of antipersonnel mines against civilians. In some areas the most common medical procedure they perform is the amputation of limbs injured by mines. Children, who watch over the animals in the fields, are often the victims. Many have lost legs or feet by stepping on mines left in the mountains.

In her summary of the effects of the Soviet-Afghan offensive against Saijawand, Logar, which she witnessed in January 1983, Dr. Odile de Bailleux of Aide Médicale Internationale noted:

> Antipersonnel mines were spread everywhere, inside houses, in the flour storage bins. . . . The people are now living forty to a room out of fear of these mines.[22]

Mines are left in mosques. Sayed Azim of Maidan told us in a 25 September 1984 interview in Peshawar about a mine left under the carpet of the mosque in his home village of Omarkhel in the autumn of 1983: "We took a long piece of wood and lifted up the carpet very carefully, so that the bomb underneath would not go off."

Dead bodies are mined.

> "Next to a place called Mustokhan nobody could touch or retrieve the body of the dead freedom fighter, because they were afraid of the body being booby-trapped. A 16–17-year-old sister went up to the body, and she was blown up with the body of her brother. We simply had to pick up the pieces and put them in a sack."[23]

Houses are mined.

> "When the Russians entered the houses, they put small bombs inside suitcases and briefcases. When children and women picked them up, they exploded. I had retreated from the village with the mujahedin. Then the Russian forces came. They entered the village and put the bombs. When we came back, we found the dead bodies and the bombs, on door frames, under couches. I saw it myself." (Mohammad Zaher, thirty-five, farmer from Qala-e Shadad, Jaghatu District, Ghazni Province; interviewed in Quetta, 3 October 1984)

Almost from the start of the Afghan conflict, reports began circulating about the use of "toy bombs," mines disguised as toy trucks or dolls, or as pens, watches, chewing gum, combs, and other everyday objects. Sardar Gul, a thirteen-year-old refugee schoolboy now in Pakistan, described how two of his friends, brothers named Rafiq and Atiq, were killed when they picked up something yellow and round, about the size of a film container. "My father saw many children killed by these toys," he added. "He was always warning us not to touch such things."

These lethal attractions, snatched up by curious, unsuspecting hands, explode in the children's faces. Sometimes they kill, but more often they maim. "The story is always the same," a doctor explained. "The children find something in the village, on the road. They play with it; it explodes. Usually it's a combination of hands, face, and eyes. Many of them lose both hands and a few lose their sight. It always looks like a little toy, a small car, something like that." He paused, then said angrily: "It is the most inhuman way of fighting. To give toys to children. To cause that crippling damage. This is very, very inhuman. And this is not something that happened once or twice, but many, many times."[24]

The practice of using toys to kill is so outrageous that many have refused to believe it. Yet we received scores of testimonies about such weapons, from credible witnesses who often had no notion of the significance of what they were reporting. It is the Afghan government itself, however, that has provided physical evidence of the toy weapons. At a press conference in Kabul, reported in the Soviet newspaper *Krasnaya Zvezda* on 12 June 1985, the Afghan government's official press agency BAKHTAR described the toy mines as "terror methods" used by "imperialism" against Afghanistan. Although victims of the toy mines have never been able to produce samples because the "evidence" self-destructs, the Afghan news agency was apparently able to mount a sizable display of lethal pens, dolls, cigarette lighters, and watches. It also exhibited miniature explosives that could be used to booby-trap keyholes and a tiny explosive that looked like an ordinary pebble.

> Kabul—At a press conference organized in Kabul by the Afghan news agency BAKHTAR, new evidence was presented of the terror methods that are a key element of the undeclared war waged by imperialism against the DRA. The instruments of terror, exhibited in the hall where the press conference was held, did not outwardly resemble weapons. However, as soon as you take off the cap of a Flowmaster pen, move an arm or a leg on a doll, try to use a lighter to light a cigarette, or attempt to set a watch, an internal explosive device will go off. There was also a set of miniature explosive devices used to booby-trap keyholes—the device explodes as soon as the key comes in contact with it—and a booby trap that looked like an ordinary pebble. . . .
>
> The press conference showed that the exhibited instruments of terror were intended for use against the civilian population. No matter what tricks the inspirers of the aggression use to feign love for the Afghan people, no matter how hard they try to masquerade as their protectors, they cannot hide their true, murderers' faces.[25]

The hospitals of Peshawar continue to receive children and others who have lost limbs owing to antipersonnel mines. The Soviets distribute such mines from the air, usually by helicopter, or have them placed by ground troops. In addition, according to reports from both Laghman and Paktia provinces, mines are also being distributed from land-based artillery shells. In an interview in Peshawar on 20 August 1985, Syed Fazl Akbar, former director of Radio Kabul and of the Pashto service of Radio Moscow, now director of the Afghan Information and Documentation Centre in Peshawar, described artillery shells distributing such mines in Paktia Province during an offensive in August 1985.

Others have also described the ways in which the mines are distributed:

> "They left mines in the shape of a watch, a pen, a thousand afghani note, a tape recorder, a radio, a camera, small balls for hockey, and a type of bird that children keep. Yes, they did it this year right up until now. When the troops leave the area they distribute these things by air and also by artillery. Mostly children and goats get hurt, but some mujahedin also lost their feet." (Testimony of Said Mohammad, son of Gul Mohammad, farmer, thirty-six, Omarzai village, Central Laghman District, Laghman; interviewed in Munda refugee camp, NWFP, 21 August 1985)

We received numerous reports of the damage wrought by mines disguised as toys or everyday objects:

"My friend picked one up and lost an arm. Then we understood why the pens were scattered all over the road. When the operations are over, they scatter these materials. . . . There are also shiny tins that explode; they look like this snuff box." (Nur Beg, an elder from Darra-e Nur, near Jalalabad, Nangarhar Province; interviewed in Peshawar, September 1986)

In the cliffside house that serves as a base for my particular band of Muj [mujahedin], a young guerrilla medic works to save the mauled hand of a local 14-year-old boy. When the Soviet armor and paratroops were here last week, they left behind some booby-trapped toys, on the off chance there were some children left in Jegdeleg [Nangarhar Province] to pick them up. This boy found a bright red plastic truck by the river and made the mistake of grabbing it. It must have been defective, because his hand—though a bloody, torn, skinless mess— still has all of its digits. The medic is washing and rebandaging it daily, trying to ward off infection.[26]

"I know it is true. It happened to one of my relations in Kabul. About eighteen months ago this eight- or nine-year-old child was playing in the street near his home, near Microraion. He picked up something that looked like a toy, and it exploded." (Testimony of Shah Mahmud Baasir, economist; interviewed in Quetta, 3 October 1984)

Dr. Jacques David of Médécins sans Frontières told us on 8 June 1984 that while he was working at the dispensary in Jaghori in 1981 he had to amputate two fingers of a five-year-old boy who had picked up what looked like a toy. The boy's parents showed Dr. David the twisted and charred remnants of a small, red, metal truck.

Edward Girardet of *The Christian Science Monitor* reported that an Aide Médicale Internationale doctor saw the metallic fragments of a booby-trapped watch that had severed the foot of one of her companions on the march into Panjsher in August 1981.

Dr. Gilles Albanel of Aide Médicale Internationale testified at the March 1983 Afghanistan Hearings in Oslo:

"Prior to the offensive [of January 1983 in Logar] we were asked to see a person 60 years old who had picked up a fountain pen on the road and the next day wanted to see whether this fountain pen actually worked. It exploded in his hands. It was an antipersonnel mine. He had lost three fingers of his left hand."[27]

Médécins sans Frontières nurse Eric Valls was told by a nurse working in the Afghan government hospital in Faizabad, Badakhshan, that he regularly saw patients who had lost limbs owing to mines disguised as pens, watches, cigarette lighters, and coins.

We also received firsthand reports from refugees in Pakistan, who pointed to our pens and watches to show us what the mines looked like. Kefayatullah, a farmer from Harioki Ulya, Kapisa Province, was describing the actions of the Soviet troops that invaded his village. "They put toy bombs in the food storage bins," he volunteered. "Some of them exploded. They were like toys, watches, pens."

Hafizullah, of the same village, said: "There is a type of bomb like a radio. They leave it on a stand with a wire. If you touch it, or if your feet touch the wire, it goes off. If I had been there, I would have been killed. But I know people injured by mines left in the houses in my village. Some were killed, and others were handicapped."

Another refugee from Bela in Nangarhar described similar mines, amid a chorus of affirmation from fellow villagers who had gathered around him during the following account: "They left small bombs like pens, knives, watches. When people picked them up, they lost their hand or leg. I saw it myself. The helicopters dropped pens, or something else that was a mine. The pens were red and green. Some were the colors of wheat fields, green and yellow. There were also combs. The pen looked just like the pen you are writing with. The watch was just like my watch."

In an August 1985 interview in Peshawar, two nurses with Médécins sans Frontières, Rudy Seynaeve and Marie Basuyan, described some civilian victims of antipersonnel mines whom they encountered in Afghanistan in 1985:

> Rudy Seynaeve testified: "It was on January 6 [1985], after a period of about ten days' occupation of the valley of Zari in the north of Afghanistan, that government troops turned back, and they left only one little post behind with about one hundred men. But before the valley, in the valley, and the bazaar, and everywhere they had been, there were mines, big and little mines. They described to me some as big as a plate you can eat out of, and when you touch the mine, when you are walking on it, it blows one foot away. . . . We have had a victim of a mine that must have been laid in the same period, in the same valley, Zari."
>
> Marie Basuyan added: "It was an antipersonnel bomb, a small one, khaki. . . . The Russians had spread a large quantity of these antipersonnel mines. They [the victims] said that it was small, like a matchbox. It was small, khaki, in different shapes, it could be square, round. And he lost his hand."
>
> Seynaeve, having found the notation in his diary, continued: "Yes, the 29th of January, that Nur Ahmad, eighteen years old, from Aq Kupruq, arrived with half of his right hand away, already twenty days ago he said. So approximately the 9th of January there had been jets above Aq Kupruk, and he said two big enormous bombs they let fall. The bombs they opened in the air, and out of them little things are falling. And he said approximately 120, he said, little, kind of khaki colored, little things, big as

a box of matches. You touch it, and you lose three fingers, half a thumb, even more, half of a hand. But he was the only one that got wounded, because all the others had been destroyed by means of sticks and stones. Children were using them, they threw rocks at them. It's approximately the same time that Alphonse [a Belgian journalist] wrote us a letter, and he said that Aq Kupruq had been bombarded as a reprisal, because a weapon transport had passed by."

Basuyan said, "There's the story of the soap, also." Seynaeve continued: "It looks ridiculous, it must have been 20 January, that in Kishindeh one man was killed by exploding soap. It means, they have a kind of rough soap they they wash the clothes with. They hold it, and they rub it in the clothes, and they said there must have been something, an explosive in the soap, and when you have rubbed a certain amount, it exploded. He was killed. It looks strange, but they have told it seriously. They were not laughing at it. We have only heard of one case like this. They say, we don't know if they are really fantastic—James Bond—or if it happens.

"Something else, we had another victim of an antipersonnel mine that must have been left by the Russian troops in January, but it only happened somewhere in May. The 9th of May in Zari an old man, a 'white beard' as they say, fifty-six years old, something like this—he had the age of my father—was digging an irrigation canal, and he found a mine, and it exploded, and he lost his leg. He lost his leg, but he had a lot of wounds, because the bones of the leg that was exploded, pieces of bomb were, you could find them everywhere in his body, in his arms, he had a lot of small injuries, but a lot of them, throughout his arms and the other leg and everywhere the bone of his own leg was flying around and made wounds all over his body. This must have been a mine that the Russian troops had left there when they went away in January." "He died," said Basuyan. "Yes," Seynaeve said. "He died also."

Arrest, Forced Conscription, and Torture

During offensives or sweeping operations, Soviet and Afghan troops often arrest men of fighting age. They may be imprisoned in temporary detention camps in the field or turned over to the KHAD for interrogation about the resistance. Most of them are ultimately inducted into the Afghan Army, often regardless of age or previous military service. Such forced conscription is necessary because of the army's high desertion rate. Men are forcibly enrolled and even killed in action without their families knowing anything, other than that soldiers took them away one day.

Some prisoners are subjected to more thorough interrogation in KHAD jails in Kabul or in regional centers, where they undergo intensive torture, followed by imprisonment or execution. Those who are released from prison may then be forcibly conscripted without notification of their families. Torture is also used by Soviet forces during offensives, sometimes with the help of Afghan interpreters, to elicit information from the villagers about the resistance.

The Afghan militia and KHAD also arrest refugees en route to Pakistan. They are imprisoned in KHAD detention centers and sometimes tortured. Those that are released (sometimes after paying large bribes) are sent back to their villages or forcibly resettled. We received reports that some internal refugees, including refugees from the Panjsher Valley, have been imprisoned for resisting forced resettlement.

"We received information that there were 'dushmans' or 'Islamic Committees' in a village. Usually we used a whole battalion. We drove in APCs to the village, and the infantry would sweep the village in a house-to-house search, looking for weapons. If we found people with weapons, we took them. The second time we arrested four men in their forties. The soldiers were pushing them and beating them, just because they were angry. We brought them to a post of the Afghan militia [run by KHAD]. We were told that the militia 'would know what to do with them.' " (Pvt. Sergei Zhigalin, Soviet Army defector; interviewed in New York City, 3 May 1984)

"On 2 Sawr 1362 [22 April 1983] I was captured in a blockade by some Russian and Parchami soldiers. I was with the mujahedin, close to the road, but I didn't have a weapon. Some spies told where we were. After I was captured, I was beaten with Kalashnikovs, and they kept asking if I was a mujahed. The Russians pointed a gun at me and took Af 1,000. Then they took me to KHAD in Pol-e Khomri. This KHAD was the center for the Russians in Pol-e Khomri. They were living there. They asked me more questions. They dug a hole in the ground and made me stand in cold water. There were two Russians and a Khalqi translator. They asked me, 'Where did you put your weapons? How many people did you kill? What party do you belong to?' After a few days they brought me to Kabul, to the office where they put you in the army. They sent me to the army base in Moqor, Ghazni. One evening they called me in to dinner, and I said I had to relieve myself and found a way to escape." (Aziz Khan, thirty-five, farmer from Dasht-e Guhar, Baghlan; interviewed in Peshawar, 25 September 1984)

"I knew a young man from my village, I know his mother, I know his wife and child. I treated his child several times. This boy was taken with other people during the searching of the houses by the Russians [in Logar Province in September 1982]. He was taken to the area of Shikar Qala. They made a camp there for a few days. When they took the people—hundreds, maybe—they started to torture them there. This boy I knew was crying because of the beating. And there was someone else in another tent, and he heard his voice, he was crying, shouting in a very loud voice, 'Anyone who hears this should get a message to my family. I have an old mother and a wife and small child. I'm sure they are killing me. My small amount of money is with such-and-such a shopkeeper. Anyone who hears my voice should inform my family so my wife can get the money.' And so he was killed there. After they left the area, the people went and got his body. The man I knew was taken to Kabul and sent to the military, and he slipped back from the military. Then he brought this message." (Dr. Ghazi Alam; interviewed in New York City, 30 March 1984)

Qadratullah, thirty-nine, a farmer and mujahed from Qala-e Murad Beg, a village just north of Kabul, was arrested by a mixed Soviet-Afghan army unit in his village in the summer of 1983 and taken in a Soviet armored vehicle to the Sedarat (Prime Ministry) Palace in Kabul, where the main KHAD inter-rogation center for the entire country is housed. In an interview in Peshawar on 29 September 1984, Qadratullah told us how he was intensively tortured by a team of two Russians and a Parchami. He was sentenced to a year in prison. Upon his release from prison he was inducted into the army and sent to Kandahar, from which, after three months, he escaped with a group of twenty-six other soldiers.

The torture methods used in the countryside are sometimes quite so-phisticated, not unlike those used in the cities. Mullah Feda Mohammad de-scribed his experience when he was taken to a temporary command center near Kandahar:

"After some beating the [Soviet] soldiers took me to a small container. There they put several straps around my ankles and wrists, then they put a small box on my head and tied it there. After that they put one string [wire] in one black box, and immediately I felt a strong shock. The shock was so huge that I shouted loudly, without any shame from my fellow villagers who were still outside in the Qila [small fort]. They repeated the shocks several times, then the translator came to the small room in the car and told me, if you do not cooperate with us, we will kill you in such a terrible way."

The Soviet soldiers also tied a noose around his neck, threw the rope over a mulberry tree, and pretended they were about to hang him. This went on for twenty minutes.[28]

In a 23 July 1984 interview, Dr. Robert Simon, an American specialist in emergency medicine who ran a clinic in Konarha Province in May 1984, de-scribed an old man who had lost his toes:

"He actually came for another complaint, but I asked him how he had lost his toes. He told me that the Russian soldiers made him stand barefoot in the snow while they asked him where the mujahedin were."

A French doctor, Gilles Albanel, treated a victim of interrogation during the Logar offensive of January 1983.

"The next night, January 23rd, in the village below our refuge in the mountains which I mentioned, we saw a man, fifty years old, who had three gunshot wounds which were over a week old, one in the wrist, the leg, and in the arm. We had to amputate in this case. The conditions of his accident of wounding: this man and three others had been interrogated by a Soviet officer—he had been interrogated through an interpreter—and he was asked where the French doctors were. After the questioning, these four old men did not reveal the information which was required, they were put up against the wall and executed."[29]

In an August 1985 interview in Peshawar, a defector from the Interior Ministry who had worked in military radio communications as well as in Pol-e Charkhi Prison in Kabul described what is considered standard procedures after a village is destroyed by planes and troops:

"Then the ambulance helicopter comes. They try to surround the village and capture anyone and put them in the ambulance helicopter—women, children, old men, they put them in the helicopter and send them to Kabul, to Pol-e Charkhi Prison, to the central zone [zon-e markazi]. Farmers, old people, and so on go first to Pol-e Charkhi. To [the central KHAD interrogation office in] Sedarat they bring the political prisoners.

"In the central zone of Pol-e Charkhi Prison there are some Afghan police and also Soviets who speak Pashto, Hazaragi, Persian. These are KGB officers trained in Afghan languages in Russia. They interrogate the people and give them electric shocks with a machine. They use electric chairs and ask them, 'Where are the ashrar?' Among those people some may be physically or mentally weak, so they tell about the mujahedin bases. Some who can control themselves don't say anything until they die. In this way they find the people who are helping the mujahedin, and they clear those with no links to the mujahedin. For this reason they also call it the 'clearance zone' [zon-e tasfiwi]. It belongs to the Ministry of Internal Affairs.

"When they find that some of them are linked to the mujahedin, they transfer them to KHAD, and KHAD has other branches and other methods of torture.

"I was working in Pol-e Charkhi as a member of the administration, and I was also imprisoned in Pol-e Charkhi, and I had colleagues who were working there. I have seen the evidence with my own eyes, and some of my Muslim colleagues also told me about it. I saw with my own eyes that to this central zone they are not bringing the ordinary criminals from the cities. They brought people from the districts and subdistricts when the troops undertook operations. I myself visited the 'clearance zone' in the center of Pol-e Charkhi."

Rape and Mistreatment of Women

Afghans are generally reluctant to discuss the subject of rape. In recent years, however, there have been a number of reports of rapes by Soviet soldiers during searches and massacres, as well as reports of other forms of brutality directed specifically against women. From the sketchy evidence we have, it appears that rape is generally not part of the systematic attacks on the villages but the result of unrestrained behavior by an undisciplined occupation army.

We have also received reports of rape and abduction in the city of Kabul. These reports, unlike those from the countryside, implicate Afghan party members as well as Soviets. There are also some reports of rape and molestation of women in the prisons.

Pregnant women have been singled out for particular brutality during massacres. Survivors of the December 1984 massacres in Chardara District, Kunduz, told Dr. Juliette Fournot of Soviet soldiers disemboweling three pregnant women with bayonets. During searches the previous week a number of women had reportedly been raped.

A man from Jalalabad testified:

> "At Charbagh [Laghman] I had a friend called Gul Haidar. In the past we hunted together. I heard about his death in the latest Russian operations. I went to Charbagh to help his family. [The man from Jalalabad broke into tears.] At Charbagh the neighbors of Gul Haidar told me that when the Russians went inside his house, his wife was in the process of giving birth to a child. After the departure of the Soviet troops, the neighbors found everybody dead: bullet holes all over Gul Haidar's body, his wife and her belly torn open and the newborn baby horribly multilated."[30]

Another refugee testified:

> "In Shahmangal, the Russians took pregnant women and asked them, 'What's in your stomach? A grenade? A mine?' The woman would turn her face away, because Afghan people don't talk like that. The Russian said, 'There's a hand grenade of mine in your stomach.' Then they took bayonets and stabbed them in the stomach, killing the unborn baby and the mother." (Testimony of refugee from Qarghai District, Laghman; unpublished interview with Rob Schultheis)

Anders Fange, director of the Peshawar office of the Swedish Committee for Afghanistan, recounted the following story, which he reconstructed from accounts by refugees he met inside Afghanistan on 29 July 1984:

"On our way out, we reached Kantewa Pass in the early morning, and we ran into a huge caravan of people, camels, old ladies, eight- and nine-year-old children carrying babies. The camels were falling down, the donkeys were screaming. We walked faster than the caravan, and when we reached the top of the pass we looked back and saw about five thousand people. I first spoke to Abdul Ma'aruf of Askalan village, Amal subdistrict of Kunduz. [The refugees were all from this area.] He said that a Russian adviser was captured and killed by the mujahedin. Other people said he had been killed by a mine. Then in April or May the Russians came to Amal in force." Abdul Ma'aruf went on to describe how the Soviet troops had burned the fields, destroyed food, robbed people of money, and, in an incident corroborated by several witnesses, cut the throats of twelve children one by one while asking villagers for money. "This was one of the few occasions when men told me that their women had been raped. They don't like to say it. I checked the story with others. It differed in some details, but mainly it was the same." (Interview in Peshawar, 16 August 1985)

Several refugees told tales of rape.

"Last year in Jauza [May–June] they took twenty-one old people from Alishang to another village—Ren village. They covered their eyes with plastic and killed them. They had some money with them, so they took the money and killed them. When they came back to the village [Alishang], they raped the ladies and killed the children with bayonets. They tried to rape Ghulam Ali's wife, but she escaped. They raped Mahmadullah's wife, Razaq's wife. When some ladies escaped from them they killed the children with bayonets [he demonstrated two upward strokes of a bayonet] and kicked the bodies, just to play with them, a girl eight years old and a boy five years old." The girl was Siddiqa, daughter of his brother, Aminullah. The boy was his own son, Mirwais. (Testimony of Ataullah, son of Mullah Abdullah, Kalacha village, Laghman; interviewed in Munda refugee camp, NWFP, 21 August 1985)

"When coming to Pakistan, in Musavi, there was someone crying. I asked, 'What happened?' He said that there was someone who had been going to Kabul. From the other direction a Russian convoy was coming, and the Soviets stopped his bus. During the search a Soviet uncovered his wife's face. As she had gotten married recently, they laughed at her and took her away from her husband. Her husband tried everything he could to get her back, but they told him, 'Tomorrow at eight o'clock we'll bring you your wife here.' The boy went home and informed his parents. Next day in the morning, he came there with a big knife, waiting for the Soviets. When the tank arrived, the woman was set down from the tank. She was injured, and her face was bruised. She told her husband, 'I have lost everything. I have lost face. Kill me.' He started to kill her. The Soviets fired at him with Kalashnikovs. His parents, who wanted to take revenge for him, were holding an ax, in his father's hand, but they could not take revenge.

Instead they were shot dead by the Soviets. All were buried there. Peace be upon them." (Testimony of Ghausuddin, seventy-three, artist; interviewed in Islamabad, 28 August 1985)

"We left [Kabul] because a group of Russians, about eleven or twelve of them, coming from Kolula Pushta and Bagh-e Bala started to search houses. Then they came to Taimani and reached Mu-e Mubarak. They were searching in Taimani [where the witness lived], and in five houses they attempted rape. There was no Afghan government guide with them, only one Hazara boy, who was seventeen or sixteen years old, and it looked like they had paid him to show them the houses. They were trying to steal the valuable things from the people and tried to rape them. So when my father found that they were searching the houses and committing these crimes, he decided to leave Afghanistan. [This was in Sawr (April–May) 1984.]

"At the beginning of 1363 [around March–April 1984], three ladies were walking early in the morning in Khairkhana to go to the hamam [bathhouse]. They were taken to a tank and disappeared for a month. Their husbands were searching for them. After that one of the ladies was found, and she lived for only an hour and a half more. She told about what happened to the others, and then she died. She said that the other two had been with her, receiving the same treatment, so they had also died. These were Russians who had taken them. The residence of these ladies was in Kala-e Najaran in Khairkhana, and I was also living there at the time. This story is the truth, but I don't know their names.

"Near Mu-e Mubarak, in Taimani ward, three girls were walking along the road, and a Russian tank came up from behind them and stopped. They tried to put the girls in the tank. When they took one girl, she fought back, and there were some boys, students, maybe from the Teachers' Training College or some faculty, and they came to help the girls. Those students got some sticks from nearby shops. Then a jeep came up behind the tank, and a crowd gathered to see what was going on. So they didn't manage to get the girls in the tank. From the Russian jeep they started shooting. Two of the girls were killed, a vegetable seller was killed, a shopkeeper, and another girl was wounded, and eleven students were killed, and some other people walking along the road were also injured. I saw this with my own eyes in Mu-e Mubarak, Taimani ward, as I told you before, in Jauza 1362 [May–June 1983]." (Testimony of Fariba Hamidi, twenty-one, nurse of Taimani ward, Kabul; interviewed in Peshawar, 22 August 1985)

"About one o'clock in the afternoon some students from Zarghuna Lycée [a well-known girls' school in Kabul] were walking home. A Soviet APC came and pulled off a Hindu girl, put her in the APC, and drove away. Until now no one has seen her again. This was in the summer of 1362 [1983]." (Testimony of former teacher from Kabul; interviewed in Peshawar, 25 August 1985)

"Another story happened in 1361 [1982]. In Deh Sabz [a village close to the Kabul airport] there is a place where the women draw water from a spring. Two helicopters flew over. One was scouting, and the other landed. They took away two beautiful young girls in the helicopter and flew away. Three days later a helicopter appeared and dropped the bodies of these girls from the air. The man who told me was my tenant farmer. I have some land in Deh Sabz." (Testimony of former military communications officer; interviewed in Peshawar, 25 August 1985)

"They committed rape many times in Kabul. In Khairkhana there were two girls going to the *hamam*.[31] Some Russian soldiers attacked them and were putting them in a tank. There were some people with donkeys, bringing vegetables to the bazaar, and they came at the Russians with shovels, hitting them. The Russians killed two men like that, but the girls got away. I saw this myself in the winter of 1981.

"Another incident was in Dar-ul-Aman. I didn't see it. They took two women and kept them for a week. Then they both were dead, and they left their bodies in the fields. Some villagers found them and went to the government, but nobody told the Russians anything. Some of these villagers came to Pakistan after that, because they were afraid for their women. All the people in Kabul know this story—they took the bodies to the Presidential Palace. It happened many, many times. They took seven *kuchi* [nomad] girls another time, and their bodies were found ten, fifteen days later." (Testimony of Ata-ur-Rahman Dadgar; interviewed in Peshawar, 22 September 1984)

Killing and Abuse of Children

Children are among the most victimized in the Afghan struggle. They are bombed in their schools and during religious instruction in the mosques. Children have been shot while fleeing to caves in the mountains or en route to refuge in Pakistan or Iran. There are reports of children burned alive in locked rooms, their charred bodies unrecognizable by their parents. Unborn children have been bayoneted to death in their mother's wombs.

"A tank exploded, the work of mujahedin. The Russians then went into a small village and began to slaughter people. Women and children were bayoneted. They asked the mothers: who placed the mine? When they wouldn't talk, they bayoneted the children. In every house, it was the same . . . children in cradles and children who could walk. I arrived right after it happened and saw it myself." (Testimony of Tajwar Kakar, a thirty-eight-year-old schoolteacher from Kabul, describing a February 1984 reprisal operation in Kunduz Province; interviewed in Peshawar in September 1986)

On 10 September 1986 Professor Felix Ermacora, the U.N. Human Rights Commission's Special Rapporteur on Afghanistan, visited the Said Gi transit camp in North Waziristan, on the Afghan border. While he was there, Afghan jets bombed a caravan of refugees that was approaching the border en route to Pakistan. The Pakistani official who accompanied Ermacora later described the scene:

> "We could hear the strafing and see the smoke. After forty-five minutes we saw the dead bodies coming in. There was a small child whose mother had died, about eleven or twelve months old. He was tied to a horse and his grandfather was riding with him." (Interview in North Waziristan, September 1986)

A *Washington Post* reporter inside Afghanistan heard the following account:

> In October [1985] the Soviets and Afghan Army troops staged a four-day sweep through Barakat [Ghazni Province] and nearby villages, killing 20 people and taking 12 young men to serve in the Afghan Army, villagers said.
>
> A young man from nearby Bedmoshk told a horrifying tale of Soviets who held a 14-year-old boy and slowly killed him when his parents would not pay a ransom. "They tied him to a tree and beat him and stabbed him with a bayonet," the man said. "Finally they shot him."[32]

Many Afghan children have become refugees within their own country, driven from their homes and villages and herded into cities, where they live confused and impoverished lives. Millions more have made the arduous journey to Pakistan, where they live in camps, without purpose or direction. Many of the children have had to walk for weeks or even months before finding refuge. They are without possessions, tired, often hungry. They bear visible scars of war—wounds, burns, amputated limbs, blindness—and there is anguish in their words.

> "My brother was taken under a tree and shot. Then they went inside. They killed my father and mother and wounded my sister. That was four years ago. I saw it all with my own eyes." (Mohammad Zaher, thirteen years old, from Shamali; interviewed in Peshawar in September 1986)
>
> "I was conscious when I saw my house burning, but after the next bomb was thrown, I remember nothing." (Abdul Qudus, ten years old, from Nuristan, Konarha Province; interviewed in Peshawar in September 1986)
>
> "When I came back, there was no village. I was the only one left. When I saw this I cried, cried and wept. When the planes left, the mujahedin

came back and said not to cry, they would be my father." (Abdul Karim, eight years old, from Taleqan, Takhar Province; interviewed in Peshawar in September 1986)

Atiqullah, a ten-year-old refugee, recently began school in Pakistan. He described how he had watched while his grandmother and aunt were stabbed with bayonets in their homes and then shot:

"We were standing right there. I was shouting and crying. He said something to us in Russian. We didn't understand. They pointed their rifles at us to keep us quiet."

Mike Hoover, a CBS television producer whom we met in Peshawar, told us he had filmed an interview with an Afghan who had formerly worked as a translator for the Soviet Army.

"He was extremely disturbed. He told how he had translated questions that the Russians were asking about the mujahedin while they held a child over a fire."

A refugee from Laghman Province told Rob Schultheis about the following atrocities during an interview in Munda refugee camp, NWFP, in May 1985:

"My name is Shir Dal, I am from the Kats area. I lost four members of my family—my sister's children, her husband, and her. The only thing left alive was one calf—they even killed chickens, pigeons, everything alive they killed. . . . When the Russians came, the children were hiding in a cave. One Parchami Communist man was with them, and helped bring the children out, and they burned them to death. . . . The children who were killed, their parents could not recognize them, because they were burned. They made fires with wood, and put the children in them, or put kerosene on children and burned them. Sometimes they killed children and then burned them, and sometimes they burned them alive. They were taking children out to the fields and burning them alive, and they put them in the rushes and burned them alive. Burned alive. . . .

"They hung one two- or three-week-old baby boy in a tree, bayoneted him and made the parents watch while they burned him; when the baby was dead, they shot the parents. One half-year-old boy and a seven-year-old girl, my sister's children, were killed. It was very cruel. They killed many people, and this is a story people should not forget."

3
DESTRUCTION OF THE RURAL ECONOMY

The Soviet-Afghan forces have pursued a determined campaign of destroying agriculture in Afghanistan. The devastation includes significant portions of at least Badakhshan, Konarha, Parwan, Kabul, Nangarhar, Logar, Paktia, Kandahar, Herat, Laghman, and Kunduz provinces. They employ various tactics, from the killing of individual farmers to the destruction of the delicate agricultural infrastructure in the Afghan countryside. These tactics not only spread terror, but also destroy the food supplies in the villages upon which the resistance depends for sustenance. Farmers are killed; food is destroyed; the means of food production is disrupted. Whole regions of Afghanistan have become barren.

This is a far cry from the image of mechanized agricultural progress that is projected in Soviet literature and the press.

> In this [column of tractors heading for Afghanistan] he saw the whole essence of the revolution sweeping the country: the tractors struck at the feudal structure, at the cooped-up potter's vessel baked in a thousand-year-old stove. And the people, turning their eyes away from the wooden ploughs, from the feudal fortresses and the mosques, would watch the big-eyed blue machines moving over the roads and would connect their appearance with their own rebirth from darkness.[1]

Killing of Farmers

Farmers working in the fields are targets for Soviet gunships or jets. Those who have not fled have had to reverse their normal work patterns, sleeping by day and working in the fields after dark.

Lala Dad, a farmer from Dasht-e Guhar, Baghlan, told us in a 25 September 1984 interview in Peshawar that Soviet jets usually came between ten and twelve o'clock in the morning, when "the people are in the fields. They kill them whenever they find them, wherever they find them. Rostam was killed—he was a farmer—while he was trying to get rid of some weeds."

Dr. Juliette Fournot of Médécins sans Frontières, in an interview in Paris on 8 June 1984, described what she saw during a July 1982 visit to the Panjsher Valley:

> "Because of the bombing, the people hid in caves during the day, and they only came out with their animals at night to work in the fields with kerosene lanterns."

Hafizullah, a farmer from Harioki Ulya, Kapisa, told us in Peshawar on 23 September 1984:

> "We have to do the agricultural work in secret. Whenever the people go to work in the fields, if the planes come, they are shot. Some have been killed working in the fields, about ten to twelve in my district."

Dr. Patrick David of Aide Médicale Internationale in an interview in Peshawar on 25 September 1986 recounted how, during the Logar offensive in early September 1984, Soviet helicopters killed harvesters in the fields with rockets.

Sayed Azim of Maidan, interviewed in Peshawar on 25 September 1984, said:

> "The mujahedin try to cultivate the earth, but the Soviets don't let them plow. The Soviets shoot the farmers in the fields."

Nicholas Danziger, a British art historian who traveled through war-torn Afghanistan, told us in a 28 September 1984 interview in Peshawar:

> "The people come to work the fields at night, they wash the clothes at night, they bake the bread at night. And they ask, 'What are we going to do this winter when the snow comes?' "

Destruction of Food Supplies

> "Right now is harvest time, and the Soviets are burning the harvests. I am also from a village, you know, and this happened to my cousin just one month ago, and now they are here. In Dasht-e Archi—this is the *uluswali*, the district [in Kunduz]—they burned more than one hundred fields of

wheat. And those farmers are refugees right now in Pakistan. They live in Haripur [refugee camp] because they haven't anything left. The main time they are attacking is this time, and also early summer. Early summer is the sowing time, to put seed in the ground, and this is the harvest time." (Testimony of a former executive of a government corporation dealing with agriculture; interviewed in Peshawar, 19 August 1985)[2]

Wheat, the staple food of the Afghans, has traditionally been grown on fifty percent of the irrigated land and most of the dry-farmed land in Afghanistan. It is also the crop that has been most heavily destroyed by Soviet attacks since the invasion. As early as 17 March 1980, an old woman from Surkhrud, near Jalalabad, Nangarhar Province, told Michael Barry, an American specialist on Afghanistan:

"The wheat! The harvest is all burnt! And they killed our children! And on our fruit trees they threw something like containers of gasoline, and all of the trees burned down!"[3]

An economist now working with one of the relief committees in Peshawar said in a September 1984 interview that he had seen the early stages of this strategy in November 1980 in northern Afghanistan, when he traveled from Kabul to his parents' home in Mazar-e Sharif.[4]

"Between Kabul and Mazar was a fertile green area with a lot of gardens. They had leveled everything—buildings, trees—and there were mines by the road. They started the hunger tactic at that time. I saw one harvest burned. There were only ashes left by the highway. This was near Rabatak. Later I took refuge in a tea house, while the Soviet post was firing with *dashakas* [machine guns]. Five kilometers from the post was a big harvest, and they burned the harvest. It belonged to a very rich man named Khwaja Kabuli. It was burning all through the night, until morning. It was four kilometers from the highway—the mujahedin couldn't ambush the convoys from there. If was just to produce scarcity of foodstuffs."

Since then the burning of wheat fields has become part of almost every offensive and reprisal operation. Every month there are a number of reports in the *Afghan Information Centre Monthly Bulletin*, each repeating the same story: a village was bombed; people were killed; the wheat was burned.

"Until we were forced we wouldn't leave our homes and country. They used napalm bombs and burned all the crops. My house was bombed, and all the property in the house was destroyed. They burned the ripe wheat fields in the month of Sawr [April–May]. In the Kats area of Laghman they destroyed about 2,000 houses. And they totally destroyed the area. Until now there is no one living there. Until now the empty beds are sitting on the rooftops, because there is no one left there alive." (Testimony of Said Mohammad, son of Gul Mohammad, farmer, thirty-six, Omarzai village, central Laghman District, Laghman; interviewed in Munda refugee camp, NWFP, 21 August 1985)

Refugees tell of wheat being burned in the field, on threshing floors, in houses, and on trucks. We were also told of wheat being poisoned in Maidan:

"In houses of famous [resistance] commanders, they put poison in the wheat flour. This September they did it in Mirza Khan's house. One year ago they did the same thing. Last year some people died—Abdullah and his family. Now we tell the people, if the Russians have been in the house, to throw away the wheat flour." (Sayed Azim, former government official; interviewed in Peshawar, 25 September 1984)

Initially the Soviets appear to have used a form of napalm to destroy the wheat. Hafizullah, a farmer from Harioki Ulya, told us about a special type of bomb that "hits the ground and starts a fire." Some farmers, he said, dig ditches around stacks of wheat gathered for threshing and keep them filled with water so that they can put out such fires quickly.

Louis Dupree, an anthropologist who lived in Afghanistan for fifteen years before the coup in 1978, has investigated the specialized weapons used to destroy crops in Afghanistan. He has described two types of bombs which, when exploded, scatter pellets of phosphorus over a wide area, increasing the amount that can be burned: One type, which is used to destroy wheat that has been gathered for threshing, drying, or milling, explodes and scatters incendiary material on contact with the ground. The other type, used to burn crops standing in the field, is dropped by parachute and explodes in midair, scattering pellets over a wide area.

We also received reports of how Soviet soldiers during offensives destroy other kinds of food—sheep, chickens, eggs, oil, and sugar.[5] Dr. Ghazi Alam, whom we interviewed in New York City on 30 March 1984, described an incident in Baraki Barak in 1982:

"There was an old woman, who had no son in the house. There was only this old woman in the house, and she had to take care of the house as well as do all the agricultural work. She had a watermelon yard. And when the Russians came to the area, they didn't pick up one or two or three or four or five or ten watermelons from the ground. They took some, and the rest of the watermelons they hit with their bayonets, just to destroy them."

Destruction of the Agricultural Infrastructure

Like all peasant agriculture, Afghan agriculture depends on a complex system of balances involving nature and technology. The land requires constant maintenance to preserve proper drainage and prevent erosion; in some areas, it is carefully terraced. Soviet-Afghan forces have tried to destroy this delicate system of food production in some strategic areas.

In areas with plentiful water, such as the plains of the far north and around the dams on the Helmand and Kunar rivers, open ditches are used to irrigate the fields. In most of the country, however, an underground channel called a *karez* in Pashto (*qanat* in Persian) is more common. The *karez* brings water from nearby hills to cultivated flatlands through a series of underground wells connected by tunnels reinforced with ceramic hoops.[6] It requires constant maintenance against silting and cave-ins and is extremely vulnerable to bombing.

Animals are another element in the agricultural system: most plowing, threshing, and transport is done with the aid of beasts of burden, including oxen, cows, camels, horses, donkeys, and mules. Animals play an even more important role in the economy of the nomads, thought to constitute about ten percent of Afghanistan's population. Livestock—extensive herds of sheep and goats—are necessary for milk and meat and the wool that is used for clothing, carpets, and tents. They are also a major way of storing wealth. Fruit trees and vines are another vital part of Afghan agriculture, requiring years to reach maturity and careful watering and pruning to survive and keep yields high. Finally, there are the homes, social institutions and possessions of the villagers themselves: a roof to shelter them, a mosque for prayer, a blanket for winter, a Koran for study, a pot to boil water for rice and tea, and a stove to bake bread.

In contested areas of strategic importance, the Soviet-Afghan forces have systematically attacked every part of the agricultural system. They have destroyed the irrigation and terracing systems, as indicated in reports by observers such as Pål Hougen of the Norwegian Afghanistan Committee, who saw the destruction of terracing during his July–August 1982 visit to the Bashgul Valley of Konarha Province:

> "The irrigation system was disturbed by rockets, and so were the terraces, built through 100 generations to make this landscape fitted for men to live in."[7]

An article in the *Afghan Information Centre Monthly Bulletin* of July 1984 also described extensive damage to irrigation systems from bombing, as well as a number of cases where Soviet ground troops destroyed *karezes* with grenades. The famous vines and fruit trees of Kandahar Province, for example, are dying for lack of water because of damage to the irrigation systems. People from Maiwand and Sangsar districts of Kandahar reported that the Soviets had established military posts along the irrigation canals, preventing the residents from repairing or using them.

Sayed Azim, a former government official, said in an interview in Peshawar on 25 September 1984:

> "When the Russians came last year, they destroyed the *karezes*. They put bombs in them to destroy them. This year they are doing the same thing, for instance, in Busragh village."

There is also a deliberate policy of killing animals. In the same interview just quoted, Sayed Azim told us that in Maidan, whenever Soviet-Afghan convoys come through on the road to Ghazni and Kandahar, helicopters accompany them and shoot at the animals, whether there is fighting or not. French journalist Alain Chevalieras, interviewed in Peshawar on 22 September 1984, saw cattle destroyed by helicopters in the Sholgarah Valley of Balkh Province.

Lala Dad, a farmer from Baghlan interviewed in Peshawar on 25 September 1984, showed us documentation of a recent bombing raid in which 118 horses and mules were killed in his village. Others interviewed during that period, such as Hafizullah and Kefayatullah of Kapisa, women from Kohistan, and refugees from Batikot District of Nangarhar, described how Soviet soldiers during raids had killed sheep, cows, and other animals.

Olivier Roy reported in *Les nouvelles d'Afghanistan* in October–November 1983 that

> Soviet armored helicopters systematically machine-gun the villages and herds within a radius of 30 to 50 kilometers of the Soviet base at Chaghcharan [Ghor Province], especially in the winter, when the flocks are concentrated in the stables.

Many orchards have been demolished. One grim photograph of the Afghan war shows a turbaned man holding an antique rifle, surrounded by an arid field filled with the cutoff stumps of apricot and almond trees. It was taken north of Kandahar in the fall of 1982, where a representative of Amitié Franco-Afghane (AFRANE) was told that government troops had cut off the trees at a height of thirty centimeters in the autumn of 1980.[8]

Refugees from Shamali told us on 23 September 1984 how bombing had destroyed vineyards and orchards in that region. Sayed Azim described the destruction of the apple orchards of Maidan:

All the fruit trees are cut down. They cut them down when they shoot everywhere with bullets or BM-13s." (Interview in Peshawar, 25 September, 1984)

Shah Mahmud Baasir, an economist interviewed in Quetta on 3 October 1984, said:

> "The Soviets are cutting down fruit trees in Kandahar. In the very place where the prison is located they cut five or six very good fruit trees— apples, pomegranates, apricots—just because the mujahedin may hide behind trees and attack them."

Theft of Property

Perhaps the most direct method of forcing peasants off their land is simply to take away whatever they have. Michael Barry told the Afghanistan Hearings in Oslo of a village in Logar:

> "[In November 1982] I saw an enormous village by moonlight which had not been bombed, and yet there is not a single human being left alive in it. It was already snowing, and you could tell that there were no footsteps in the snow. It was a freezing night, and with my companions I explored the village, and all we found living in the villages was a single dog. One month later I was able to track down the people who had originally lived in this village in a Pakistan refugee camp, and they explained their story. . . . On August 30, 1982, the village was surrounded in the classical way by tanks, helicopters flying above. Young men of military age had been able to run away into the mountains on time, so all the people who were collected by the Soviet troops were elderly villagers, farmers, women, and children. The soldiers did not kill anybody this time, they simply stripped every single person in the village that they could lay their hands on of anything valuable he had on, whether jewelry or wristwatches. Houses were searched, and all transistor radios were confiscated. The granaries were emptied, all sacks of grain, finally all the sheep, all the goats, all the cattle were loaded onto military lorries and taken away. By nightfall the population of Aochakan [Ab-e Chakan in standard Persian] had to take stock of the fact that they had nothing left with which to survive the coming winter. An assembly was held that evening. It was feared that the Soviets could come back this time to pressgang the young men into service, and it was decided that the best thing for the villagers to do would be to abandon everything and go to Pakistan."[9]

Afghan villagers we interviewed in Peshawar in September 1984 described systematic theft and destruction of property by Soviet soldiers sweeping through their villages. Bibi Makhro of Chardara, Kunduz, told how Soviet soldiers had stolen sewing machines, watches, and money. Lala Dad of Baghlan said that Soviet soldiers "broke china and all expensive possessions." Kefayatullah of Kapisa said the Russians "took all the expensive things, tapes, watches, money, and fruits. They walked up to old men and said, 'Give us bakhshish [alms or a bribe].' " He added that "they also burned the mosque and tore apart the Holy Koran. They tore up my own copy of the Holy Koran! I found the torn pages in my house."[10] A woman from Kapisa told us: "The Russians came while I was cooking dinner. They asked, 'Where is your husband?' They broke dishes and glasses, killed animals, and burned the rugs."

This is not the first time an invader has used these tactics in Afghanistan. In the thirteenth century Genghis Khan swept through the country, leaving silted irrigation canals and devastated cities as his monuments.[11] There is an ominous resemblance between the devastation of Genghis Khan and the destruction of today, as in this description by Dr. Fournot of a village in the Panjsher Valley:

> "In the village you could not find one house intact. No doors, nothing left; just walls were standing. It was smelling horrible, of dead bodies. It was smelling of death. It was the season of the apricots. Apricots were all falling down, and there was nobody to pick them. And everywhere there was . . . putrefaction."

4
TORTURE AND KILLING OF PRISONERS OF WAR

Prisoners of war must at all times be humanely treated. Any unlawful act or omission by the Detaining Power causing death or seriously endangering the health of a prisoner of war in its custody is prohibited and will be regarded as a serious breach of the present Convention. . . . Measures of reprisal against prisoners of war are prohibited.

Geneva Conventions

The war in Afghanistan is a war without fronts. It is also a war without rules. From reports we have received, it seems apparent that combatants on both sides assume they will be killed if taken prisoner. And there is evidence that they are correct. Attempts by the International Committee of the Red Cross (ICRC) since 1981 to negotiate prisoner exchanges met with some initial cooperation from the resistance forces but were informally suspended when there was no reciprocity on the Soviet-Afghan side.

Abuses by Soviet and Afghan Government Forces

According to Sgt. Igor Rykov, a Soviet Army defector interviewed in *Le Monde*, 3–4 June 1984: "We did not take any prisoners of war. None." The testimonies of other former Soviet soldiers confirm this statement. Former Soviet Army Pvt. Nikolai Ryzhov, when asked how Soviet forces treated Afghan prisoners, replied, "They destroy [*unichtozhayut*] them"[1]

Former Soviet Army Pvt. Garik Muradovich Dzhamalbekov witnessed the following incident in February 1982, while he was stationed with a company of the 121st Brigade, headquartered in Mazar-e Sharif, at a post on the road between Rabatak and Samangan in Samangan Province in northern Afghanistan:

"Three Afghan trucks were coming with dried fruit toward Mazar-e Sharif. Our commander, Captain Rudenko, from Zhdanov in Donbas, Ukraine, and some soldiers stopped those trucks and asked for a report. The truck driver, who was a spy, said, 'There are twelve Afghans standing by the road, two of them with weapons, ten of them without arms. They stopped the trucks, and they asked to go to Samangan.' Capt. Rudenko took some APCs, went toward Rabatak, and captured those twelve Afghans. He brought them back close to the garrison. Capt. Rudenko was drunk. It was about four or five o'clock in the afternoon. They took their weapons and ammunition, searched them and took some knives, everything they had. Then they tied them up, laid them down in the road, and Capt. Rudenko gave the order to drive the APCs over them. I saw the vehicles coming back all covered with blood. Once they kill them, they are just meat, and they left them for the jackals to come at night. They just cleared them off the road and dropped the bodies beside the road. At nine o'clock the commander was even more drunk, and he went back again. He cut off the head of one body, a mullah with a long beard. He brought the head back and said, 'Look, I've brought some fish.' He gave it to one of the soldiers with some gasoline. The whole night they were pouring gasoline on the head and burning it, and in the morning it was just ash." (Interview in Peshawar, 21 September 1984)[2]

Former Soviet Army Pvt. Vladislav Naumov had just finished repairing two combat vehicles in a post on the Kabul-Jalalabad road in May 1983 when he heard some cursing.

"Two soldiers were chasing a man whose hands were tied. The man's face was swollen, there were fresh scratches, his mouth was bleeding. They brought the Afghan prisoner to the tanks and forced him to his knees. 'Well, what shall we do with him?' Two noncommissioned officers had arrived. They were drunk. One of them looked at the Afghan and said with a wicked smile, 'This beast is unworthy of prison. He must be shot.' 'No,' mumbled the second one, 'He should be hung upside down in the sun. Then he'll realize who he attacked.' But then a lieutenant arrived. The soldiers reported they had arrested a *dushman*. 'Good,' said the officer. 'We'll settle accounts. Shoot him. Bring an automatic rifle.' The Afghan understood what was about to happen, and he started to say something in his language, but no one listened to him. We were all around, waiting to see what would happen. One of the soldiers came back and said that all the rifles were locked up. 'Too bad,' said the officer. 'We'll have to manage without bullets. Bring him over to the cannon.' The officer climbed up on the turret. The soldiers stuck the tied hands of the Afghan into the barrel of the gun. 'Move aside,' hollered the officer. 'Fire.' When the smoke dissipated, there was no trace of the Afghan. Everyone left. I was waiting in line for tea to eat with my porridge, when suddenly a sergeant next to me started yelling, 'Go away, you filthy beast!' I didn't understand right away. Then I saw a dog with a piece of meat in his mouth. It was the arm of the man we had just killed."[3]

Former Soviet Army Sgt. Igor Rykov testified:

> "Generally we killed [prisoners] on the spot. As soon as we caught them, the officers ordered us to slaughter them. I'll tell you one story. Lt. Gevorkian was the commander of my unit. When I arrived, he had already been in Afghanistan for a year. He told us that he had seen a lot, and that now he had become like ice, he had learned to kill absolutely anyone, and he had to teach the same to the soldiers. One day he brought in a boy, an Afghan kid about fourteen years old. He told us that the boy was certainly a *dushman*; he had tried to run away when he saw the soldiers. There was one soldier in our unit, Oleg Sotnik, who could not stand the sight of blood. Then Gevorkian took out a sort of bayonet—it had been mounted on a carbine; it looked like a dagger, and Gevorkian always carried it. He gave this knife to Sotnik and told him to kill the boy. Sotnik's face was unbelievable. He was planted to the ground, shaking all over his body. The boy was sitting peacefully on the ground. Finally Sotnik got control of himself, went up to the boy, and stuck the knife in his chest. The boy started to shriek, and he grabbed onto Sotnik's hands. Then Gevorkian started yelling, 'You idiot! What do you think you're doing? Watch how it should be done!' He pulled out the knife, kicked the boy in the face, and when the boy fell backward from the kick, he stuck the knife in his throat, once, twice. We were all around watching, but no one said anything."[4]

Kefayatullah, a farmer from the Kohistan region of Kapisa Province, interviewed in Peshawar on 23 September 1984, described what happened after a Soviet-Afghan offensive in his region two and a half years ago:

> "The Russians came with a few Parchamis. They took authority and captured people. Those who escaped attacked them again. The Russians took more prisoners. The people who didn't surrender to them they took to the bank of the river and shot."

Tur Abbas, a twenty-two-year-old farmer from Keraman in the Panjsher Valley whom we interviewed in Peshawar on 27 September 1984, had spoken to a boy who had just come from Panjsher with this story:

> "Last spring [1984, during the seventh offensive in Panjsher] the Russians landed paratroops in Keraman. The mujahedin fought as long as they could, but they ran out of ammunition. Most of them were killed. About ten were caught by the Russians. They put them in a line and tied some kind of electric bombs to their bodies and blew them up."

Abuses by the Afghan Resistance

It is almost meaningless to discuss human rights violations by the Afghan resistance as a whole. Despite the establishment of an umbrella organization, the Islamic Alliance of Mujahedin of Afghanistan, in 1985, the seven parties represented in the alliance, and others as well, have operated independently of each other throughout most of the conflict. Moreover, those fighting within Afghanistan often have no more than tangential links to the political parties based in Pakistan.

The Afghan government has accused the resistance of many crimes which we were unable to investigate because the government ignored our requests to visit Kabul to seek additional information. Nevertheless, we received evidence that indicates that at least some elements of the Afghan resistance have committed acts forbidden by the Geneva Conventions, including the execution and torture of prisoners of war. Some such practices appear to be widespread, while others are occasional.

In their treatment of prisoners, the Afghan parties in Peshawar and Quetta (we could not speak with those in Iran) and most of the resistance groups operating within Afghanistan appear to distinguish three groups: Soviet prisoners, Afghan officers or party members, and Afghan conscripts.

Until 1981 most of the Afghan resistance forces, acting on the basis of their traditional concept of *badal* (revenge), executed captured Soviet soldiers. During 1981, however, the resistance parties in Pakistan agreed to allow the ICRC access to Soviet prisoners, and word apparently went out to commanders in the field to try to keep Soviet prisoners alive. The ICRC began negotiations and worked out an agreement:

> Negotiations carried out by the ICRC with, successively, the USSR, the Afghan opposition movements, Pakistan, and Switzerland led to partial success. The parties agreed to the transfer and internment in a neutral country of Soviet soldiers detained by the Afghan opposition movements, in application, by analogy, of the Third Geneva Convention, relative to the treatment of prisoners of war.
>
> On the basis of this agreement, the ICRC has had access to some of the Soviet prisoners in the hands of the Afghan movements and has informed them, in the course of interviews without witness, of the possibility for transfer by the ICRC to Switzerland, where they would spend two years under the responsibility and watch of the Swiss government before returning to their country of origin. . . .
>
> To date, eleven Soviet soldiers have accepted the proposal. The first three were transferred to Switzerland on 28 May 1982. Eight others arrived in August and October 1982, January and October 1983, and February and April 1984.[5]

The ICRC has had only "partial" success, however, for several reasons. One is that it can have access only to those prisoners held in or near Pakistan, as it has not been able to operate in Afghanistan or Iran. British art historian Nicholas Danziger, in an interview in Peshawar on 26 September 1984, told us about problems faced by a Jamiat-e Islami resistance group that he encountered in Herat, near Iran:

> "They realize that it is good for them [Soviet prisoners] to go to the West, but the problem for them is to actually get the prisoners to Pakistan—I saw it myself—it is an impossibility to do that. So I fear the worst."

The main problem, however, is that the Soviets and the Kabul government, at least until 1987, refused to let the ICRC even interview their prisoners. ICRC official François Zen Ruffinen told us in an interview in Peshawar on 22 September 1984 that "the leaders of the resistance groups understand our needs and try to cooperate with us, but they tell us they are under a lot of pressure from their men, since there is no reciprocation from the other side."

> "They [the resistance fighters] were very upset by a BBC report whilst I was there that said that two Russian prisoners were going back to Russia, had decided to go home, after a period of two years in prison [in Switzerland, under the ICRC agreement]. I spent the next week trying to explain this, because they felt that two years in prison was nothing—*they* obviously are shot to death immediately once they're caught, if the Russians realize that they're mujahedin." (Nicholas Danziger)

With the admission of the ICRC to Kabul in 1987, however, the possibility of implementing the agreement on prisoners may be reopened.

After their initial experience, the resistance groups became reluctant to cooperate with the ICRC. Some once again began killing Soviet prisoners, while others have been holding them but not permitting them to be transferred abroad. Some resistance groups tried to hold prisoners in Pakistan, but this stopped after late April 1985, when a group of Soviet soldiers and Afghan Army officers held by the Jamiat-e Islami resistance party at a storage depot near Zangali, fifteen miles south of Peshawar, were killed in an escape attempt. Sources differ on whether the prisoners were seeking asylum in the West or were loyal to their own side. The international repercussions of this incident, principally pressure from the Soviet Union, led the government of Pakistan to insist that all Soviet prisoners be moved back inside Afghanistan.[6]

Following the transfer of Soviet prisoners back to Afghanistan, the ICRC began discussions with the Islamic Alliance on the possibility of a prisoner protection visit to resistance detention centers inside Afghanistan. These talks became public knowledge in August 1985 with the following news report:

> The International Committee of the Red Cross (ICRC), with headquarters in Geneva, will make use of its "right of initiative" to enter Afghanistan without visas at several points in order to survey and inform itself about Afghan and Soviet prisoners held by the resistance, according to a reliable source Thursday [22 August] in Islamabad.
>
> According to sources close to the guerrillas, the ICRC delegations, which will visit Afghan territory from Pakistan after the conclusion of negotiations currently in progress with all the parties, will also investigate the conditions of life and the consequences of the war for the local population. . . .
>
> The right of initiative is granted to the ICRC by the Geneva Conventions. No reaction from the Kabul authorities was known as of Thursday afternoon.[7]

The Kabul authorities reacted three weeks later:

> Chargé d'affaires of the Embassy of Pakistan in Kabul was summoned today to the Ministry of Foreign Affairs of the DRA and the following was conveyed to him by the deputy foreign minister.
>
> According to Swiss News Agency, the military Government of Pakistan with the help of the counter-revolutionary bands is seeking to get the representatives of International Red Cross infiltrated illegally and without visas from Pakistan into the territory of the DRA.
>
> This illegal action is to take place with the accord, permission and the assistance of Pakistani authorities. The Democratic Republic of Afghanistan (DRA) like any other countries considers the illegal trespassing of any foreigner through the Pakistani soil into the territory of the DRA a gross violation to its sovereignty and territorial integrity and reckons the military Government of Pakistan responsible for it.
>
> The international organizations including the Red Cross International Committee can take contact with the DRA authorities through the diplomatic channel.
>
> The Democratic Republic of Afghanistan lodges its severe protest with the Pakistani authorities on the illegal intention and the accord of Pakistani authorities about the trespassing. The DRA cautions that the dangerous consequences of this illegal action will be borne by the military authorities of Pakistan.[8]

The ICRC subsequently visited prisoners held by resistance command-er Mawlawi Jalaluddin Haqqani of Hezb-e Islami (branch led by Yunus Khales) at his base in Zhawar, Paktia Province, just across the border from Pakistan. In April 1987 representatives of the ICRC witnessed the freeing of 138 Afghan army prisoners by Commander Jalaluddin in the tribal areas on the border.[9]

When Afghan Army officers are captured, they are investigated by resis-tance representatives or an Islamic court to see whether they are party mem-bers, after which they are tried. The sentence most often is death, and it is usually carried out.

Jeff B. Harmon, an independent film producer who visited resistance bases near Kandahar, described the following scenes, which he also cap-tured on film:

> In Malajat [outside Kandahar, at the headquarters of resistance leader Haji Abdul Latif of the National Islamic Front of Afghanistan (led by Gailani)], I saw 12 Afghan army prisoners lined up in chains before a judge named Mawlawi Abdul Bari, who was awaiting orders to execute them from the guerrillas' high command in Peshawar, Pakistan. Bari claims to have executed 2,500 prisoners.
>
> The judge told me: "I have personally slit the throats of 1,000 *khalqis*. I have sent 500 Russians infidels to the gallows." Other prisoners, he said, were shot, decapitated or stoned to death.
>
> This information was given in front of the 12 prisoners, whose own fate seemed certain. They listened impassively, while the judge's chief executioner, Muhammad Juma, fondled an axe and grinned. "This is no ordinary axe," he said. "This is for *halal* [execution by blade]."
>
> But Bari's brand of justice is swift and formal compared with that of the mujaheddin at Markazee Apo [*sic*], a Hezbi-Islami [Hekmatyar branch] guerrilla camp in Kandahar province. There, 12 prisoners, presumably Russian, were recently bayonetted to death. The stench from their decomposing bodies, buried in makeshift graves, permeates the camp.[10]

Aziz was a high school student from Kabul who ran away to join the resistance in Paghman after members of his family were arrested for connec-tions to the Hezb-e Islami. The Paghman resistance group, affiliated with the Ittehad-e Islami party of Abd-ur-Rabb-ur-Rasul Sayyaf in Peshawar, sus-pected him of being a KHAD agent, interrogated him, and put him to work as a cook.

> "They had some prisoners of war. There was one of them who belonged to the party [PDPA]. He had a card, and they decided to kill him. But the commander of the mujahedin said to me, 'Shall I kill him, or would you like

him to help you cook?' I said I needed the help, so he helped me cook. Another time they captured one army officer and two soldiers. They killed the officer and released the soldiers. The commander of the mujahedin told me to kill him. He was sort of testing me, and I agreed, but then I found that he had already been killed." (Interview in Peshawar, 25 September 1984)

Agence France Presse correspondent Michel Martin-Roland witnessed the following scenes in May 1983 in the Barri Fort in Paktia Province, which had just fallen to one of the resistance groups (he did not state which one):

Under a tent sit six Afghan officers, tank drivers trained in the Soviet Union. Pale, frightened, they listen to a *mawlawi* (Muslim scholar) teaching them and agree in a trembling voice to all of his criticisms. Outside, an unbearable odor: fifty prisoners have been shot in the last three days, then thrown into a mass grave covered with a few shovels of earth. "The irredeemable Communists were executed. Others were shot while trying to escape," stated one of the guards.[11]

In July 1981 wire services reported a large battle in the Paghman area of Kabul Province between resistance forces and a military force that included several hundred cadets from the Kabul military academy. Some of these cadets were captured by the resistance.[12] Anwar, a former office worker, knew one of them.

"There were some military students in the military university, and the Russians advised that they would take them to practice shooting. And they were taken to a famous district called Paghman. They took these young kids—they were taken out from the bus and told to start shooting. And there were thousands of automatic rifles [of the resistance] shooting at them, and they stopped shooting. One of my friends was there, and he told me. My friend was running through a street in a small village, trying to find a house to hide, and he was caught by mujahedin. He was taken to a mujahed court immediately and was asked if he was a member of the Communist party. He said he is not. 'What are you doing here?' He said he was a student, and then he told the facts to the people there, like 'We were told we were going to practice. I've only been a student. One or two years and I will graduate, and I couldn't quit, because if I quit, then they would kill me. They would realize I quit the military because I came to work with the mujahedin, so I had to stay there.' So he told all the facts to the mujahedin, and he said he was kept in the night, because they went to many folks to find out if he was a member of the Communist party. Since they didn't find his name, he was released so that he came back home." (Interview in Chicago, 15 April 1984)

The resistance often treats captured Afghan conscripts as potential allies rather than enemies. Mike Hoover, whom we interviewed in Peshawar in September 1984, described an incident he had recently witnessed in which fighters of the National Islamic Front of Afghanistan (Gailani's group) carefully disarmed a group of Afghan prisoners near Sarobi, Kabul Province:

> "They were telling them to lay down their arms very carefully, because they didn't want to harm them. They were so careful that one of them got killed. It was early evening, when visibility is really bad, and there was one guy who was guarding these prisoners. But it turned out that one of them was an officer, a real party member, and he fired at the guy who was guarding him, and hit him right in the head. I saw him go down. He was dead. Then everybody started shouting and firing all over the place, but in the confusion, the officer escaped. The other ones, they did what they always do. They took their weapons and then let them go home to their families."

We also heard reports of the resistance giving soldiers pocket money to pay for the expenses of their trip home.

From time to time the Afghan resistance groups take other kinds of prisoners, usually people suspected of spying for KHAD. Sometimes these prisoners are tortured. We heard of cases in which torture has resulted in false confessions of guilt. We also received reports from various resistance parties that suspected spies have been sentenced to death by Islamic courts and executed. Spies are not considered prisoners of war under the Geneva Conventions, but they are protected against torture and entitled to fair trials and humane treatment.

Besides the prisoners of war mentioned above, Jeff Harmon also saw a suspected spy in the custody of the Hezb-e Islami in Kandahar.

> At the camp, a stooping figure in a tattered uniform was led around by a heavy chain. He was a *khalqi* prisoner who, after 30 days there, seemed no longer human—the guerrillas called him *char* (donkey). The soles of both his feet had been sliced by daggers and one of his knees had been crippled during torture. The mujaheddin pulled up his eyelids, spat in his face, playfully ran a dagger across his neck, competing to get a reaction. The man's face remained expressionless, his trembling lower lip the only sign of pent-up rage and humiliation. In the month since his capture, he had not spoken.
>
> "This communist spy is an infidel," the camp commander said. "He does not even pray. The day that he speaks, I will cut his throat."[13]

Stephane Théollier, a French student interviewed in Peshawar on 27 August 1985, described a prisoner of fighters belonging to Khales's Hezb-e Islami in Kabul Province. He saw the prisoner while on a mission to provide humanitarian assistance to civilians inside Afghanistan.

"It was about ten days ago. There was a prisoner who was himself an ex-mujahed who had killed some other mujahedin. The commander showed me the prisoner in a room, and it was terrible, because the prisoner had been there, according to the mujahedin, for six months, but actually, after I talked to him it turned out he had been there for nine months.

"He claimed he was innocent, that it was his cousin who had killed the two other people but he had escaped, and that he had been arrested, and that since he was considered as a criminal, a profiteer, someone who had sold his weapons without any scruples, they kept him.

"He was in very bad physical condition, because he was in a dark room, with no windows, and he almost never went out. So I saw him, I spoke to the commander, and after that they took better care of him. Starting from the day I went there the prisoner was taken out every afternoon. He was shaved; he had had very long hair, with fleas, lice. He was washed, and I gave him injections of serum, gave him some vitamins to make him more energetic. Then he began to eat, and so on. He was always asking when I was going to leave, because he thought that when I left his situation would go back to what it had been.

"I told them, 'According to Islam you should bring together the family, the witnesses, the people who arrested him.' But they told me that since it was a tribal area, Pashtun, it was up to the family of the two people killed to avenge their deaths. They told me that if they let him go, he would be killed at the first crossroads by someone from the family, and they were protecting him from that. Also I think there was no judge in the area."[14]

Aziz, the former high school student mentioned above, described how he became a prisoner of an Afghan resistance group affiliated with the Ittehad-e Islami (led by Sayyaf):

"After my brother was arrested [by KHAD in Kabul], my father told me and my other brother that we also might be arrested, so we should leave Kabul and join the mujahedin. So we went to Paghman to join the mujahedin, but they made us prisoners, because they thought we had been sent by KHAD. They didn't trust us, because they have a big problem with KHAD, and also they had found that students of my age from the government schools may be on the side of the government. So my brother and I were prisoners of the mujahedin for thirteen months. They also tortured us by beating us on the feet. But we didn't blame them. Some of the people *are* agents. Finally we confessed we belonged to KHAD. Then they kept beating us for a while. Eventually they stopped and let me work as their cook." (Interview in Peshawar, 25 September 1984)

There are many other reports about the treatment of those suspected of spying.

> Gul Mohammad [a resistance commander in Logar] said that towards the end of April [1983], four leading figures of the local informants' network were arrested at Zaidabad, Nazarkhel, Kotikhel, and Pol-e-Kandari; documents seized from them showed their close connections with the Soviet-Kabul authorities and the extent of their activities in the province. After having been tried by an Islamic resistance court, they were executed.[15]

> The leader of the Afghan resistance in the Panjsher Valley, "Commander" Ahmad Shah Massoud, has reportedly undertaken a vast purge among his resistance fighters, unmasking about fifty agents infiltrated from Kabul by the secret police ("KHAD"), Western diplomatic sources revealed Tuesday in Islamabad. According to this same source, these agents of the "KHAD" were imprisoned in Rokha, in the southern part of the valley, on 4 April, where they are awaiting trial. Some of the communist regime's spies had portable radio transmitters. A source close to the resistance in Peshawar indicated that the mujahedin of Panjsher were continually on guard against infiltrators. The agents of the "KHAD" who are discovered are killed, turned into double agents, or imprisoned.[16]

> "In the summer of 1982 I saw a trial near Herat, in a village controlled by the Jamiat-e Islami. The resistance had arrested an agent of the KHAD and imprisoned him in a house. This agent managed to escape, and, when they caught him, they beat him pretty badly. The next day a qazi [Islamic judge] was summoned, because the family of the KHAD agent had gone to the resistance court and entered a complaint against the mujahedin. The family of the KHAD agent actually went to the resistance court! And I was there the next day, when the qazi came in and started yelling at the commander. He said, 'Torture is forbidden by Islam. We should not adopt the practices of our enemy, or we will have no right to fight against him.' The resistance chief really tried to excuse his men; he said, 'We didn't really torture him—he was escaping,' and so on. But the qazi examined the prisoner and saw he had cut lips and a black eye and rebuked the commander again.

> "Then the qazi convened a court of four judges and held a trial. This trial lasted over a week, maybe eight or ten days. I attended many of the sessions. The prisoner was charged with having caused the death of a member of the resistance. The qazi called a lot of witnesses, including the family of the accused. In the end the prisoner was found guilty and executed." (Testimony of Olivier Roy, French political scientist and expert on Afghanistan; interview in New York City, 25 April 1984)

5
REPRESSION IN THE CITIES

The city is in the grip of fear, which was visible in all the Afghans we managed to meet. This fear, they said, is methodically maintained by the secret police of the Afghan regime, the KHAD, "a veritable octopus which is continually spreading its tentacles" over the capital. . . . Stories of disappearances, arrests, spying are plentiful in Kabul . . . where the KHAD has become not just a state within a state, but the state itself.
Yves Heller, Agence France Presse

The Afghan regime and its Soviet allies maintain and enforce control in the cities through the fear of a terrorized population aware of the ever-present possibility of arbitrary arrest, torture, imprisonment, and execution.

The system is enforced by the largest agency of the Afghan state, the State Information Services, known as KHAD.[1] The KHAD has a larger budget than even the military and is reported to be directly financed by the Soviet Union.[2] Organized in 1980 under the guidance of KGB advisers, it remains under close Soviet supervision. KHAD informers sit in almost every office and classroom in Kabul. A former high official of the KHAD told us in Peshawar that the KHAD aimed to have "a spy in every family."[3]

House Searches and Arrests

The KHAD arrests people in a variety of ways. Sometimes the militia surrounds a house at night and proceeds to search it before making arrests, ripping apart pillows, tearing clothes, and going through all books and papers. In another common procedure, young men are stopped by street blockades and whisked away to join the army. Troops have been known to blockade an entire neighborhood while KHAD agents search the houses.

Students have been called from libraries or classrooms only to find themselves in a jeep on the way to a torture center.

> "My neighbors, everyone was afraid in their homes. They were putting two locks instead of one, and they were afraid that tonight maybe Russians will take me. Usually we could hear kids crying from all neighborhoods, especially when it was dark at night, and we could hear them more clearly. Then the following day we learned that a neighbor was taken from his house." (Anwar, former office worker from Kabul; interviewed in Chicago, 15 April 1984)

Most arrests in central Kabul are made by KHAD agents in plainclothes, sometimes assisted by the militia or Afghan soldiers. In some cases, Soviet agents are also present.

> "There was a Russian-made car called Volga. I got to the car, and I saw two armed Russians sitting there in the back seat. They were wearing just very normal clothes, not in military dress, just ordinary suits, with ties." (Anwar, quoted above; arrested November 1980)

In outlying areas or in massive searches, Soviet troops themselves may conduct house-to-house searches, as they do in the countryside.

There is no due process.

> Arrests take place for the most part without warrant or even identification of the arresting officer. These arrests usually take place at night. No reasons are given for the person's arrest, and the family is not informed of where the prisoner is taken.[4]

When people are arrested outside their homes, their families may not even know that they have been arrested. The elder brother of Razia, a university student arrested in 1981, told us in Peshawar in a 23 September 1984 interview that "nobody in the house knew where she was."

> "Finally a friend in her class came to the house and said the KGB had taken her. Then we tried to find her, and after five days we finally learned that she was in the women's prison in Sedarat."

An Afghan woman in Kabul wrote to a friend in France:

> The following summer [1982] a husband had to take his wife to the maternity hospital to give birth. Since he had no one to leave them with, he locked his 3 children (1, 3, and 4 years old) in the house. At the

hospital, when complications arose during the birth, the doctors asked the husband for certain medicines, which he had to go to the pharmacy to buy. Between the hospital and the pharmacy the husband was arrested by soldiers who demanded his papers. The soldiers did not listen to any explanation or plea, and he was sent off. After three days, he had the good fortune to find an understanding officer, who let him go. When he returned to the hospital, the poor man found that his wife and newborn child had died, for lack of the medicines. At home the one-year-old had died, and the other two children were in comas from lack of food. I must stop; I do not have the courage to go on.[5]

Arrests are based on "evidence" received from spies and informers, from suspects interrogated under torture, or, occasionally, from electronic eavesdropping.

Anwar-ul-Haq, a physics student at an advanced institute whom we interviewed in Peshawar on 29 September 1984, was arrested while driving his car early in the morning. During interrogation, KHAD agents told him they had received a report from an informer that he was a member of the Hezb-e Islami.

A former employee of the Pashtuni Tejarati Bank told how he and his brother were arrested in September 1982 after others gave their names under torture:

"One of my brothers was active in the Hezb-e Islami, distributing night letters.[6] Some of his friends were arrested while they were distributing night letters, and after a week about fifteen to twenty KHAD agents came to the house in the early morning. They arrested my elder brother and also me. I had thought about joining the Hezb-e Islami, but actually I had not, because I was afraid of getting caught. But I had discussed it with my brother's friends. During the interrogation, some of them said that I was going to join them." (Interview in Peshawar 25 September 1984).

"They said I had said in front of people that I hate the government, and my Afghan people lacked freedom, and Afghanistan would be a free country soon, and Afghan people are freedom lovers, and they would never come under Russian yoke. I said I hadn't spoken these words. They said, 'We have your tape, and we have it with us.' I said, 'Why don't you turn it on so I can listen?' They turned on the tape, but after I heard the tape I denied I had spoke, because the tape seemed to be a Russian tape and did not catch the sound very well; you could hardly tell that it was my voice." (Interview with Anwar, quoted above)

"We have some kind of instruments. We would park the car and we would drop something like a microphone to listen from a distance. But it was difficult to put the microphones, because in Afghanistan the houses are very close together. Anyway, we had a lot of other programs." (Testimony of a former officer of the KHAD; interviewed in Peshawar, 30 September 1984)

Sometimes the KHAD arrests people for the sole purpose of obtaining information from them about another member of their family. Torture is used to get them to talk.

> Shahnaz and Natila Ulumi, believed to be 21 and 18 years old respectively, were arrested with 11 other members of their family in the first week of June 1983. The 13 members of the family were taken to the KHAD interrogation center in the Sedarat in Kabul. The family is said to have been closely questioned about the activities and whereabouts of Khozhman Ulumi, the brother of Shahnaz and Natila, who is reputed to be a leader of Rahayee, a Maoist group that is active in the resistance to the government of President Babrak Karmal. . . . Amnesty International has received allegations that Shahnaz and Natila Ulumi were ill-treated and tortured with electric shocks whilst they were detained at the Sedarat.[7]

House searches accompanying arrests are thorough and vindictive.

> "They did not say who they were, but we knew they were KHAD because we saw they had a Volga car with a double antenna and a license plate 22000. . . . They sent someone to search every room, but they could not find anything. Then they called with a radio to their central office. They waited at the house, and after some time a second group of men came, all in some uniform, and they made a more precise investigation. They tore open everything in the house, pillows, cushions, mattresses. They took all these things off the beds and cut them open. They tore all of the clothes hanging in the closets. They made a complete search of the kitchen. They looked in the sink, the chimney, the well. And they went over the whole inside and courtyard of the house with some electric machines [apparently metal detectors]. They were doing this for four hours, until three o'clock in the afternoon." (Testimony of a former accountant from Kabul whose brother was arrested in August 1982; interviewed in Alexandria, Virginia, 22 March 1984)

When the resistance carries out an assassination or some other operation in a city, the security forces often respond by searching houses or shops in the area and arresting people who are sent to jail or, in the case of young men, to the army. Sometimes mass searches are conducted for no apparent reason.

> "During Ramazan [June–July 1984] the mujahedin killed an Afghan soldier in Topkhana Bazaar in the old city [of Kandahar]. His body was lying there for an hour or so. . . . For this reason, about five or six shops

away from where he was killed, the militia . . . took a small boy and an old man and imprisoned them. Nobody knows what happened to them. I saw it myself." (Shah Mahmud Baasir, economist; interviewed in Quetta, 3 October 1984)

"There is much fear of attacks by mujahedin. Whenever there is an attack, they [the security forces] encircle a whole neighborhood. They start to search the houses. That is a time when they can catch the young men for military service. And in the streets there are systematic searches. Every five or ten minutes you are stopped by people who ask to see your papers. My own house was searched several times." (Mohammad Gul, former student at Vocational High School, Kabul; interviewed in Peshawar, 30 September 1984)

With all of its doors flung open, the antediluvian yellow Volga is blocked up against the sidewalk: its occupants are pulled out by 3 armed soldiers who check their identity papers. A few meters away, in a military truck, two young Afghans are prostrated. Captured several hours earlier in a taxi that resembled the old Volga, they will end up in an army barracks that same day. These blockades are daily occurrences in Kabul, where every young man is treated as a suspect.[8]

"They took us to Kandahar Jail in the Sarpuza quarter. Inside the prison they had a separate place for those arrested for military service. There were about 150 people there. Then they took us to another room, with about 40 to 45 other people. There was no carpet, and the floor was wet. It was Ramazan; we were fasting and could eat only at night, but they did not give us any food. For about twenty days we were just given a piece of bread in the evening, nothing else. Then some Russian advisers along with Afghan soldiers registered us for military service. We were sent to Mazar-e Sharif. We spent four days there, and then twelve of us escaped. We came back to Kandahar—it took us twenty-four days." (Mohammad Ashraf, eighteen, former high school student from Kandahar; interviewed in Quetta, 3 October 1984)

Torture

The torture of political prisoners was brutal under the governments of Taraki and Amin, but only under Babrak Karmal and Najib has it been fully integrated into an interrogation process that is part of a sophisticated intelligence apparatus. Amnesty International describes torture since December 1979 as "systematic."

Amnesty International has received persistent reports of widespread and systematic torture of political suspects in Afghanistan under the government of President Babrak Karmal, who came to power in

December 1979. Testimonies and other information received by the organization indicate that torture is inflicted in detention centres throughout the country which are administered by the State Information Services, *Khedamat-e Etela 'at-e Dawlati*, known as the KHAD. . . . Although Amnesty International has received reports of torture under all three governments since the "Sawr" revolution of April 1978 . . . it was only after the formation of the KHAD in late 1979 that the practice was reported to have become systematic.[9]

"I was arrested three times, once under Taraki, once under Amin, and once under Babrak and the Russians. Before, they were killing a lot of people without any investigation. It is much better organized, because of the Russians." (Mohammad Nabi Omarkhel, civil engineer; interviewed in Peshawar, 27 September 1984)

All political prisoners are subjected to lengthy interrogation by the KHAD and its KGB advisers. Interrogation procedures invariably involve torture. Amnesty International has described the pattern of torture as follows:

Numerous reports have indicated that the treatment meted out to suspects by KHAD agents has followed a pattern: they are arrested and taken to one of many KHAD detention centres—Amnesty International knows of eight in Kabul alone—where they are first subjected to various forms of deprivation and then soon afterwards intensively tortured.

Suspects are reportedly deprived of all contact with family, lawyers or doctors, or even other prisoners, by being held incommunicado and in solitary confinement. During this period they may be continuously interrogated, threatened, and be deprived of sleep or rest; cases have also been reported of detainees having been deprived of food.

Former detainees have told Amnesty International that suspects who fail to cooperate with the KHAD are then tortured—the methods reported have included electric shocks, beatings, burning with cigarette ends, and dousing with water.

Detainees are also known to have been kept in shackles or bound hand and foot for prolonged periods. In some cases prisoners are reported to have been forced to watch their relatives being tortured.[10]

The largest KHAD detention center in the country is in the Sedarat Palace in Kabul.[11] Sedarat contains the central interrogation office. Another major KHAD interrogation center is in the Sheshdarak District. The Khalqi-dominated Ministry of the Interior has its own security force, the *Sarandoy*, in whose offices torture has also been reported. Besides these three, Amnesty International lists other detention centres in Kabul where prisoners have reportedly been tortured: the office of the military branch of KHAD, *KHAD-e Nezami*; KHAD "Office Number Five," responsible for counterinsurgency, in

Dar-ul-Aman; other departments called offices three and four; two private houses near the Sedarat, the Ahmad Shah Khan house and one in the Wazir Akbar Khan District; and the KHAD office in Hawzai Barikat District.[12] Amnesty International also reports torture in Pol-e Charkhi Prison. Former prisoners we interviewed had been tortured in various places; Sedarat, Sheshdarak, KHAD Office Number Five, the house in Wazir Akbar Khan, and Pol-e Charkhi.

There are other centers in Kabul as well. A former bank employee whom we interviewed in Peshawar on 25 September 1984 reported being taken to a KHAD center in Kart-e Seh. A former KHAD agent described a new detention center: "In Shahrara there is a hill, and they have made rooms inside by digging tunnels. There is an underground jail there."[13] A former prisoner interviewed in New York in August 1986 had been interrogated by KHAD in a "big garage."

Amnesty International reports that each provincial center has its own KHAD office and detention center.

> Amnesty International has also received reports of torture at KHAD centres in the provincial cities of Bamian, Ghazni, Jalalabad, Kandahar, Lashkargah and Pol-e Khomri, and in the prisons of Kunduz and Mazar-e Sharif, although some people arrested in other cities were taken immediately to Kabul for interrogation in Sedarat.
>
> In Kandahar, the headquarters of the KHAD are said to be in the former house of Abdul Rahim Latif in Shahr-e Nau district, but most torture is reported to be practiced in a building known as the Musa Khan building. Another KHAD center in Kandahar from which torture was reported was described as Darwazan (Herat Gate).
>
> In addition to KHAD centres and prisons, Amnesty International has interviewed people who said they were tortured in military posts.[14]

We also received reports of torture in Herat and at the Soviet air base at Shindand, Farah Province.

People arrested in Kabul are usually taken first to one of the smaller detention centers for a preliminary investigation. They are asked to confess their crimes and are left alone for various periods of time. If they do not confess, the torture begins, sometimes immediately, sometimes after a few days.

Usually, the prisoner is transferred to Sedarat after a relatively short period of time (perhaps only a few days).[15] In Sedarat the prisoner may again be given a chance to confess, but sooner or later there is likely to be more intensive torture.

Prisoners are held completely incommunicado throughout the interrogation. The frequency and intensity of the torture appear to be carefully calibrated to the political importance and physical stamina of the prisoner. When the KHAD has finished the interrogation, the prisoner is transferred to Pol-e Charkhi Prison. In some cases, the interrogation continues there.

Some of the most important prisoners are apparently interrogated in a special section of Pol-e Charkhi Prison. Some are kept in tiny cells where they cannot stand up or stretch out and are tortured daily for as long as a year by Soviet officers aided by a few Afghans.

In the provinces, arrested persons are brought first to the local KHAD office for preliminary interrogation. The more important prisoners are then transferred to a detention center in Kabul for intensive interrogation. Most are sent to Sedarat, but some apparently go to the special section of Pol-e Charkhi.

The most commonly reported methods of torture are sleep deprivation, prolonged beatings, and electric shocks administered by a variety of devices and sometimes intensified by dousing the prisoner with water. There are many other methods as well, as illustrated by the following extracts from testimonies which also illustrate the pattern of interrogation described above.

Testimony of Shafaq Torialai, twenty-eight, an army officer working for one of the resistance parties (Harakat-e Enqelab-e Islami) when he was arrested in February 1982 at his base in Ghazni and taken to the KHAD office in the Ghazni citadel (interviewed in Paris, 17 June 1984)

"I stayed there for four or five days. They brought me into a room. There was a bench, and they had us [the prisoners] sit down. They brought captured resistance fighters before us, and they tore out their fingernails, saying 'This is what will happen to you, if you don't confess.' The Russians and the Afghans both did this. The majority were Russians, and there were a few interpreters. The person whose fingernails they tore out fainted several times.

"Once some of the Russians and the Afghan interpreters took us at night into the gardens of Ghazni, where there were poplar trees. They pulled down the tops of two poplars and tied ropes to them, and they tied one arm of one of the prisoners to one of the trees and the other arm to the other tree. Then they released the poplars, and the prisoner's arms were pulled off, and he was killed. They call that, 'making vests.' They told us, 'If you don't confess, this will happen to you too.'

"The afternoon of the fifth day they told me my interrogation was over, and that I would be shot. But that night they took me to Kabul. They started to torture me again in Kabul. I was in a room with such a low ceiling that it was impossible to stand up, about 1 m by 1.5 m, and I was there with two other prisoners. It was in Pol-e Charkhi. These were underground rooms for the most dangerous prisoners.

"The torture there was always by electricity, with electric shock batons. One day during the interrogation, one of the Soviets got angry and hit me with his Kalashnikov in the mouth, and I lost three teeth. I was tortured two to four hours a day, every day, for about a year. There were different people torturing me. There were Afghans who spoke Pashto and there were Soviet officers. The Soviets tortured more, and they asked more questions. They did not let you sleep.

"They gave the shocks between the toes, between the fingers, on the temple. I often fell unconscious. One day they hung me up on a wall, where there were big hooks. They didn't let me sleep, eat, or drink for forty-eight hours. My arms were stretched out wide, and the hands were tied to the hooks, and there were rings around my feet. This caused a great pain in the stomach and kidneys. The next morning they took me down and brought me a piece of bread and some water. Then they hung me upside down by the feet all day." (A few days later Soviet officers told Torialai that he had been sentenced to death, but resistance agents inside Pol-e Charkhi smuggled him out.)[16]

Testimony of Razia, a student at Kabul University when she was arrested and taken to Sedarat in 1981, where she stayed for a year (interviewed in Peshawar, 23 September 1984)

"I saw many people tortured, and I was tortured myself. Electricity, standing in cold water, keeping you from sleeping, beating, these are very normal things. They made a man stand on a board with nails coming out and beat him with chains or cables. They hung a man by the legs from the ceiling. All the men were tortured.

"For women, they would keep them from sleeping, or they would make them stand in cold water, then add a chemical, and after a half hour the skin would start to come off their feet. They made them stand barefoot in snow, gave them electric shocks, pulled out their hair, beat them with electric shock batons.

"For both women and men they have something like earphones. They attach wires to it and put it on your head and give you a shock, a harder one for the men. They attach wires to the hands and feet.

"There were men supervising the torture of the women. Sometimes they tortured them separately, sometimes together in the same room. This was a form of mental torture. For instance, they took one girl to a room, and the men from KHAD were all around her. They brought a man, a mujahed. Then the KHAD men molested this girl, they fondled her all over the body. Then they beat the man in front of the girl. They beat that man to death, and then they left the girl alone with the dead body. This girl, Jamila, was in prison with me. She became deranged. For a whole week she could not move.[17]

"When they took me, they gave me a paper, and said, 'Write your complete biography.' Then they asked, 'Did you write all your antigovernment activity?' They took out a pistol and said, 'If you don't want to tell us, we will kill you.' They left me alone in a room for three or four hours. They came and saw I hadn't written anything, and they said, 'Now we will torture you, but electric shocks are not good for you, nice girl.' They asked me questions for eight hours, 10:00 A.M. to 6:00 P.M., and then they started the shocks."

"There was something like a ruler—they hit me on the knuckle, and I jumped back with the shock. They made me stand in cold water. They put some chemicals in the water and after thirty to forty-five minutes the skin was coming off. They showed me a picture of myself in the demonstration. They tried to get something from me, but they couldn't. They tortured me for two months, with no sleep, and also with mental torture. They told me, 'We will bring your sister here and beat her and rape her.'"

"The first day my interrogators were three women, Nazifa, Zarghuna, and Nahib. Malia was the woman in charge of the women's jail, but they were all controlled by men. Then there were two men, Amin and Taher. The Russian advisers were also coming and telling us that Russia is a very good place, and that they were helping us. Sometimes the advisers were with uniform, sometimes without. The adviser organizes the interrogation. When they finish asking the questions, they go tell the adviser the answers. Then they come back and ask new questions. We heard from the men that the advisers sometimes give the torture for men, but we didn't see it."

Testimony of Qadratullah, thirty-nine, a farmer from just north of Kabul who was arrested in the summer of 1983 (interviewed in Peshawar, 30 September 1984)

"In Sedarat they put me in a small room. I was alone there from 9:30 in the morning to 9:00 at night. Then two Russians and an interpreter came, and I was under investigation. The Russian told me, 'You are an *ashrar* [bandit].' They accused me of burning the school in my village. They were beating me and hitting me against the wall. They had a table. They put my fingertips under the legs of the table and hit the table. Then they repeated this after ten minutes. My nails were bleeding, and some of them were broken. [They asked a series of questions about his participation in the resistance.] Then they told me to stand. When I stood they told me to sit. Then they told me again to stand, and they were beating me on the shins while I did this. Then they left me alone till 9:00 the next night.

"For five nights they repeated the same questions. The Parchami told me, 'Your people have already confessed, and we have ways and means of making you confess.' I said I didn't know anything. Then the Parchami hit me in the stomach, and I had to lean against the wall. The Russian said to bring the wire, and the Russian connected the wires to my toes. They gave me a shock, and I fell unconscious.

"After an hour I woke up, and they told me to confess, or they would connect the wire again. [They asked many more questions, but Qadratullah did not confess to anything.] There were two tables. They turned me upside down. They put my head between the two tables and pushed them together. They leaned my feet against the wall and made me stretch out my arms on top of the tables, and the Parchami was beating my hands. They asked, 'Would you like to confess or not?'

"After half an hour my legs began to feel light, and my upper body felt heavy. My eyes and neck were swollen. My hands were trembling, and I lost control. I fell unconscious for a long time. When I woke up, at first I couldn't open my eyes. When I did, I saw a lot of blood on the floor. My mouth was so swollen I could not eat."

Testimony of Ghulam, thirty-eight, a shopkeeper in Kandahar, arrested in September 1981 (interviewed in Quetta, 3 October 1984)

"First they took me to the headquarters of KHAD in Kandahar, which is in the house of Abdul Rahim Latif in Shahr-e Nau. For torture they took me to another house nearby, the house of Musa Khan. They told me to give the names of those I was helping. I refused and denied knowing anything about the documents. Then they started the electricity. They connected four wires to my toes, fingers, and tongue. The wires came out of a machine with a crank like an old-fashioned telephone. It was operated by hand. They turned the crank, and I fell unconscious from the shock. Then I was thrown in the water. Then they tied my hands behind me and tied my legs. I had to stand for seven days. I just had five minutes rest in the evening. The KHAD people were torturing me, but every morning at ten o'clock many Russians would come and say, 'Give me the names of people, and I will set you free.' The Russians were instructing the KHAD people what to do. Every morning the KHAD people reported to the Russians to find out what to do. We heard them talking on the telephone; it was a small place. Then I was locked in a room alone for forty days and interrogated just once or twice. Then they let me go."

Testimony of K., a student in the eleventh grade when he was arrested in 1980 (interviewed in Peshawar, 24 September 1984; name withheld on request)

"I was first taken to the KHAD office in Wazir Akbar Khan. At first they gagged me and hung me on a wall with both arms out and my legs tied, and they lashed me with a cable from 8:30 to 12:30 at night. The question was, 'Tell to what organization you belong, and how many people you have killed.' I stayed in Wazir Akbar Khan four nights. But in the day they also tortured. They took a bandolier, a belt for holding bullets, and someone came and strangled me with that. They tried to hang me, and without asking me any questions.

"I was not given electric shocks, but I saw another boy. They tied some wires to his body, and I saw him jumping up and falling down.

"I was taken in the daytime to Sedarat in the minibus with about twenty-five other young people. They took us into a yard and told us, 'You will be talked to later. These are the last minutes of your lives.' The next day they took papers and questionnaires and started the interrogation. I stayed in Sedarat for twenty-five days. Each day they interrogated me. They put my hand under a chair's leg and sat on the chair. They were beating me with Kalashnikovs and sticks. They told me, 'This is your last day.' Russians were coming in the room with their weapons and saying, 'You are *basmachi*' [bandits, a term originally used by the Soviets in referring to Central Asians who resisted their rule in the 1920s]. The most horrible thing of all was being strangled. I lost consciousness, and my face was all swollen. Then I went to Pol-e Charkhi."

We also received descriptions of torture from people who were not torture victims themselves.

"They hang the prisoner by one hand and one foot on the wall, and then they connect the wire to the toes or testicles. The wire comes out of a machine that plugs into an outlet. There is a switch, and a meter that shows the amount of current. There is a terminal with wires that have rings on the end to connect it to the body. You can control the amount of current. It looks like a telephone box. They put cotton in the prisoner's mouth, and start to turn the crank. When he nods his head, it means he will confess." (Testimony of a former KHAD agent, describing practices in the Sheshdarak KHAD office; interviewed in Peshawar, 30 September 1984)

"We heard the moans and crying of the political prisoners being beaten by soldiers or party members in a separate building inside the prison compound. They were weeping, screaming. Once we managed to go to a canteen where we could purchase something. It was near where the political prisoners were. We could see the corridor—the walls were covered with blood, dirty and wet. There were people who had been locked in their rooms for many months." (Mohammad Ashraf, eighteen, former high school student from Kandahar, describing conditions in Kandahar Jail, where he was detained before being sent to military service; interviewed in Quetta, 3 October 1984)

There are reports that many prisoners have died under torture. Of those that survive, many suffer psychological and physical aftereffects: sleeplessness, irritability, inability to concentrate, anxiety, and lack of trust.

"My office was outside the city. One time in early 1981 I was coming to the city, and I saw a truck loaded with some people near the KHAD office in the prefecture. The driver of the truck said, 'We need some gasoline,' and we called somebody to bring it. Then I got out of my car, and I saw the truck was loaded with dead bodies. One of them, the hands were chopped with an axe or beaten with a hammer. One, I saw the blood come out of his mouth, and the other one had his head broken. Blood was all over. Usually, when the KHAD killed some people during interrogation, they carried the bodies to one of the military bases, and in the night they would bury the bodies far from the city." (Testimony of a former high police official from Kandahar; interviewed in Alexandria, Virginia, 23 March 1984)

Specialized items, such as those used for administering electric shocks, are not manufactured in Afghanistan. A former police official from Kandahar told us that during the monarchy, the Afghan police had imported electric shock batons from West Germany for use in controlling demonstrations. Sometimes, he said, they had also been used to torture criminal suspects. Col. Mohammad Ayoub Assil, a professor of criminology at the Kabul Police Academy until his defection in 1982, told us in an interview in New York City on 21 April 1983 that since 1978 shock batons had been imported from East Germany. The "earphones" and the "telephone box" described by various torture victims are manufactured in the Soviet Union or East Germany, according to the former KHAD agent we interviewed in Peshawar on 30 September 1984. He said that he had seen markings on the equipment indicating their country of origin.

Several witnesses also described a torture device imported from the U.S.S.R. or East Germany for the first time in 1984. An eighteen-year-old girl was tortured with it for fifteen days after her arrest in the fall of 1984 for distributing opposition leaflets.

"I was arrested on the fourth of Aqrab last year [27 October 1984]. Two days before, I had gone to Khairkhana to distribute *shab nameh*, and I was marked absent from school. On Saturday I returned to school and took an examination. After I left school, they followed me, and when I got home, I found that a group of people had searched my home. They arrested us [her and her cousin] and took us to KHAD in Sheshdarak.

"During the day I was not tortured. At night, between one and two, I was tortured. They used electric shocks, held our feet and beat them, and asked about our relations with mujahedin, with what group we were working, where we got the leaflets. Despite all this I did not confess.

"For the electric shocks there was a new machine brought from the Soviet Union. They fixed wires around the wrist. There was a chair on which they made you sit. They tied us to it and connected the wires to the electricity. Then they pushed a switch. The chair turned around in a circle. When they connected it to the electricity, the chair moved so fast it made me dizzy. I was tortured like this for fifteen days, between one and four in the morning. All the interrogators were men.

"We felt it was a Soviet-made machine, because the members of the KHAD were talking about it among themselves, saying that the new imported machine works well and really makes the people confess easily." (Testimony of former student from Zarghuna High School; interviewed in Islamabad, 28 August 1985)

"They have changed the method of torturing. They have a new machine from East Germany for torturing. The new machine was brought in 1984, very modern machines for torturing. There is a chair, a very comfortable chair. The accused must sit in the chair. When they turn the switch, it turns at 1,800 RPM. Then there is another type of machine, going zigzag, knocking the people on the ground. A man came here who showed a broken arm. He saw a doctor in Lahore. He told me he could not drive more than one hour now. I also heard about these machines from another driver. He was from Jaji [in Paktia]. He had a transport company, he had many lorries, and he was coming always to Peshawar with grapefruit and other fruit, and also he brought things to Kabul from Peshawar. He was under the eyes of police. I saw him five months before. He was tortured in January 1985 and left the jail in March. After a few days he came to Peshawar." (Testimony of Col. Mohammad Ayoub Assil, former professor at the Police Academy and director of the passport department, Ministry of the Interior; interviewed in Peshawar, 17 August 1985)

"I heard from my friends who worked in the prison that there was an electric chair. There are wires, lines in the chair. You push the button, and the electricity comes. The chair also turns at 1,000 RPM." (Testimony of a former official of the security apparatus; interviewed in Peshawar, 17 August 1985)

The high school student's uncle mentioned that "they had beaten her so badly her eyes could not be seen. And from so many electric shocks, she has many problems." He described her hypersensitivity to noise and stress. When asked if she had any problems sleeping, she replied, "I am afraid of sleep."

Another woman, former science teacher Fahima Naseri, described how women were being tortured both in 1981, during her first arrest, and in 1984, when she was arrested again. Much of her testimony confirms the reports of other Afghan women torture victims such as Razia (see above), whom we interviewed in 1984, and Farida Ahmadi, who testified in 1982 at the Permanent Peoples' Tribunal in Paris.[18] Indeed, Fahima Naseri recalls seeing Farida Ahmadi in the Sedarat interrogation center.

Testimony of Fahima Naseri, former science teacher, arrested in April 1981 (interviewed in Peshawar, 27 August 1985)

Arrested on 23 April 1981 for her work in organizing demonstrations against the Soviet invasion, Fahima Naseri was taken first to party headquarters in Microraion, where men and women party activists beat her under the guidance of Soviet advisers. She was then taken to the KHAD office in Sheshdarak: "What struck me most at the entry of the KHAD was the music—all sorts of very, very loud music, European, Asian, Afghan. And after the first moment I heard the cries of women, men." She was kept alone without food, listening to the loud music and the cries until late at night, when a woman and a man came to interrogate her. After they left, she was watched to be sure she would not sleep.

Some time the next day she was taken to another place, which she learned later was the main interrogation office of the KHAD in the Sedarat Palace. "They left me in a room where on the walls I saw spots of blood and all kinds of insects and rats. I have never seen so many insects." That night she was taken to a "well-decorated room of the old regime" and interrogated by a seated man named Kaiwan as well as women named Alamtab [also mentioned by Farida Ahmadi] and Rahila Tajzai. "They started to beat me and pull out my hair. Alamtab was the one who pulled my hair most often. This method of questioning continued until 3:00 A.M. Then they took me to a room where there were other women sleeping on the floor, and told me to sleep there. I asked where, and they said, 'Here, with the other bitches.' " Two of the prisoners turned out to be undercover KHAD agents. Fahima was preoccupied with worry about her parents, her husband, and her two children.

"The third night they came and took me. They kept asking questions, but this time they brought an instrument with wires. There was a sort of collar of iron they put around my neck. They took off my shoes and made me put my feet on the floor. They brought my notebook with names in it and asked, 'What is your organization, what is your connection with bandits, who are these names in the book?' I said they were my friends, it doesn't mean anything. They gave me an electric shock, and I jumped up. They repeated it the same way. On the third day of electric shock torture, I realized that if I raised my feet, the current was less. So when I saw they were about to push the button, I raised my feet. The wires were attached to my hands, and there was a button on the machine. Each time the electricity passed through me, I fell flat, like a corpse. My heart palpitated, and I was nearly numb. The fourth night they tried several times more, and then they stopped.

"Then they took me to a dark room with tables, not so big a room, and a woman and a man were there. They again started to pose questions and pull my hair. I had already lost three fingers of hair. [She pulled back her hair to show how it had receded by the width of three fingers.] They made me stand and slapped me. This was the worst, because it did not hurt very much, but it was very insulting. They made me stand on one leg, and when one foot fell down, they would beat me.

"When they finished making me stand on one foot, they took me into another room, where there was some bluish water. They told me to stand in it. And my feet felt like there were needles in them, like ants eating them. It felt like needles, and my feet started to swell as if they would burst. Since then I have pain and a swelling in the toe from that, and an infection. [She showed a swelling on her foot.]

"After I think the thirteenth night they took me to another room [she began to weep], that smelled, it was very dark. In this room it stank. I saw a corpse, and there were cut fingers, cutoff limbs, blood." [Overcome at this point, she had to leave the room.][19]

After this she was left alone, except for psychological torture consisting of false news about misfortunes befalling her family. Four months later she was sentenced to one year of imprisonment and one and a half years of parole.

Fahima noticed in the prison:

"One of the things that struck me the most was that when pregnant women were taken to the hospital [from prison] to give birth, they were brought back with their children, but as soon as they came back, they started interrogating them again. As a result of tortures, they had problems and couldn't nurse their babies."

Soviet KGB advisers control the activities of KHAD. According to a former KHAD official:

"The Soviets have an office in Kabul controlling the KHAD. The ordinary work, like collecting information, can be done by Afghans. Then they take it for analysis by Soviets. The office is in a former private house on Dar-ul-Aman Road, between Habibia High School and the Soviet Embassy." (Interview in Peshawar, 20 September 1984)

Soviet advisers are also present in the interrogation centers. Our evidence is the same as Amnesty International's.

Many of the testimonies available to Amnesty International refer to the presence of Soviet personnel when prisoners are being interrogated under torture. In many of these cases, prisoners state that Soviet personnel are present during torture and participate in or direct interrogation while the physical application of torture is left to Afghans.[20]

In provincial cities, where there are sometimes not enough Afghan personnel, the Soviets conduct the interrogations themselves. As mentioned above, they also take direct charge of the interrogation of important prisoners, both in the special section of Pol-e Charkhi and in Sedarat.

> In a few cases, allegations extend to some actual participation by Soviet personnel in the physical application of torture. . . . Allegations that Soviet personnel are present during torture and give orders for it to be inflicted have been made not only regarding those present in KHAD centers but also regarding military personnel in the field.[21]

> "The very important people are taken to be questioned by the Russians. There was someone like that in my room in Sedarat. He was a Khalqi. Part of his family was captured by the Russians, and they said that he was active with the mujahedin. They searched his house and found some acids." (Testimony of a bank employee interviewed in Peshawar, 25 September 1984)

> "Two of the people with me in the cell in Sedarat were interrogated by Soviets. They were more 'guilty' than I was. They had been employees of the U.S. Embassy, and they took them for CIA agents. Of course, they were just typists, and they had been working there with the consent of the Afghan government." (Anwar-ul-Haq, former physics student in Kabul; interviewed in Peshawar, 29 September 1984)

Qadratullah, a farmer, reported being tortured by two Soviets with an Afghan interpreter, and a former bank employee reported that the head of the KHAD office in Kart-e Seh is a Russian who speaks Pashto and Persian.[22]

A resistance fighter under Commander Abdul Haq of Kabul Province was arrested around 12 February 1983, the morning after he had helped destroy an electric pylon. He was tortured first in the Fifth Office of KHAD (the counterinsurgency office) and then in Sedarat. He described the role of Soviets as follows:

> "In the KHAD Fifth Office Russians were coming and interrogating us. The Russians asked, 'Where is your center? Why did you join the *ashrar*? Why did you use rifles against the government?' He had a translator, but he spoke Persian. I said, 'I don't have a center.' He asked, 'Why are you an *ashrar*?' I said, 'We are not *ashrar*, we are people working the land.' If we agreed we are *ashrar*, they would have killed us. During that session I was not tortured. The Soviets gave the order, and then the Afghans gave the torture.

> "In Sedarat there were many, many Soviets. There were many Soviet advisers supervising the interrogators, giving advice on how to give torture. They were working as sort of inspectors of the interrogators. One adviser interviewed me there. He asked me, 'Why did you oppose the government and join the *ashrar*? What was the main reason?' But if I told him, they would execute me. So I said, 'I am poor, a peasant's son, and I

have never been an *ashrar*.' He had an interpreter who spoke Persian. That time I was beaten, slapped, and kicked. The Soviet adviser beat me with his hand and kicked and punched me. Only Afghans gave the electric shocks, but the Soviets were ordering them to do it.

"The Soviets asked more complicated questions. The Soviets would ask, 'Why did you destroy the pylons? Why did you want to cut off the electricity? Why did you become an *ashrar*? Why do you destroy mosques, villages, government buildings?' The Afghans only asked simple questions, like, 'Where is your center? Why are you against the government?' " (Testimony of Nader Khan, son of Mohammad Anwar Khan, twenty-three, of Tangi Gharo area, Deh Sabz District, Kabul Province; interviewed in Peshawar, 21 August 1985)

Most observers agree that many KHAD agents learn their trade during three- to six-month training courses in the Soviet Union.[23] We were also told that the Soviets have established a school near Kabul to teach interrogation techniques.

"I saw torture in Sheshdarak, and I also saw that some people are trained how to torture. The class was somewhere between Kabul and Paghman, in 'Company.' [An area where the headquarters of the American company that built the Kabul-Kandahar highway was located, which has come to be known as 'Company.'] I went there with someone important and saw them writing something on the blackboard. There are soundproof rooms where they beat and torture people there. They have these in the Ministry of the Interior, too. They show them theoretically and practically, and some have also gone to the Soviet Union." (Testimony of a former KHAD agent; interviewed in Peshawar, 30 September 1984)

Conditions of Detention and Imprisonment

Interrogation and torture take place in KHAD detention centers, where abysmal conditions become an integral part of the torture process designed to break the prisoner.

"I was in a small room [in Sedarat] with forty-eight people. We could hardly sit down. There was nothing in the room—no mattress, carpet—it was completely empty, except for forty-eight people. There were small parasites, lice, everywhere. We had the right to go to the toilet one time in twenty-four hours, at 2:00 A.M., in groups of five. There was no water to wash our hands with afterward.[24] There was no respect for us as human beings. The government people compared us to animals. Since once in twenty-four hours was not enough, we made a hole under the door to urinate. Often there were prisoners who had diarrhea. Since they couldn't wait until 2:00 A.M., they defecated in a small bowl. I was there for two months in these conditions." (Anwar-ul-Haq, former physics student; interviewed in Peshawar, 29 September 1984)

"I was arrested in Daulatabad on February 28, 1982. They took 80 peasants to Andkhoy prison. Throughout the journey we were blindfolded, and for the whole month I was imprisoned in Andkhoy it was the same. My cell was dark, without any light, 3 m by 2 m. . . . Then [after beatings] they took me to a subterranean prison, also in Andkhoy. There were five cells underground. There were 130 prisoners in my cell. We did not wear blindfolds, but the cell had no light. All we had to eat was dry bread."[25]

After interrogation by the KHAD, most prisoners are transferred to Pol-e Charkhi Prison, about twelve kilometers outside Kabul, where they often wait for many months without being charged or tried. British journalist Anthony Hyman described the prison:

Pol-e Charkhi is a great wheel composed of eight multi-storied blocks, with watchtowers and high walls cutting off the prison from the main road south to Jalalabad and the border, just a mile away. The prison was not completed in the spring of 1978, when the new regime's wave of arrests made it essential to use its ample accommodation for 5,000 prisoners, so as to relieve pressure on Kabul's old Deh Mazang prison. Intended as a modern-style, progressive prison by its designers, Pol-e Charkhi failed from the first to satisfy elementary rules of hygiene, quite apart from its other defects; floors were unfinished concrete, water pipes had not been connected, and there was no water closet, and all other necessary works were suspended after occupation.[26]

The exact number of prisoners in Pol-e Charkhi Prison is not certain. According to Amnesty International, "estimates of the total number of prisoners vary, but Amnesty International believes that it is probably well in excess of 10,000. One block is said to be occupied by ordinary criminal prisoners, but they are estimated to be not more than about 1,000 of the total in prison."[27] John Fullerton, who has interviewed both prisoners and former prison personnel, wrote in 1983, "Pol-e Charkhi holds some 12–15,000 prisoners."[28] The Kabul regime claimed to have released 6,000 prisoners in the first six months of 1987, including 1,200 from Pol-e Charki, but the number has not been verified.

Conditions vary among the blocks. There is a separate section for women. Testimonies from former prisoners give some idea of the miserable conditions to which prisoners are subjected. Fullerton describes the experience of Tobah Hamid, a former university student who had been imprisoned in the women's section of Pol-e Charkhi after forty-six days in the KHAD:

She joined 34 other women in a large cell, including a nine-year-old girl and two female informers. The place was bare save for the constantly burning light bulb and a few blankets the more fortunate inmates had managed to obtain on the all-too-rare family visits to the jail. Washing was not permitted. All the women suffered from body sores. Tobah still bears the scars. Most of them were sick most of the time. All had been tortured with varying degrees of severity. They were forbidden to talk to each other. They could not see out of the room and sunlight did not penetrate the small, barred window. The highlight of their existence consisted of a twice-daily visit to the lavatory.[29]

Qader, a former university student who was imprisoned in Pol-e Charkhi Prison in 1980, told us in an interview in Peshawar on 29 September 1984:

"There were a lot of strange and criminal stories. There was a retired army officer, an old man. One day he had blood diarrhea. The diet gave everyone diarrhea; it was rare to have a normal stomach. Once he tried to go to the bathroom, but it was morning. The guard told him, 'Shut up! You are *ashrar*! You burned schools and the Holy Koran.' The old man was nearly dying. He forced open the door and ran to the bathroom. The guard took a belt and hit him, and when he came back, his face was all covered with blood.

"For seven or eight nights I was alone in a very dark room. I couldn't see anyone but the guard, who threw me a piece of bread now and then. Then I was brought into a room with about twelve people. Once one of them had his whole back on the ground, and this caused a quarrel. People asked, 'Why are you putting your whole back on the ground?' There was not enough room! At night, when we wanted to turn on our shoulder, we had to wake all the other prisoners.

"In twenty-four hours we could go once to the bathroom for five minutes, at six o'clock. You know, defecation is a natural thing. Some people were in urgent need of it, so we stood up and held our *patous* [a type of cloak worn in the winter] around them, and they did it in the cell."

We were told of cells where "dangerous" prisoners are kept chained in cages.

"In Pol-e Charkhi there is a special block of cells for dangerous prisoners. [He drew a diagram, showing that it was a three-story building to the left of the main gate, next to the circular arrangement of the eight principal blocks.] In these cells, there is no room to stand up. As soon as the prisoner sees them, he loses his morale. I saw them. I was imprisoned there [under the Taraki regime]. I was the commander there, and then I was imprisoned there. I spent eight months there, because I permitted some prisoners to walk in the sun. At that time the construction had not been completed, but now it is completed. There is no central heating. Actually, it has a heating system, but they don't turn it on, because they want the prisoners to be cold." (Testimony of former official of Pol-e Charkhi Prison; interviewed in Peshawar, 25 August 1985)

"We were in a cage in Pol-e Charkhi. In this cage, you can't stand up, and we were handcuffed to the side of the cage." (Testimony of Mohammad Hasan, former employee of the Ministry of Water and Power in Kabul, where he worked as an agent of the Jamiat-e Islami resistance party; interviewed in Islamabad, 28 August 1985)

These conditions set off a hunger strike by some of the prisoners in May 1982. Two of the former prisoners we met, civil engineer Mohammad Nabi Omarkhel and high school teacher Dad Mohammad, had participated in the strike. Dad Mohammad was considered a leader, and hence his sentence was lengthened by six months.

"In Jauza 1361 [May 1982] we started a movement in jail over the difficulties in prison. There was no good food, too many were sick, there was no medicine. There was one bathroom for five hundred people. The condition of the food was so bad that many had dysentery. The electricity didn't work because the mujahedin had cut the power lines. The water was scarce, and we couldn't wash. In each block there was one doctor, and he was for the KGB agents, not the prisoners. The worst torture was the lack of bathrooms. Prisoners could not speak to each other. Every Friday night we were all searched. There was psychological torture: they would wake us up at night and check us. There were so many prisoners we could not lie on the floor. Most couldn't walk, from sitting on their knees for a long time on the concrete floor. There were many parasites, lice. We started a hunger strike. Twenty of us were punished—our sentences were increased. Most of the people were just beaten." (Dad Mohammad, interviewed in Peshawar, 26 September 1984)

"They warned us, 'If you don't eat the food, you will be responsible for what the government will do.' Soldiers came with guns and started beating us in the rooms. They moved people from the second block [where the strike began] to the third block. They tortured people in the first and second blocks. Then they started the investigation. They put about seventeen persons they considered leaders in a small room. They took their *patous* and shoes away. The room was all wet with water. They brought more water two or three times. In the morning they started the investigation. But they punished us before the investigation." (Mohammad Nabi Omarkhel, interviewed in Peshawar, 27 September 1984)

The presence of informers among the prisoners made it difficult for them to speak to each other.

"In Pol-e Charkhi there was a man who brought me tea and cakes. I asked him who he was. He said, 'I escaped from the army and killed twenty people and burned down four mosques. You haven't done anything, so why are you so upset?' After a few minutes, he told me to tell the truth. Then he got angry and shouted, 'Do you think I have nothing better to do than ask questions?' He stayed with me that night, and then I was transferred to another place. There were already six people there, and one of them gestured that I should keep my mouth shut. One of the people asked me why I was taken to prison. He said he was an army deserter. Each one was telling me they were sentenced to six years, seven years. In the morning we were allowed to go out of the room for a half hour. The man who had gestured to me told me not to speak. The people who had been talking were all spies." (Qadratullah, a peasant from Qala-e Murad Beg; interviewed in Peshawar, 30 September 1984)

As in the detention centers, there is a Soviet presence in Pol-e Charkhi Prison.

"There are [Russian] advisers there, sometimes wearing Afghan uniforms and sometimes not. It seemed to me that they were inspecting the prison. Those who don't have uniforms have offices in the first block. I don't know what they are doing, probably advising the chief of the prison." (Mohammad Nabi Omarkhel, quoted above)

"I saw Russians in Pol-e Charkhi. One came into my room. The Russian, who was wearing a suit, was in front, and a group of Parchamis were following him. They walked around the room. They didn't speak to anyone. They left our room, and then they went into the next one. They were inspecting the rooms.

"The control of Pol-e Charkhi is in the hands of the Soviets. They have a Center of Afghan-Soviet Friendship in Block 1 of Pol-e Charkhi Prison! Of course, it is for the personnel, not the prisoners." (Anwar-ul-Haq, physics student, quoted above)

We received a report that some prisoners are sent to the Soviet Union to serve out their terms:

"After interrogation, they decide where to send the prisoners, some to Pol-e Charkhi, some to other units of KHAD, and some to the U.S.S.R. Most of the old people are kept here, but young people sentenced to prison for a long time are sent to the U.S.S.R. They put them in special trucks after the curfew is imposed at night. They are blindfolded and taken to the airport. On one occasion, I was there. I separated some people to be sent to the airport. Dr. Baha [head of KHAD's Fifth Office] was also there, and so was Jaman Mohammadi, who is now the head of KHAD in Sheshdarak. I don't know exactly where they were going, but people were saying they were being sent to Siberia." (Testimony of a former KHAD agent; interviewed in Peshawar, 30 September 1984)

Trials, Sentences, and Executions

After waiting in prison, often for months without charges or a trial, some prisoners, presumably judged "not guilty," may then be released without explanation.

"I had no trial, because I had not done anything. But when I was released, my brother and his friends were taken before the judge. Of course, the judge has no power. The Russians write on the back of the file how many years to give. My brother got fourteen years." (Testimony of a bank employee, arrested and tortured because of his brother's political connections; interviewed in Peshawar, 25 September 1984)

"One night in the washroom [in Pol-e Charkhi Prison] I saw a small piece of paper in the mirror. It said, 'Brother, be careful. They took two people from their rooms and must have killed them last night. Fight on the way.' Then at 1:00 A.M. at night someone came and knocked on my door and said, 'Take your clothes. You'll be released.' They took me to sign a form, that I wouldn't be in demonstrations or be against the government, and that I would report anyone against the government. And I signed it.[30] And I remembered this guy's letter. And I was thinking, 'Let's see where they take you. I know the directions.' When they left the prison it took a while to get to the main road. I was thinking, 'If they turn left, that's to Kabul, where my house is. If they turn right here it means they'll take you to KHAD again,' and then the driver asked me, 'Where do you live?' " (Statement of Anwar, former office worker; interviewed in Chicago, 15 April 1984)

Those considered guilty are presented with a document called the *Surat-e Da'awa*, a "statement of accusation" issued by the KHAD. Former high school teacher Dad Mohammad showed us his "statement of accusation." Under the KHAD letterhead, it lists the conclusions of the investigation, names the laws under which the defendant was charged, and recommends a sentence to the Revolutionary Court.

A prisoner cannot meet with family members or lawyers, confront witnesses, or prepare a defense. In many cases the main evidence is a confession obtained under torture. Sometimes a prisoner is not informed of his trial until the night before it is to begin. He is then taken in a windowless van from Pol-e Charkhi Prison to the Sedarat Palace, where the Revolutionary Court holds its secret sessions in the precincts of the KHAD.[31]

> No accounts suggest that prisoners tried by special revolutionary courts
> have had access to defence counsel or that either defence or prosecution
> witnesses are present. . . . Members of special revolutionary courts are
> PDPA members and in some cases recruited from the KHAD itself; most
> do not have a legal or judicial background. Hearings are not public and
> relatives are unaware that trials are taking place, although a few trials are
> filmed for showing on television.[32]

Except in a few trials staged for political purposes, no one is present in the court except the prisoner (or group of prisoners) and the officials of the court. The charges are read, but the prisoner is not allowed to defend himself and may be reprimanded if he tries. It is the KHAD, rather than the court, that determines innocence or guilt. The court confirms the KHAD's "guilty" verdict and determines the sentence in accordance with the recommendation of the KHAD. In the course of our interviews, we did not hear of a single case in which someone judged guilty by the KHAD was found not guilty by the court. There is no appeal from the decision of the Revolutionary Court.

Engineer Omarkhel was charged six months after his arrest.

> "They sent me a copy of the *Surat-e Da'awa* from the investigation office.
> It said, 'You did such and such antigovernment activity in violation of such
> and such number of the law, and for this you might be in jail ten or fifteen
> years.' I said, 'I don't accept this.' But they said, 'Whether you accept or
> not, you have to sign.' So I signed, but I said, 'I don't accept this fifteen
> years, because they tortured me, and there is nothing that proves my
> membership in Afghan Mellat [a nationalist party]. The only evidence
> against me was one *shab nameh*, that anyone can pick up in the street.'
> [The KHAD had found one leaflet during a search of his house. He wrote
> on the *Surat-e Da'awa* that he had been tortured. He was sent to see the
> prison doctor, who without examining him wrote that he had not been
> tortured. A new *Surat-e Da'awa* was issued, asking for only five to ten
> years.]
>
> "After one and a half months, at midnight, they called me and said, 'You
> will be taken to the court tomorrow morning.' They had a special bus
> without windows carrying the prisoners to court in Sedarat. The judge
> would not listen to the defense I had written out. Instead he gave three
> reasons for my guilt: 'You are from Maidan [Wardak] Province, and Mr.
> Ghulam Ahmad Farhad [founder of Afghan Mellat] is also from Maidan
> Province; this proves that you are a member of the Afghan Mellat Party.
> You don't work for the government. The third reason is that members of
> Afghan Mellat and mujahedin attacked Russian and Afghan government
> troops in the Kabul-Jalalabad road about a month ago [while Omarkhel
> was in prison]. This means that Afghan Mellat is completely against the
> government, so you have to be in jail.' I said, 'There is no document that
> proves my membership. Please show me a document such as a card, my
> photo, or my signature, and I will accept that you put me in jail.' But he

didn't give me any answer and just wrote there, 'five years.' The whole procedure took about twenty minutes." (Omarkhel was released in an amnesty in April 1983 on the fifth anniversary of the 1978 coup. We interviewed him in Peshawar on 27 September 1984.)

Others described similar experiences:

"After the end of the interrogation, they sent me the *Surat-e Da'awa*. Two months later I went to the judge to answer the charges. The court was in Sedarat. There was the president of the court, a judge, and two *saranwals* [state's attorneys]. The *saranwals* brought the *Surat-e Da'awa*. For defense there was only me, no representative. I was not allowed to defend myself. All four didn't ask questions like a judge but like a boss. Whatever you say, the sentence is determined in advance. They got angry whenever I said anything. I was sentenced to five years, but the sentence was reduced by eighteen months last year." (Anwar-ul-Haq, physics student; interviewed in Peshawar, 29 September 1984)

The procedure appears to be similar in the provinces, except that there are no regular sessions of the revolutionary courts there. From time to time judges of the Revolutionary Court come from Kabul to hold sessions. Abdul Wahid, who was in prison in Jalalabad for two years and seventeen days, described the following to Syed Fazl Akbar, former director of Radio Kabul:

"During the month of March 1984 members of the so-called Revolutionary Court of the Communist regime visited the Jalalabad central jail, and the Communist judges ordered the execution of the 12 detainees who were lying there without trial for the last more than two years. . . . 200 more detainees were punished with from 3 to 20 years of imprisonment because they defected from the army. With some of them they had captured cards of the mujahedin groups. I was also imprisoned for 3 years without knowing the crime and the charge of my imprisonment. All the comments by the KHAD department regarding these detainees were confirmed by the judges."[33]

"A judicial delegation of the Special Revolutionary Court which had gone to Faryab, Jowzjan, Balkh, and Samangan Provinces to assess and investigate cases within the jurisdiction of the court today returned to Kabul. . . . Thousands of citizens of Maymana and Mazar-e Sharif attended these open sessions and welcomed the decisions of the court concerning these criminals."[34] (Kabul Radio home service in Pashto, 27 May 1984)

These courts can also impose the death penalty, which must be confirmed by the Revolutionary Council, but which cannot be appealed by the defendant.

When Babrak Karmal became President of the D.R.A. in 1980, he stated that the government deemed it its urgent duty to "abolish executions under favorable conditions."[35] He repeated these assurances to representatives of Amnesty International in Kabul in February 1980.[36] Nevertheless, the government continued to announce executions for several years, and the number increased dramatically after September 1984. Moreover, former prisoners, defecting officials, and defecting prison personnel all claim that actual executions far outnumber those publicly announced.

In 1980 the Kabul government announced eighteen executions, including seventeen former officials of the government of Hafizullah Amin and Abdul Majid Kalakani, leader of the leftist organization SAMA (see chapter 6, n.26). In 1981 Kabul identified fourteen people who were executed. Sixteen executions were announced in 1982 and thirteen in 1983.[37] In 1984 the government announced sixty-eight executions and seventy-seven death sentences. In 1985 the government announced forty death sentences but seemed to stop announcing executions. Amnesty International believes that "these represented only a proportion of the total number of cases in which death sentences were imposed and carried out."[38]

Professor Abdul Ahad of the Agricultural Faculty of Kabul University saw three hundred men taken out for execution at night, their mouths gagged and their hands tied behind them, during his seven-month stay in Pol-e Charkhi from June 1982 to January 1983.[39] Assad, an engineering student at Kabul University, was in Pol-e Charkhi twice, with a hiatus between December 1982 and April 1983. When he returned in April 1983, prisoners told him four hundred people had been executed while he was gone.[40] K., a high school student, told us on 24 September 1984:

> "Many people are taken out and executed. In 1981 I saw twenty-five people taken and executed in fifteen days. They killed them on Polygon Field." [Polygon Field, behind the military academy, is a well-known execution ground.]

Engineer Omarkhel, interviewed in Peshawar on 27 September 1984, told us:

> "Under Babrak many of the prisoners have been killed. They wrote it on the *Surat-e Da'awa*—killing. I knew many of them. Silently, during the night, they were transferred for killing. Only a few persons are announced, the most famous. Sometimes they don't inform the person he is to be killed. At the trial the judges say, 'We will deal with your case later.' Then they come and kill them. Thousands have been killed. This process is current."

On 26 April 1985 Reuters reported from New Delhi:

A Supreme Court judge who fled Afghanistan for India said today that his country's legal system had been reduced to what he called organized "terror" by the Soviet-backed authorities. . . .

[Mohammad Yusuf] Azim said he knew of at least 100 cases in which it had been announced that people had been sentenced to death by the special courts. Many others were executed and their sentences recorded by the courts after the executions. "Many of these victims never appear in court, and in these instances the special courts do not even know them," he said.

Former prisoners indicated that dozens, perhaps as many as a hundred or more prisoners a week, are taken at night from Pol-e Charkhi for execution, and that executions, including sometimes extrajudicial ones, continue in other prisons around the country.

"There were many people executed in Pol-e Charkhi: a commander of a group of mujahedin from Hodkhel [northeast of Kabul near Pol-e Charkhi] named Azim Jan; Jalil from Ghazni Province, who was chief of finances of the mujahed front of NIFA [National Islamic Front of Afghanistan]. They were executing people sometimes every day, sometimes every other day, sometimes every third day, thirty or forty people. When they were taken to execution, they were first taken to the first floor of block one. Their faces were covered, and their hands were chained. Then they were put in a special truck and carried to the executions. We watched from the windows. Some were crying 'Allahu Akbar' [God is great], but some were gagged." (Testimony of Nader Khan, son of Mohammad Anwar Khan, twenty-two, resistance fighter of Hezb-e Islami (Khales's group), of Tangi Gharo, Deh Sabz District, Kabul Province; interviewed in Peshawar, 21 August 1985)

"From the beginning of this year, from Hamal [in late March, the Afghan new year] after sunset two vehicles without doors and windows would come to pick up prisoners sometimes every day, sometimes every two days, and they took the prisoners and carried them to Polygon Field, code no. 15. [This is the military code for the brigade stationed at Polygon Field behind the military academy near Pol-e Charkhi.] First they had doctors take out all their blood, because they need a lot in the hospital, and then they were shot. Then tractors and bulldozers came and covered them with mud.
"When the prisoners were taken to be executed, they would cover their eyes, gag them, chain their hands, and put them in the vehicle and transfer them to Polygon no. 15. The prison was four stories high, and the prisoners upstairs could see where they were going. At the beginning a soldier would stand there to keep the prisoners from seeing them execute people, but sometimes the prisoners could see them in the distance. When they were transferred, on that night the prisoners in each block would pray for the dead and recite verses of the Holy Koran. We knew

about the blood because some of the soldiers were also Muslims. We got the information from different sources, from the soldiers and from some other people, workers in the prison, or lower ranking army officers.[41]

"They took twenty, twenty-five, up to thirty people at a time for execution, sometimes every day, sometimes every other day and always after two days, at least three times a week. There were seventy people with me in a cell in block one of Pol-e Charkhi in Ramazan 1362 [around July 1983], and afterward I only found twenty, and the rest were executed." (Testimony of Zmarai Shikari, son of Mian Gul Shikari, twenty-one, resistance fighter of Hezb-e Islami (Khales's group), of Gazak village, Bagram District, Kabul Province; interviewed in Peshawar, 21 August 1985)

"Every day they were taking about eight prisoners and killing them in Miali Samarkhel [a nearby military post]. All the Khalqis and Parchamis were very, very cruel. Some of them were killing the people, they were saying, 'I know this prisoner, he killed my brother, he shot at me.' They killed them without proof, without judgment." (Testimony of Din Mohammad, son of Gul Mohammad, of Charbagh District, Laghman Province, who was released from prison in Jalalabad in May 1985; interviewed in Panyian refugee camp, Haripur, NWFP, 23 August 1985)

In May 1984 the Chief Justice of the Kabul Civil Court, Sayyed Gharib Gharibnawaz, defected to Pakistan and described the role of the Soviets in the Afghan court system:

In an interview, he said that only 50 of Afghanistan's 230 courts were functioning; the remainder had been closed because the majority of judges had either fled or been jailed or killed. Soviet advisers were working in the Supreme Court, and no judgment was pronounced without their permission. A 30-member committee of Soviet advisers called the Revolutionary Court was entrusted with investigation work in political affairs and in the affairs of the mujahedin.[42]

6

SUPPRESSION OF CIVIL LIBERTIES AND INDEPENDENT INSTITUTIONS

The Afghan Communists and their Soviet allies have tried to construct a new Afghan society in the cities, especially in Kabul. It is a society in which all sources of information are directly controlled by the government and the ruling People's Democratic Party of Afghanistan (PDPA), which, in turn, are under the close supervision of Soviet "advisers." Criticism of the government is not allowed.

Freedom of Expression

In order to maintain power, the Afghan government and its Soviet advisers have created a climate of fear.

> "You couldn't talk to someone in your office unless you knew him very well, that he was a good person, not a member of KGB [KHAD] or was not a member of Communist party [PDPA]. If a visitor was coming to the office for work, then no one could talk. Everybody was silent." (Anwar, an office worker arrested for a remark to his coworkers; interviewed in Chicago, 15 April 1984)

Those in Afghanistan who attempt to collect information about human rights abuses do so at great risk. If caught, they face arrest, torture, and imprisonment. Even those who have fled often decline to testify for fear they might cause harm to relatives or associates still in the country. For this reason, the names of some of the people we interviewed have been withheld. One such witness, a former official in the security apparatus interviewed in Peshawar on 18 August 1985, refused even to have his voice taped, explaining, "I know a lot, but I am afraid to tell you in Peshawar." He recounted the following incident.

> "I am afraid for my mother. Some of my relatives gave an interview in Peshawar, and therefore I was under police surveillance. They told me, 'Someone in your family spoke about Afghanistan.' I said, 'I don't know anything about it.' Every day I had to present a report that I was there. I was watched whenever I left the house or the [office—the witness named his specific place of employment]. In each apartment building of Microraion there are KGB agents, and I lived there, so I wasn't safe there either. It was the deputy [head of the office] who asked me about it. He said, 'Someone from your family reported on the situation in Afghanistan.' "[1]

In early 1982 a group of professors at Kabul University founded the Organization for the Defence of Human Rights and Academic Freedom. The organization planned to distribute pamphlets protesting the lack of freedom at Kabul University and the arrests of students and teachers. In April 1982, before the group could carry out any of its plans, five of its members were arrested.

A leading member of the group was Professor Hasan Kakar, a historian trained at London University, who had also been a research associate at Harvard. His best-known book is *Government and Society in Afghanistan: The Reign of Amir 'Abd al-Rahman Khan*, published in 1979. Those who know him describe his work as a natural extension of his love for his country. Rasul Amin, former professor of political science at Kabul University, told us in Peshawar on 28 September 1984 how Kakar had wept when he saw Soviet soldiers in Kabul after the 1979 invasion:

> "On the day of the invasion [Hakim] Taniwal and [Sayd Bahauddin] Majrooh and Hasan Kakar came to my house. [All were professors at Kabul University.] And Kakar suggested that we go see Kabul. He said, 'We have lived to see the Red Army in Kabul, and we may start hating our Kabul, because when you see the army, you won't remember the sweet Kabul from before.' And we took a car and just went to see all the soldiers. They were standing on both sides from the premier's office to Salang and those places. And Hasan Kakar was very emotional. He started to weep. I said, 'But Kakar, it is not a question of weeping. It is a question, a big question, what should be done.' He talked to the Russians, 'Why have you invaded?' And I said, 'O.K., you may be shot dead, he does not know your language, he is a soldier.' But he was really very emotional, and when we went back, he was the only person to whom

we disclosed that we were leaving. And Majrooh came after three months. But Kakar was not willing at that time to leave."

According to Majrooh, "Kakar was a most politically innocent man." At Kabul University he openly opposed attempts by Soviet advisers to eliminate Islamic influences from the curriculum. These efforts, combined with his activities in the short-lived human rights group, led to his arrest, along with four other group members, some of whom were severely tortured. Kakar was kept in solitary confinement and denied reading or writing material for fifteen months, during which he was allowed only one half-hour visit from his fourteen-year-old son in the presence of a soldier.

> In the interview in April of this year [1983] Professor Kakar declared, "My conscience is clear, and I sleep well," expressing, however, great concern about the future of his family. As tokens of his anxiety and love for his family, he passed on two stones—each laboriously carved with their names. One stone had the name of his wife and five children, the other only the name of his eldest daughter, twenty-four-year-old Palwasha, seriously ill with a disease of the arteries, which has worsened since her father's arrest. Each stone had been carved out by a means of a nail, after endless pains.[2]

One of the professors arrested with Kakar was released. The other four were sentenced to long prison terms for "distributing antistate literature": Professor Hasan Kakar (history), eight years; Professor Osman Rostar (law and political science), twelve years; Professor Habiburrahman Halah (journalism), ten years; Professor Shukrullah Kohgaday (history), seven years. Amnesty International adopted Rostar, Kohgaday, Halah, and Kakar as prisoners of conscience.

A former student had seen these four men in Pol-e Charkhi Prison during the first week of September 1984, just two weeks before we interviewed him in Peshawar on September 24.[3]

> "I met all the professors. I saw Shukrullah Kohgaday. I saw Osman Rostar. I saw Kakar. I saw Halah. Osman Rostar's hair has turned all white, and he has lost his mind. [Subsequent reports indicate Rostar's condition may have improved.] Halah is entirely deaf from the beating. Kakar's hair is entirely white, but he is still surviving."

In the summer of 1984 a representative of the political office of KHAD named Karim met with Kakar in Pol-e Charkhi Prison and, in a repetition of a previous offer, informed him that he would be released if he would write a retraction of his views and appear on television to announce it. Similar offers were reportedly made at the same time to Rostar and Kohgaday. All refused.

Kakar was reported to "look very happy in jail, laughing and joking. He says, 'I am happy to be in prison at a time like this. My conscience is clear (*ruhan aram hastam*).' "[4]

In March 1987 the government released Kakar under an amnesty decreed in January. Rostar and Kohgaday were released later in the year. Halah remains in prison as of January 1988.

There is a National Committee for Human Rights in Afghanistan, an organization based in Peshawar that collects information on human rights violations within Afghanistan as well as from refugees. The group has documented over eight thousand cases of human rights violations in Afghanistan since 1978.

The arrests of the Kabul University professors were only a small part of a vast effort to bring all communications under state control, enforced by Soviet advisers.

> "There are many Russian advisers at BAKHTAR News Agency, the government news agency, and the Kabul *New Times* [the English-language daily newspaper]. They are all run by Russian advisers. According to their advice they publish certain articles. It is difficult to write an article that would express the ideas of the people. It is not possible. And in Radio Kabul sometimes the broadcast is written by the Russians and then sent there. Many of my students were from the department of journalism, and they are working there now. They were telling me that there is no question of press anymore. Everything is under the Russians' control." (Professor Sayed M. Yusuf Elmi, formerly of the Faculty of Social Sciences at Kabul University; interviewed in Peshawar, 21 September 1984)

The imposition of ideological uniformity has created other victims among cultural figures. In 1982 a number of sources, including Amnesty International, reported the death under torture of Ghulam Shah Sarshar-e Shomali, a well-known poet and former editor of the daily newspaper *Anis*.[5] He was reportedly arrested in February 1982, together with about forty writers and artists working for Afghan Radio-Television or the Ministry of Culture, including Azam Rahnaward, Latif Nazemi, and Wassef Bakhtiari.[6]

All forms of publication, including literature, are subject to strict censorship. Works that do not agree with the policies of the Soviet-Afghan regime are not published or sold. In addition, the regime actively promotes publications from the Soviet Union.

> "There is a bookstore in Kabul called Baihaqi Bookstore. Baihaqi was a famous scholar of the tenth century. This bookstore is the main bookstore of Kabul, in the center of Kabul, in a big building. Before the coup it was meant for Islamic publications or other sorts of books, from Europe, or from America, from Iran, India. Every sort of books, Islamic, un-Islamic, all

> sorts of books were there. But after the coup it was changed. All Islamic
> works were removed from there. Now all the whole bookstore is filled with
> Russian books, with Russian pamphlets and periodicals." (Sayed Elmi,
> quoted above)

Some writers have become nonpersons because of their opposition to the regime. The poet Khalilullah Khalili, seventy-nine, widely regarded as the leading writer in Afghanistan, was ambassador to Iraq at the time of the 1978 coup and did not return to Afghanistan. His books, which had been regularly published by the government printing house, are no longer available in Afghanistan.

> "Many of our writers now must be published in foreign countries, and we
> send their works into Afghanistan. . . . There are two kinds of literature:
> free literature and compulsory literature. The poets living outside of
> Afghanistan or at the fronts try to keep the people's real literature and
> religion, which is Islam." (Khalilullah Khalili; interviewed in Islamabad, 1
> October 1984)

The Afghan regime has organized a Soviet-style Writers' Union to safeguard the ideological purity of Afghan literature. The chairman of the union is Ghulam Dastagiri Panjsheri, Minister of Higher Education and a member of the Politburo.

Because all legal channels for publishing literature of protest are closed off, the residents of Kabul and other cities have turned to clandestine literature. The most common form is the pamphlet or "night letter" (*shab nameh*), mimeographed or copied by hand and secretly left in public places. Distribution or even possession of antiregime night letters is a crime in Afghanistan. Many high school and college students have been arrested, tortured, and sentenced to prison terms of several years for possession or distribution of such pamphlets.

Mohammad Nabi Omarkhel, a civil engineer and member of Afghan Mellat (a Pashtun nationalist party that describes itself as social democratic), told us in a 27 September 1984 interview in Peshawar that he was arrested after a team of about twenty KHAD agents found a single pamphlet during a search of his house. A student we interviewed, who asked that his name be withheld, had served a sentence of four years in prison after being found in possession of a single leaflet. The interpreter during our visit with the poet Khalilullah Khalili in Islamabad told us that he had left Kabul three months before because some friends with whom he had been distributing night letters had been arrested, and he was afraid that they would give his name under torture.

KHAD monitors the spoken word as well through a network of spies. Anwar, a former office worker now in the United States whom we interviewed in Chicago on 15 April 1984, was arrested in his office in September 1980. On the third day of his interrogation, a Soviet interrogator and an Afghan interpreter played a tape of private remarks he had made in his office and asked him to confess to ties with the CIA.

A former top government official told us that the government installed spies in his office:

"When Russians come, they trained more young girls as typists, and they sent these girls to offices. These girls were trained by the government. They were sent to Russia, but when they come back, they don't say that they were trained in Russia. The KHAD also had courses in Kabul, and they trained girls, but they didn't know how to type. But they send them with a letter, she must work there. When we saw that they cannot type, nobody can say something to them, that you are not a good typist. For example in my office they sent me two 'typists' but they cannot type! When I learned that they were from KHAD, and they have pistols, I did more and more work by myself. I typed it. Sometimes when they came to the office, they were very tired and sleepy. And I asked 'Why are you sleepy?' They said, 'We had a job last night. We checked some houses.' After we knew each other for a year, they said some things to me. They checked what I was doing, what my friends say. Before that in the office some friends talked to each other about government, about Russia. When they sent these girls to the offices, all Muslim people were quiet. They could not speak." (Jahadyar Aminullah Wardak, former civil servant and cabinet secretary; interviewed in Peshawar, 24 September 1984)

Freedom of Association, Assembly, and Movement

Association with foreigners, especially Americans, is considered prima facie evidence of criminality. Anwar, a former government employee now in the United States, was questioned under torture by Soviet officers about his friendship with an American Peace Corps worker who had been his English teacher when he was fifteen years old.

In May 1982 the KHAD arrested all Afghan clerical employees at the U.S. Embassy. Anwar-ul-Haq, a former physics student from Kabul whom we interviewed on 29 September 1984 in Peshawar, told us that he had met two of them in jail and that they were being interrogated under torture by Soviet officers who accused them of being CIA agents.

Fr. Serge de Beaurecueil, a French Dominican monk who taught at a lycée in Kabul until he returned to France in August 1983, had educated many abandoned children in his home over the years. In June 1983 six of these boys and two of their friends were arrested by KHAD agents and accused under torture of being spies for Fr. de Beaurecueil. One, who was found with a resistance party membership card, was sentenced to ten years in prison, the others to several months.[7]

Many of the former prisoners we interviewed had been sentenced because of their association with other Afghan citizens.

> "In my room was a woman, Rahima. She was tortured for one month. She had been in jail before me, and she had harder torture than I did. Her story was, she was working in the Ministry of Agriculture, and in this ministry one man tried to kill one of the party members there. Then they took this man, and they were torturing him, and he said, 'Rahima is my friend.' So they took her too." (Testimony of Razia, former student from Kabul; interviewed in Peshawar, 23 September 1984)

The Afghan government prohibits all forms of public demonstration against the government. Demonstrators are fired upon and killed or wounded; they are also arrested and interrogated to elicit information about organizations responsible for the demonstrations. In 1980 and, to a lesser extent, in 1981, hundreds were killed and many thousands arrested as the Kabul government, with Soviet help, suppressed mass public demonstrations.

A strike by shopkeepers on 21 February 1980 led to a week of mass demonstrations in Kabul in which hundreds of thousands of people participated. Afghan Army troops fired on the crowds with machine guns and tanks as Soviet helicopters hovered overhead. The Afghan government officially acknowledged a death toll of five hundred. A number of Shia religious dignitaries were reportedly arrested and summarily executed, including the scholar Maulana Zabibullah. Thousands of others were arrested as well.[8]

In March 1980 demonstrations continued, mainly organized by Kabul University students. A former student, Qader, whom we met in Peshawar on 29 September 1984, described the government's suppression of a demonstration by surrounding students with horsemen and tanks, while helicopters flew overhead. Several students died of gunshot wounds and hundreds were arrested.

In April 1980, on the second anniversary of the coup, hundreds of high school girls organized their own demonstrations and were soon joined by other students. Throughout April and May, troops fired on these demonstrators and arrested participants by the thousands. About fifty students were killed, more than half of them schoolgirls.[9]

Schoolgirls called anti-Soviet demonstrations again in September 1981 to protest the mobilization of reserves. At Pol-e Bagh-e Ommumi in central Kabul, they were met by a line of Soviet and Afghan tanks, telling the girls to stop.

> "It was coming from inside a tank like a tape through loudspeakers, announcing, 'Stop the demonstration, don't go ahead, go back to your

classes, otherwise you'll be shot.' There was a small speech like 'You are the property of the country, and you young girls don't know that this is the hand of imperialism, and imperialism is never happy for you to have a happy life, and you shouldn't be fooled to listen to imperialism, and Russians are here to help us, and Russians are here to support revolution,' and stuff like this. The girls continued shouting, 'We know you Russians! We know you, sons of Lenin! We know you are murderers, and we don't want to go back! We'd rather prefer to be killed than to go back to our classes. We want you Russians to get out of Afghanistan.' That's what they were shouting. Then there was firing from the Russian tanks. Six girls were killed. The six bodies, I saw that they were not able to move. Their hands and legs stopped moving, and they put them in a Russian jeep." (Testimony of Anwar, quoted above; interviewed in Chicago, 15 April 1984)

In 1984 the Afghan government enacted regulations, restricting private gatherings and travel within Afghanistan.

The inhabitants must have new identity cards.

If they want to leave the city, the security office of the party must be informed as to where they are going and how long they intend to stay. Only after receiving written permission will they be allowed to travel.

If they receive guests, the party office must be informed about their identities. The guests must not stay more than three days.

Any large gatherings such as funeral processions or wedding parties must be announced in advance to the party office, and the gathering must be kept as small as possible.[10]

Academic Freedom

The Soviets have made the schools—from kindergarten to the university—a major focus of their pacification efforts.[11]

"Once the Soviets entered our country, they demolished everything. They wanted to change our way of writing. They introduced their writing and alphabet. Each year they send students to the Soviet Union for brainwashing. They want to introduce a new culture to a new community." (Khalilullah Khalili, Afghan poet; interviewed in Islamabad, 1 October 1984)

"There are Russian advisers in every office of every ministry, including the Ministry of Education. They were controlling all the curriculum and teaching materials. They also brought a lot of changes in the texts." (Shah

Mahmud Baasir, economist, formerly with the Ministry of Education; interviewed in Quetta, 2 October 1984)

High Schools:

New history textbooks, written by Soviet scholars, praise not only the Soviet Union, but even Czarist Russia as the only true friend of the Afghan people.[12] Russian has replaced English as the required foreign language, and each school has a "Friendship Room." There is constant pressure to join the party and mass organizations.

"There was a room called the 'Friendship Room,' where there were Soviet newspapers, Soviet books. This 'Friendship Room,' among other things, distributed certain books and newspapers, sometimes newspapers of the day before, which were translated into Persian so we could use them in class. We used to make book covers out of the newspapers." (Mohammad Gul, former student at Kabul's Vocational High School; interviewed in Peshawar, 29 September 1984)

"Their main activity is that they have a subject called politics. In that subject they described all the Communist terms and activities. We were asked, 'Why are you not joining the party?' Every day during the politics period they were asking, 'Why don't you join?' "

"If you join the party, then you will succeed in school, and your conditions of living will be good. Those who were ranked as first or second in the class were always members of the party, even though they were not really the first and second. Every year there were scholarships to go to Russia. Only those who belonged to the party got these scholarships." (Taher, former student at a commercial high school in Kabul; interviewed in Peshawar, 25 September 1984)

"In Ahmad Shah Baba Academic High School there was a lot of political pressure on the students. They were pressing us to become members of the party. They were threatening us. We were called to the principal's office, and the principal would tell us that we should join the party, or else they would take us to KHAD." (Mohammad Ashraf, former student at Ahmad Shah Baba Academic High School in Kandahar; interviewed in Quetta, 3 October 1984)

The party brings this pressure against teachers as well.

"There are very few left of the teachers we had before. All the rest of the teachers are new. And some of them are completely unqualified. Often they are simple high school graduates. They don't have the education to be teachers. But the former teachers, some of them are in prison, some of them have fled, and some have been killed." (Mohammad Gul, former student, quoted above)

The Democratic Organization of the Youth of Afghanistan claims 125,000 members.[13] The members of this organization act as the eyes and ears of the KHAD in the high school by spying on students, interrogating them, and even arresting them.

"Another time in the politics class we were talking about Sabra and Shatila in Palestine. [Sabra and Shatila are two Palestinian refugee camps in Beirut where Lebanese Christian gunmen protected by the Israeli Army massacred hundreds of civilians in September 1982.] One of the students said that he would rather learn about our own country, where there were hundreds of Sabras and Shatilas that no one was talking about. He said he would be more interested to talk about our own country than about others. After the class he was arrested by two guards, two students who were members of the [youth] organization. He was imprisoned for four months, and after four months he signed a paper saying he would no longer speak in class."

"There was a youth organization in the school. Its main work was that in each class there were one, two, or three students who reported on the students' talking with each other. In addition to this youth organization, there was also a unit of KHAD in the school, among the students, and we knew it. Every time there were discussions or something against the government there would be arrests of the students. Simply because they had talked about something. We knew who was a member of the youth organization, but we didn't know who was in the second one, the KHAD unit. It worked in secret. We knew about this secret organization, because it happened several times when we had discussions among friends, which normally no one should hear about, but when we got to the [office of the] youth organization, they asked us about it. The secretary of the organization interrogated us." (Testimony of Mohammad Gul, quoted above)

Teachers cannot be trusted.

"Another thing that put pressure on the students was that we couldn't discuss things too much with our teachers, even technical things, because if the teacher ever got angry with us, he could take away our high school registration and send us to the army." (Mohammad Gul)

Universities:

Before the coup there were two universities functioning in Afghanistan, in Kabul and in Jalalabad. Since 1978, according to some estimates, seventy percent of Kabul University's staff has left, been arrested, or been killed.[14]

> "When I was in Afghanistan, in Zaher Shah's time, we had one thousand staff in the university. Now at present there are about two hundred or three hundred in Kabul. But what happened to the seven hundred? Probably one hundred were killed or executed in prison. The rest, most of them defected, they disappeared, finished. They are in different parts of the world." (Professor Sayed M. Yusuf Elmi, interviewed in Peshawar, 21 September 1984)

The student body has also shrunk, although reports differ on its current size and composition. Most recent observers agree that the student body is now over half female. Young men of university age do not receive exemption from military service for attending the university; until 1986, however, security work for the party did provide an exemption, as did studying in the Soviet Union.[15] In 1986 Najib's regime tried to strengthen the army by removing these latter exemptions as well.

Kabul University comprises twelve faculties, each led by a dean. Since 1978 the government has appointed new deans to each faculty, all of them young and without academic qualifications. Professor Elmi identified the new dean of the Faculty of Social Sciences as Inayat Sharif, a Parchami whose academic background consists of an M.A. in journalism from Cairo University. Previously he had worked in the broadcasting unit of the Ministry of Information. The others, Elmi said, are "similar or worse."[16] The new dean of the Faculty of Literature, Abdul Rashid, is a former broadcaster for Radio Afghanistan and the brother-in-law of Suleiman Layeq, Minister of Tribes and Nationalities.[17] The new dean of the Faculty of Law and Political Science is a former high school teacher, Sameh Qarar, who was elevated to professor of education after the coup, and later to the position of dean.[18]

Faculties are increasingly dominated by Soviet staff. In 1983, according to the Kabul New Times, sixty percent of the teachers at Kabul University were from the "socialist countries."[19]

> "Our Afghan professors, as I told you, some of them were killed and defected, most of them defected, and so they were replaced by Parchamis, Khalqis, and of course Russians were there, advisers. Sometimes they were called professor, but they were not professors, they were illiterate, some of them. They were going to the classes and teaching in Farsi [Persian]. Some of them had Persian interpreters. They taught in Russian and had interpreters. In different faculties the number varied. For instance in our faculty there were twelve Russian advisers and lecturers and teachers. The bulk of the Russians were in the philosophy department. They taught, of course, philosophy of Marx, Engels, that sort of job." (Professor Elmi, quoted above)

Like the high schools, the university distributes materials from the Soviet Union and the Socialist bloc.

> "In every faculty there is a 'Friendship Room.' In this room they put the pictures of Lenin, Marx, Engels, and all Communist works, periodicals, magazines from Russia, from Eastern European countries, from Cuba." (Professor Elmi)

There have been many changes in the curriculum, despite the resistance of some of the Afghan professors.

> "I taught in Kabul University in the Faculty of Social Sciences for about twenty-five years. I am the most senior professor of that faculty. After the coup of April [1978] the Russian advisers came to the different faculties, and they came to our faculty, and they changed the whole curriculum. They dropped some subjects and they introduced new subjects. Particularly, they dropped history of Islamic art. This subject was taught by me for the last twelve years. They said these subjects are not very important, they are not 'scientific.' Particularly history of Islamic art and history of Islamic civilization. I am the Professor of History of Islamic Civilization. So they dropped history of Islamic art. I told them that this is not good. We are Muslims, and students like to learn and understand something about Islamic art. It should not be removed from the curriculum. But they didn't listen. They said, 'No, no, this is not important. Anyhow, we will teach this subject as part of the other subjects. For instance archeology, ancient and modern. We will teach Islamic art in these subjects. There is no question of a separate subject for Islamic art. . . .
>
> "New subjects were introduced. For instance, dialectical materialism, history of the worker's movement, history of Russia, Spanish language, and Russian language. A lady and a gentleman from Cuba taught Spanish language, history of Cuba, and history of Latin American literature." (Professor Elmi)
>
> "Before the coup we hired people just like everywhere else, in particular our system was similar to the French. But after the Communist coup, they would give preference to hiring professors who were Marxists. It was very clear. The rector, the council of the professors, the Ministry of Higher Education, they said it openly. Since, during the time I stayed there [after the coup] the number of former professors, the staff that we had built up over a long time, kept diminishing, the faculty was being emptied out of professors, they recruited new professors, young students, who were not the best, but who were faithful to Marxist ideas. They hired them as lecturers, teachers. But they were not the best." (A former rector of Kabul University; interviewed in Peshawar, 24 September 1984)

The professors who remain are constantly watched and pressured to conform ideologically in their teaching.

"It was difficult for me to live in Afghanistan, because I taught history of Islamic civilization. So I was under great pressure. They were telling me, 'You should teach scientifically, according to Marxist theory.' The dean of the faculty told me this. He was always calling me, and asking me, 'Why are you doing like this?' He was telling me that our faculty belonged to the Central Committee: 'Do you know what you are doing in the class?' I said, 'Yes.' He said a report had been sent to the Central Committee and that they were asking, 'Who is this teacher? Why is he teaching like this?' I said, 'What can I do? I can't change my subject. I can't change history. I can't fabricate history. This is the truth. How can I teach wrong ideas?' So we were always in conflict. I was under police escort. After the coup police were always following me everywhere." (Professor Elmi)

"Before the coup, under the monarchy and also under the Daoud regime, the professors could express different points of view about different matters of law and political science. But after the coup the professors could defend only one point of view, the Marxist explanation of social phenomena. What they call 'scientific.' They enforced it by very subtle means. In each faculty, in each class, we had some stooge, some Communist spy. When he heard that a professor was teaching something that did not conform to the official ideology, he would sabotage the professor, protest to the secret police that this professor is antiprogressive, antinational, he is in the pay of the CIA. I tried my best to conform, but I felt that they didn't believe me." (Former rector of Kabul University, quoted above)

Students in the party organization at the university spy on their professors and also on other students. During 1980 and 1981, students organizing public demonstrations and circulating night letters were often called out of classes, dormitories, or the library to find the KHAD waiting for them with a jeep to take them for interrogation. Open protest is no longer possible.

At the University, other problems await young Afghans. . . . Students recounted them in a few words, whispered quickly, out of the presence of our official "guide." "Blackmail, spying, lack of freedom." Thanks to constant surveillance, the regime seems to have gained control of the University.[20]

As in the high schools, party members enjoy many privileges.

"In admission, preference is given to the students who have party cards. The party students can choose to go to whatever faculty they wish. . . . Of course he may be illiterate. He can't study. He doesn't know a word about science, botany, chemistry. But he can be admitted to the Faculty of Science. And he will be promoted. Because the teachers know he is Parchami. And moreover, these students are absent from the class for three or four months. For instance in my case, my students were absent. Five or six students were absent for four months. When they returned, I asked, 'Where have you been? How will you take the examination?' Then he showed a letter from the [party] committee that he was doing 'social work,' he was on duty, so please give him a passing grade. So he will pass the exam!" (Professor Elmi)

"When the civil war intensified, most of the party cadres were students, and they had to go to the countryside to fight against the resistance. So they proclaimed a decree according to which students who spent three months at the front would be promoted automatically. That is the term: automatic promotion. They didn't have to take the exams." (Former rector of Kabul University)

The Minister of Higher Education of the Kabul government announced at an official meeting in August 1983 that twelve thousand Afghan university students were in the U.S.S.R. This is over twice the number of students then at Kabul University. Some of the students have been forced to go against their will.

In 1980 I participated in some student demonstrations and a student strike at Kabul University. . . . Some of the Soviet officials noticed my participation at these events. They reported them to my father. It was decided that my behavior and appearance at these functions were becoming an embarrassment to my father's political position. As such, the Soviets applied a great amount of pressure to have me sent out of the country. As a result, I was offered a scholarship to attend the Second Medical Institute in Moscow. I was forced to accept this scholarship. In March of 1982 I became ill, and I returned home. I was only able to leave the Soviet Union and return home to Afghanistan because I had a doctor's letter describing the nature of my illness.[21]

All aspects of cultural policy have been Sovietized. French Afghanistan expert Olivier Roy claims that cultural policy for Afghanistan is formulated in Tashkent and points out that the director of the Academy of Sciences in Tashkent, Azimov, visits Kabul twice a month to supervise policy. For example:

A Swiss architect (Mr. Bücherer de Liestal), who proposed in 1974 the construction of an ethnological museum in Kabul, received a positive response in the spring of 1983 from . . . the Academy of Sciences of Tashkent.[22]

Only Russian (and a few Indian) films are now shown in Kabul, and schoolchildren are bused to see the Russian ones.[23] One of our interpreters in Peshawar in 1984, who had returned to Kabul to see his family a little more than a year before, told us that it was becoming increasingly difficult to live in Kabul without some knowledge of the Russian language.

Political Freedom

Political parties had not yet been fully institutionalized in Afghanistan before the coup.[24] The parties that had grown up were largely centered on such publications as *Parcham, Khalq,* and *Afghan Mellat* and enjoyed varying degrees of toleration, depending on the political situation.

Today, however, there is one official political party, the ruling People's Democratic Party of Afghanistan, the PDPA. Membership in the PDPA is required for a wide variety of jobs, whereas membership in other parties has been a crime. In 1987, as part of the program of "national reconciliation," the government offered official positions to leaders of other parties. Subsequently the government of Dr. Najib announced a new law to register multiple political parties. The law contains no effective safeguards for freedom of expression, and no parties have applied for registration under the law. As of this writing, we know of no change in the situation described below.

Anyone possessing a membership card in any of the Islamic parties based in Peshawar has, of course, been subject to arrest, regardless of whether a specific unlawful act has been committed.[25] One of the young men who had formerly lived with Fr. de Beaurecueil received a ten-year sentence for possession of a card of the Hezb-e Islami. Farid, who had studied nursing at a vocational school in Kabul, told us in Peshawar on 23 September 1984:

> "They arrested one guy in my school. They found he had a card of the Hezb-e Islami. I have no idea what happened to him. He was arrested about fifteen months ago, and he is still in prison."

The largest leftist party in the armed resistance, which also organized many of the student demonstrations in Kabul, was called SAMA, led and founded by Abdul Majid Kalakani.[26] Kalakani was executed in June 1980. In July 1982 the KHAD succeeded in capturing nineteen members of SAMA's central committee. The family of one, Engineer Zamari Sadiq, subsequently learned of his execution; the fate of the others is presumed to be the same.[27] SAMA no longer functions in Afghanistan.

A campaign of arrests directed against the "extreme" left beginning in August 1981 led to the arrest of several hundred people. Among those arrested was Osman Landai, leader of the Maoist Shola-e Javed (Eternal

Flame), which advocated armed resistance, although it is unclear to what extent this tiny group managed to practice it. Agence France Presse reported from Islamabad on 12 August 1981 that seventeen members of this group had been sentenced to sixteen years in prison the week before. The KHAD has also arrested members of Rahai (Liberation), a splinter from Shola-e Javed. In May 1984 BAKHTAR News Agency announced that two members of this group had been tried for "subversive activities."

Afghan Mellat (Afghan Nation) is a Pashtun nationalist party that describes itself as social democratic. It was founded by Gholam Ahmad Farhad, a former mayor of Kabul. In December 1982 a number of members of Afghan Mellat were arrested. Five months later the Afghan news agency announced that all members of the "core" of the party had been arrested. Amnesty International has published the names of eighteen members arrested at that time. Mohammad Nabi Omarkhel, a civil engineer and member of Afghan Mellat whom we interviewed in Peshawar on 27 September 1984, described a special section of KHAD, run by Russian advisers, that was in charge of interrogating him and other Afghan Mellat prisoners.[28]

The KHAD has also arrested members of the Khalq faction of the party suspected of anti-Parcham or anti-Soviet sentiments. Amnesty International published the names of two government officials, Pal Mohammad and Mohammad Hashem, arrested along with twenty schoolteachers in May 1983, reportedly for Khalqi activities or sympathies.[29]

Membership in the PDPA, on the other hand, is virtually compulsory for those in positions considered important. In government offices civil servants are subjected to pressures similar to those applied to teachers and students. Shah Mahmud Baasir was director general of economic analysis in the Ministry of Planning when the coup occurred, but his refusal to join the party cost him his job.

> "Many times I was asked to join the party. I was deprived of my rights. I had a good job. They made me a school inspector in the Ministry of Education with a much lower rank than before." (Interview in Quetta, 2 October 1984)

Sometimes even seemingly insignificant jobs require party membership. One of our interpreters told us that she had been working in a new computer center, learning to use an IBM under the guidance of an Indian engineer. Six months before we met her in Peshawar on 23 September 1984, she had lost her job in Kabul because of her refusal to join the party.

Religion

Islam is the religion of ninety-nine percent of Afghanistan's citizens.[30] Under Babrak Karmal and the present government of Najibullah, there have been no open attacks on Islam. These leaders have attempted to woo religious Afghans to their side. They praise Islam in public while exercising control through the Ministry of Religion (formerly the Department of Islamic Affairs). There are reports that the KHAD works among religious teachers to pressure them to interpret the Koran and other texts in a way favorable to the regime.

> The PDPA employs Islam in attempts to gain credibility both internally and externally. The Religious Affairs Directorate is funded by the KHAD and a special liaison committee, known as "KHAD-66," has been established to supervise the progress of religious manipulation. Three Soviet advisors specialize in this work in Kabul. All the directorate's religious tracts are vetted by these advisors, while an association with the KHAD is a condition of membership of the Afghans' Supreme Council of Ulema in Kabul. The KHAD has also created the Society of Islamic Scholars and the Promotion of Islamic Traditions, headed by Maulavi Abdul Aziz.[31]

Observance of Islam, moreover, is an obstacle to success in school and in government employment and at times may lead to persecution, punishment, or arrest.

> "The minister got some information about me—very bad things about me. . . . There it was written. 'He is not interested in the government. But the most important thing is that he is an idealist and prays in his office every day.' If Afghanistan is free, I will show you the report." (Testimony of high-level defector, interviewed in Peshawar, 18 August 1985)
>
> "We are not allowed to speak about religion in the school. If we speak about religion, the *Peshahangan* [Pioneers, the mass organization for elementary school students] send reports to KHAD. The *Peshahangan* are responsible to report about the teachers. If the teachers speak about religion, they must report it. I had some trouble myself. They interrogated me and sent me a letter, that next time I speak about religion I will get in more trouble. This was a warning. If it happened a second time, I would be sent to prison." (Testimony of former teacher, interviewed in Peshawar, 25 August 1985)
>
> "Two years ago I was in prison. I was going to Mazar-e Sharif, and I came through the deserts and reached Aliabad [subdistrict in Kunduz]. It was very small, and I didn't know that it was a government-controlled place. I made ablution to pray, in a stream, when one person came. They saw I was a religious person, and when they found out I was not from the

government, they took me to the subdistrict headquarters. A clerk there was the KHAD officer, and I was interrogated. They beat me with Kalashnikovs and asked, 'Are you a mullah? Where did you study?' I denied that I was a mullah. I said, 'I cannot read or write, I am illiterate.' " He then described how he escaped with the help of a soldier from Faryab Province. (Testimony of Abdul Baqi, mullah, of Dasht-e Archi, Kunduz; interviewed in Panyian refugee camp, Haripur, NWFP, 23 August 23 1985)

"About one month before I graduated from Kabul University, there were four Parchamis following me and three other girls because we were wearing chador, and they recognized that we were Muslims." (Testimony of Fariba Hamidi, nurse, twenty-one, of Kabul; interviewed in Peshawar, 22 August 1985)

"It happened once that some of my relatives and I and Bashir prayed in the school. After that for about a week the police wouldn't let us come to school. This was last year in Deh-e Naw school." (Testimony of former student from Kabul, eleven; interviewed in Peshawar, 21 August 1985)

"My wife was a teacher. She studied in the Faculty of Theology of Kabul University. She was under pressure, they asked her why she was hinting in favor of Islam. Because in the twelfth grade they study *tafsir* [interpretation] of the Holy Koran. In the class were some Communist students, and they wanted to insult her. They posed some hard questions. Sometimes you are forced to combine *tafsir* with the political situation. You have to attract students to Communism through *tafsir* and the Koran." (Testimony of former government official; interviewed in Peshawar, 20 August 1985)

Medicine

Since 1978, most of Afghanistan's doctors have been arrested, killed, or pressured into leaving the country. Many of them were under suspicion because they had been educated abroad or had contacts with foreigners.

Richard Reeves, in an article in *The New Yorker,* 1 October 1984, quotes Dr. Mohammad Mohmand, a Kabul surgeon now directing a hospital in Peshawar, as saying that of 1,200 physicians in Afghanistan before 1978, only 200 now remain. Abdul Wahid, a former student from Jaghori, told us in Quetta on 3 October 1984 that all the doctors in Jaghori had been arrested. General Naik Mohammad Azizi, former head physician of the Military Medical School in Kabul, who defected in early 1983, said that two-thirds of the military doctors had left the country since 1978 and that of twenty military doctors trained in the Soviet Union in the previous two years, eight were in Pakistan, three were in West Germany, and three had been killed.[32]

Some doctors left because of impossible working conditions due to the war.

> Alikhel [an Afghan doctor who had escaped to India] said he could not tolerate conditions at the Afghan children's institute in Kabul where he worked. Because of fighting and mortar attacks in and around the city, he said, the hospital frequently was without electricity. "There was no way to sterilize instruments," he said, claiming that operations sometimes were performed with unclean instruments. "It was horrible to see small children with their fingers and arms and legs blown off by antipersonnel mines" in Kabul, he said.[33]

Civilians wounded in the countryside, unless they are fortunate enough to be near one of the rare clinics run by Afghan or foreign doctors in resistance-held areas, must go to Kabul or a regional center for medical attention. Often, however, they are afraid that they will be arrested or interrogated there. Dr. Patrick David told us in an interview in Peshawar on 22 September 1984 that the parents of four boys wounded by an exploding shell in Baraki Barak, Logar Province, were afraid to send them to Kabul.

Some doctors have placed their skills in the service of torture.

> "They sent me to a doctor. So six months after the torture they were checking me, is there any mark of the torture on my body. There was a doctor in Pol-e Charkhi in the jail hospital. But he didn't check anything. He just wrote, 'He was not tortured. There is no mark of torture.' So I showed some places, but he said that, 'You maybe fell from a tree. This does not prove.' " (Testimony of Mohammad Nabi Omarkhel, engineer and torture victim; interviewed in Peshawar, 27 September 1984)
>
> "They would follow these tortures until they nearly die. Then a doctor would come and give an injection to make them feel better. Then they would start again." (Testimony of Razia, former university student and torture victim; interviewed in Peshawar, 23 September 1984)

Law

Before the coup the Afghan legal system was a combination of Islamic and secular law. There were simple religious courts operating in the countryside and a number of levels of appeals courts. Lawyers, judges, and other legal officials were trained abroad—in the West, especially France, for secular law, and in Pakistan, India, and Egypt for religious law—or in the faculties of *shari'a* (Islamic law) and law and political science at Kabul University. In response to complaints of corruption, efforts were underway to improve the training of *qazis* (Islamic judges) and to introduce a number of reforms.[34]

Like members of other professional groups, lawyers were subjected to arrest, torture, and killing under Taraki and Amin. M. N. Zalmy, a U.S.-trained lawyer who was then working in Peshawar as executive councillor of the National Committee for Human Rights in Afghanistan, told us in 1984 that the legal system has been completely politicized. Professor Majrooh of the Afghan Information Centre noted that many lawyers had been arrested under Taraki and Amin.

After the invasion, members of the legal profession who remained found themselves with little to do. Several former members of the legal profession have described the degeneration of law in Afghanistan:

> "To me it seems very strange to talk about the legal system or the law in Afghanistan, because everything is done in service of Russia's strategic interest. There are courts in Afghanistan, but we cannot say there is any justice. Everything is in the hands of the KHAD." (M. N. Zalmy; interviewed in Peshawar, 29 September 1984)

Col. Mohammad Ayoub Assil, a professor of criminology at the Kabul police academy who defected in 1982, described changes in the legal system:

> "After the Soviet invasion of Afghanistan the structure of the police was changed, and the nature of police duties as well. . . . Punishment, torture, insulting citizens, searching homes, shadowing and harassing people and the confiscation of their properties were all the order of the day. The different legal guarantees and the practice of the penal code has practically disappeared. The authority of judges and the public prosecutor has been transferred to the police. . . . The famous principle that 'no act can be considered a crime unless it is proven in a court of law' has disappeared from our system. The fact that a crime is an individual act has also disappeared, and members of families and close relatives of the accused, contrary to legal procedures, were also involved in the crimes. The legal definition of crime lost its meaning and importance; instead any act against the interest of the Russians was considered a crime."[35]

Laws are enacted by decree of the Revolutionary Council. Professor Abdul Salam Azimi, head of the Ministry of Justice's legislation and research institute, who defected in 1982, said on 27 October of that year in an interview on Karachi Radio that laws being enacted in Afghanistan were translated from Soviet texts, and that the Afghan Cabinet had no power to reject them.[36]

The administration of the system of justice has been brought under Soviet influence.

> "At the beginning, there were no Russian advisers, but when Babrak came to power, the advisers came not only to the state's attorney's office but to all the departments all over the country. One man, Dzhabarov, was the adviser in charge of the whole Ministry of Justice. He was hiring all the different officers based on their party membership, not their talent. Then we got a letter from the Ministry of Justice saying that we would have to follow new procedures, based on a book written by a Russian judge. I asked, 'What happened to Islam?' Based on their philosophy, they did not consider as criminals those who acted against society. They could use these criminals to do their spying. For them the only crime is to be anti-Communist and antigovernment. I decided to leave." (Testimony of Aminullah Sepahizadeh, former state's attorney; interviewed in Peshawar, 30 September 1984)

Sayyed Gharibnawaz, formerly a chief justice of the Kabul Civil Court, said that the country's Supreme Court has been taken over by Soviet advisers and that only about 50 of Afghanistan's 250 courts are functioning.[37]

7

CREATION OF A NEW, SOVIET-TRAINED GENERATION

For several years now the Afghan government has been administering a variety of programs under which children are encouraged or pressured to go to the Soviet Union for training periods ranging from months to years. It is not a violation of human rights to send Afghan children to the U.S.S.R. on scholarships or subsidized vacations, of course. But it is a human rights violation when small children are forcibly separated from their families and sent abroad to be trained in a foreign culture or when children are trained as spies or commandos to serve in the Afghan conflict.

Short-Term Study Programs in the U.S.S.R.

Various methods have been used to induce children to go to the Soviet Union for visits of up to six months, including promises of good food, clothes, and improved living conditions. Nevertheless, the program has apparently met with considerable resistance.

"Mostly when we line up before going to class, the principal would show us pictures of students who have gone to the Soviet Union, what things they are doing there.

"The *Peshahangan* went to Russia in time to pick apples or corn. Three times I ran away from the school to keep from going to Russia. They took students two or three times to the airport, or somewhere, and brought them back. Each time I ran away, I didn't show up. I used to give some money to the servant who was working over there, and he would let us go for drinking water, and we left the school. We threw our bags out the window and picked them up. We were scared, because they took some other students in a separate car, and they were told that they were going to be sent to Russia. So we were scared we would be taken to a car." (Testimony of eleven-year-old former student at Deh-e Naw school, Kabul; interviewed in Peshawar, 21 August 1985)

"When we were in Afghanistan, in 1362 [1983], more than three hundred students were sent to the Soviet Union. Their age was seven, eight, nine years old. When they were in the Soviet Union, they were getting food, clothes, everything, good living conditions, and also they were telling the families without enough income, they had to send their children, because they were not able to give proper food or clothes to the children. So they gave these children to the government, and they sent them to the Soviet Union. And in the Soviet Union they were trained to join *Padarwatan* [the Fatherland Front]. In Russia they were brainwashing them and constantly telling them that if we succeed in Afghanistan, we will make you the same kind of dolls, playgrounds, and give you the same kind of food. They showed these children on Kabul TV. One of the neighbors who was sitting in our house, his son was in the Soviet Union. When he came back, I asked him these questions, and he told us." (Testimony of Fariba Hamidi, nurse, twenty-one, of Taimani ward, Kabul; interviewed in Peshawar, 22 August 1985)

"They were sending seventh and eighth grade students to the Soviet Union. When they came back, they were weak, worn out. I asked them why. They said, 'They were taking us by bus and forcing us to work in a garden or to wash carpets. We were forced to work a lot in Russia.' They were sad and upset. They were also from our school." (Testimony of former teacher from Kabul; interviewed in Peshawar, 25 August 1985)

Force or deceit is sometimes used either to get the children to go or to lengthen their stays.

"They were forcing students to join *Sazman* [the Youth Organization] and *Peshahangan*. When they join *Peshahangan*, there is no need for parents' permission—they are sent to Russia. For instance some boys about eleven or twelve years old, Ilyas and Iqbal, went to Russia without their parents' agreement." (Testimony of former teacher quoted above.)

"They were sending children from kindergarten, about three years old up to nine years old, they were sent to the Soviet Union. Kindergarten and preprimary school children were sent, too. The parents had to send their children, because if there was a group of twenty children, if maybe five were willing to send their children, because they were party members, fifteen of them were opposed, but they had no right to refuse. They had to send them because of the fear that the government will punish them. I don't know their names, but some people were coming to work [at a hospital in Kabul] and talking about this. When I asked them, 'Why do you send your small children to the Soviet Union,' they said they had to, because there was no other way. I heard this personally from many patients I examined, from teachers, from nurses in the hospital. The children stayed twenty days, one month, up to six months." (Testimony of Dr. Zakia Bayati Safi, obstetrician-gynecologist, twenty-nine, of Kabul; interviewed in Peshawar, 22 August 1985)[1]

"From my class, two classmates went to the Soviet Union. There were fifteen or twenty who went, but I know only two, Shah Jehan and Naqib. They were taken to a private room, and they were told that if they go to the Soviet Union, they will get a lot of good things, like a bicycle and other good stuff, so they went home and discussed it with their parents, and finally their parents let them go.

"They were told that they were going to go for only three months, but when they went there, they sent letters to the class. They said that they would be there for ten years. So the students went to their house and told their parents that we got a letter from your sons, and they say in their letter that they are going to stay there for ten years. Then their parents got mad, and they said that probably they would come to the school and talk to the people who had taken their sons for only three months or five months, but now they are going to stay for ten years. How come? I went to the houses of both, I even had lunch over there. [Naqib returned after one and a half years. Shah Jehan had not returned. This occurred about two and a half years before the interview, when the witness was in third grade.]

"The students who went to the Soviet Union in first, second, or third grade, after they graduate from eighth grade, they are supposed to go to the Soviet Union to study. Some who finished eighth grade were taken by force. A policeman came to the school, and they were taken by force to the Soviet Union. This happened when I was in third grade in Deh-e Naw school [in 1983]. There was a guy named Bashir, he was from Panjsher. He was taken by force. Bashir's mother was there, and some of the classmates went downtown with her. Then the police rented a taxi and took Bashir and his mother to go to the airport. There was no place in the taxi for us, but the police asked us, 'If you really want to go to Russia, come on, get in.' But we refused, so we went home. Later on we found out from Bashir's mother, she told me, 'The police gave me a picture of my son, and after that I didn't see him again.' Bashir's father was dead." (Testimony of eleven-year-old former student quoted above)

Long-Term Study Programs in the U.S.S.R.

In 1984 the Soviet Union and the Kabul regime started two related programs for the long-term Sovietization of the youngest generation of Afghans. In May 1984 they founded the *Parwarishgah-e Watan*, or Fatherland Training Center. Ostensibly a residential school for orphans whose parents died fighting for the "revolution," it is both an intensely ideological training center and a conduit into the other program, announced in November 1984, for sending children to the Soviet Union for ten years of education.

In addition to collecting orphans, the Soviets and the PDPA use a variety of means, from persuasion to kidnapping, to recruit students into these programs. Poor families are told that sending their children to *Parwarishgah-e Watan* or the Soviet Union will provide economic security. The authorities threaten to arrest parents and exclude their children from school if they refuse to give them up. There are reports of parents being arrested, and of children being kidnapped from their homes or even on the street by soldiers and party members.

"They started sending first graders for ten years in 1363 [1984]. It was an emergency program. The party members were saying that although the Soviets had tried to convince the older people, it was not possible, because of their ideology. So they started an emergency program to start with children and train them. From my first-grade class ten students out of twenty-two were sent. The teachers who were members of the party sent even more, not only from first grade, but from second and third grade, too. When they are older than nine years, they don't send them."
(Testimony of former teacher, interviewed in Peshawar, 25 August 1985)

"There are some children who have become orphans. They have lost their parents or fathers or guardians. Either their relatives were killed by Khalqis and Parchamis, and they have no living relatives, or they are children of Khalqis and Parchamis who were killed, but they have no relatives, or their relatives will not accept them, because they are not Muslims. There is an institution for them in Wazir Akbar Khan on the north side of Kabul. This is the *Parwarishgah-e Watan*, or Fatherland Training Center.

"This institution for the orphans is run by KGB and KHAD together. They have their own separate schools, hostels, dormitories, and a different syllabus for their teaching. The majority of these orphan students are sent to the Soviet Union, because they don't have any relatives. The Soviets and the KHAD think they will be the hard core of Communism in the future. Other children might cry for their mother and father, but these children have no one to cry for.

"In other schools they don't come directly to talk about Karl Marx, socialism, because they don't want the students and parents to revolt. But the curriculum for the orphans is different, because it is a curriculum based completely on the Communist way of teaching. Children in other schools might take the books home to their parents, but these children don't have any parents.

"There are very few people who know about this. I get the information from different sources, from people who are still in Kabul. People come here who are close friends—I don't like to disclose their names.

Especially there are people from the Ministry of Education, the Ministry of Planning. The Planning Ministry is the central office for sending people to the Soviet bloc." (Testimony of Rasul Amin, former professor of political science, Kabul University; interviewed in Peshawar, 17 August 1985)

"This agreement was signed with the trade union organization for ten years. It states that the U.S.S.R. will accept at least two thousand children each year for ten years. If there are more, it doesn't matter.

"Most of them are from *Parwarishgah-e Watan*. This was established two years ago with the aim of educating fatherless children, members of the party. These children are under the care of the government, and all are directly sent [to the U.S.S.R.].

"Some volunteer, because it is free. Mostly they are poor people. They find them through the school. The director of the school knows if a child is poor and has no father. He reports to the government that in this school there are such children. They encourage them, saying you will go to the Soviet Union for ten years, and you will be educated, fed, and you will come back and get a high position. They have to allow them. They use sweet words to encourage the parents.

"There are two parts [of *Parwarishgah-e Watan*]. One is in Wazir Akbar Khan, and one is in Kart-e Seh [two neighborhoods in Kabul]. The one in Wazir Akbar Khan is right behind the American Embassy.

"The first group was sent to the Soviet Union before I came here. When they were sent to the airport, the majority of them were crying that we don't want to go there. They shouted, 'Take me back home.' But they were taken. The second group, when I was here, I heard that more than two thousand were sent.

"In the U.S.S.R. they live alone, by themselves. They are located in some special places, and they are provided with everything. It is in Central Asia. The majority of them are taken to Tashkent—they can speak Persian there. Also, infants can be sent." (Interview in Peshawar with a high-level defector from the Foreign Ministry in Kabul, 18 August 1985)

"Some parents were arrested. He was my close friend. He had three children—I forgot the school's name—In Kart-e Parwan. Two times they said, leave these children to send them to Soviet Union. They were eight and eleven. The name of their sons, one was Hamed, and the other was Seddiq. They were sent by force to the Soviet Union, and their father, Wali Jan, and his wife [named Seddiqa], they are in jail right now. Wali Jan was an ordinary man in private business, in the bazaar. He was in the business of spare parts for automobiles. First they arrested the parents, and then they sent the children. They were arrested about forty-five days ago. You know, this story happened, I saw it happen, and also there was a question to me, and this was the cause that I came to here.

"I don't know exactly for how long they are sent, but they have a special godown [warehouse] for children. They call it *Parwarishgah-e Watan*. We say this is a godown for children, to make groups and send them to Soviet Union. And they took them there, and from there they sent them." (Testimony of former executive of government corporation, interviewed in Peshawar, 19 August 1985)

"Everyone knew in Kabul that they are sending all the children to Russia. In Kabul they had the *Parwarishgah-e Watan*, and they were transferring the children from *Parwarishgah-e Watan* to Russia. Mrs. Karmal is the head of it. They are sending seven year olds straight from first grade for ten years, up to college. Then they go for further study. Some of my colleagues told me, they were at Kabul airport, and when they loaded the students at the airport, the parents were crying. The children were smaller than my youngest. These were the ones sent for ten years." (Testimony of former military communications specialist, interviewed in Peshawar, 25 August 1985)

"Some students went to Russia. Some went for ten years. These were first-grade students. Maybe their parents were party members; I don't know. When the fathers were in Parcham or KHAD, they would come to class. They were asked to take their sons away from the school so that they could be sent to the Soviet Union. So they came to school and said goodbye to the school. But their mothers did not know—they had divorced their husbands, because the women were Muslims. The children were crying, they didn't want to go. Some children lost their morale in Russia and were brought back.

"When the parents lost their lives, killed by mujahedin or in a bombardment, if they had relatives in Kabul, they came and went to school. Or if there was a heavy bombardment, and the parents were lost, if the child had any relatives in the party, they would move him to Kabul and send him to school. Some of these were sent to Russia. Some of the ones sent for a long time were orphans, who were forced to go, some agreed, and some were against. In the *Parwarishgah*, all the teachers are Soviets, Mahbuba [Karmal, the wife of Babrak] is the only Afghan there." (Testimony of former teacher, interviewed in Peshawar, 25 August 1985)

"Last year [1984] in the month of Sunbulah [August–September] one of my colleagues who was working for me was forced with some other girls and three or four boys to go to the alleys of Deh Mazang and Jamal Mina. They had the duty to search the houses, and find all those children who had no fathers and were being kept by their families. Their families were very sad and unhappy, and the mothers were crying. They took some kind of note from all of them and made a list. Then some soldiers came with a vehicle and took the children out from the houses by force, took them to the airport, and flew them to the Soviet Union. Of course, this was by force, not by their own will. No family, no matter how poor or hungry they are, could willingly send their innocent children to the Soviet Union, where they have no future.

"When this colleague of ours came, this colleague of ours was one of those party members, and she was working for them, and she herself told us with her own tongue, 'We have collected three thousand children from the houses in one month.' She was a girl with human feelings, and she was crying and saying, 'We took people by force from their houses and sent them to the Soviet Union.'

"I also heard that a girl had disappeared, and her mother went to look for her. A military officer met her and saw that she was crying. He asked, 'What has happened, madam?' She said, 'I have lost my daughter, and I am looking for her.' He answered, 'Madam, do not cry too much. Your daughter was taken away by soldiers. You can go there, to the military camp [he stated which one], and you can see your daughter. She is there.'

"When she arrived at the camp, she had many difficulties, and she was leaving. But her daughter saw her from a window, and started calling, 'Mommy, mommy, I'm here.' The mother complained to the soldiers, and they gave her back her daughter, but they said, 'If you make trouble about this, you will be punished. Not only you will be punished, even all of your family will be punished.' I heard this story from a patient who came to the hospital in Kabul. She had a daughter, and she told me, 'Keep hold of your daughter, don't let her go out in the street, because unfortunately it sometimes happens that the Russian soldiers take small children and send them to the Soviet Union.' It is the truth. It is not propaganda."
(Testimony of Afghan obstetrician-gynecologist, interviewed in Peshawar, 26 August 1985)

"I know of students sent to the Soviet Union. I myself am a teacher, and they took students from my own classes, between seven and twelve years old. One of my students, Shah Wali, about twelve years old, was taken to the Soviet Union. His parents came and asked the principal, 'Where is our son?' The principal said, 'I don't know. He is lost.' This was last November [1984] in Ahmad Khan School in the Rika Khana neighborhood [of Kabul].

"Then there was an old man, the school watchman. He had two sons, and he was a rather poor man. His wife, the mother of his sons, had died, and he had remarried. They asked him to send his sons to *Parwarishgah-e Watan*. They told him, 'You are poor, and they will be well taken care of there.' Finally he agreed and took them to *Parwarishgah-e Watan*. One day I greeted him and asked, 'How are your sons?' He said, 'Madam, a misfortune has struck me. They have sent my sons to the Soviet Union.' "
(Testimony of Fahima Naseri, teacher; interviewed in Peshawar, 27 August 1985)

Training Children as Spies and Assassins

Both sides in the Afghan conflict use children to spy and assassinate.

Sometimes children trained by the Soviets are captured, deprogrammed, and sent to spy for the resistance.

There is a Soviet-Afghan program to train boys aged about ten to fourteen as spies. These children, sometimes orphans, are recruited through the *Peshahangan*, or Pioneers, the mass organization for elementary school children. They are sent to the Soviet Union and trained in weaponry and espionage. The Soviet-Afghan authorities then send them into resistance-held areas with various missions, such as collecting information or assassinating commanders.

"They have an organization called Pioneers, for teenagers or younger children. They send them to the Soviet Union. Then after six months' training or so they come back, and then they are sent to different areas to collect information. Last year about ten of them were captured in Panjsher, and some were also captured in Ghazni and Herat, and other places. Farid Mazdak is the chairman of the Pioneers, and another man, sometimes called Yusuf and sometimes Nur Agha, is another leader." (Testimony of a former KHAD agent, interviewed in Peshawar, 30 September 1984)

"They are using children. And mujahedin are setting them free. The Communists are using them against mujahedin, but after some time the mujahedin are giving them back to their families, in Kabul. So this is a very humanitarian gesture, but it is one-sided, because they are not stopping that. They are doing it over and over and over. And some of these children are under the age of twelve, or ten, so it's very difficult to try them. And when they send them, they don't think about their safety at all. A boy who is from Paktia [a Pashtun area] is sent to Panjsher [a Tajik area]. He is immediately recognized. These people have been sent to the Soviet Union as Pioneers, and these people have been sent to Peshawar as well, and these people have also been captured. But this is a problem. Because some of them, their families do not know about them. They have been taken by force and sent somewhere." (Engineer Mohammad Eshaq, representative of Panjsher Valley resistance commander Ahmad Shah Massoud; interviewed in Peshawar, 24 September 1984)

Soviet forces in Afghanistan are abducting and indoctrinating children and returning them as spies to rebel strongholds, according to a Briton recently returned from the country. Adam Holloway, 18, told the *Daily Express* newspaper he met one of the child spies, a 10-year-old boy named Naim, in a rebel base near the Soviet-held town of Urgun. The boy said he had been taken from his parents a year ago and flown with 200 other children to a Soviet town. He was given a Soviet foster mother, lectured in Marxism, given firearms training and taught how to infiltrate rebel camps and direct Soviet bombers to their targets by lighting fires, according to Holloway's account. When he returned to Afghanistan, he was taken in as an orphan at a rebel base. . . . [Holloway] said Naiem demonstrated his skill with a captured Soviet Makarov 9-mm automatic pistol and said he had been trained to use Soviet TT pistols.[2]

A number of these children have been captured by the resistance and are being held illegally in re-education centers in Pakistan. We had the opportunity to interview some of them.

The boy named Naim mentioned above, by then about twelve years old, told us in Peshawar on 18 August 1985:

> "I was going to school in Kandahar, and my father was the head teacher of the school. A Russian Army officer came to my school, and they took me along with three other kids. They took us to the *Sazman* in Kandahar, and we were there for seven months. For seven months they were teaching us about the Soviet Union. Later, when we were in the Soviet Union, we were taught how to use a pistol and a Kalashnikov. During this time I went home only on Friday. The office was in the military garrison. This was three years ago.
>
> "After seven months I went to the Soviet Union. My father was in favor of it. He said I should go, because it's a nice place. I went to Tashkent, outside of Tashkent city. There were seven kids in each room from different parts of Afghanistan, Mazar, Tashqorghan. Some of them said that their fathers forced them to go, and some of them said that they were there without the permission of their parents. They were taken from schools. They were not orphans. The parents didn't know they were there.
>
> "I was in Russia for six months. They taught us that when we came across mujahedin, we should kill them. The teachers were a lady named Leila—she was from Bukhara—and another was from Tadzhikistan, I forget the name. We were told, when there are mujahedin around, we should inform the Youth Organization.
>
> "After breakfast, we were taken by vehicles to an army base. There they taught us to use pistols, Kalashnikovs. We learned that we should go to the centers of mujahedin and tell them that we are orphans, ask for money from them, spend the night there with them, and then come and report. They taught us that the Americans and the Chinese were in Afghanistan. In the afternoon they took us for volleyball.
>
> "For one week we were given vodka, and then the next week we were given beer, in cans. They said, 'It's a good thing to drink.' We were all forced to drink, by Leila and the other teacher.
>
> "After six months I came back to Afghanistan. I was looking for mujahedin, so I asked some kids if they had seen any mujahedin. They said, 'Yes,' there were some of them. I tried to open fire on them, but a mujahed caught me and took away my pistol. I was wounded here because the pistol got caught on the skin. [He showed a wound on the

back of his hand.] This was seven, eight months after I came back from the Soviet Union.

"I was living in *Sazman* behind the Afghan division in the base, in Chawk-e Shahidan, in Kandahar. [He drew a map.] I visited my father and mother on Friday. I got one thousand afghanis per month. And the other kids, who had not been to the Soviet Union, were getting eight hundred. I was their commander. My father was making two thousand, and my elder brother, in the military, was getting six thousand. I got the money for the other kids and would give eight hundred to each of them.

"We were trying to kill mujahedin, ambushing them. There were a group of kids with me, hiding somewhere, and then, when there were any mujahedin passing by, we would open fire on them. If any of the kids got wounded, I would take them to the hospital. These kids were seven to nine years old. They were using a different kind of pistol than me, a smaller one. I was maybe nine or eleven years old.

"One time there were two hundred kids, and one hundred of them were wounded by bombs. I was hit here [indicating over left eyebrow]. Some of them were killed, I don't know how many. This was in Mahalajat, three kilometers from Kandahar. We were going in front of a Soviet convoy. The Soviet forces were going after the mujahedin, and we were going in front. Then fighting started between the mujahedin and the Russians. And all of a sudden the jet fighters came and bombed that area. We were just walking in front of the Russians, with our pistols out. The secretary of *Sazman* told us to go to Mahalajat, because the Russian forces were going there, to get reports about where the mujahedin were. I remember a few names of boys who were killed: Nasir, Bashir, Wali Mohammad, Torialai, Gol Jan, Gholam Ali, Nangialai."

Masud, a fourteen-year-old child spy from Kabul, had been captured fifteen days before we interviewed him in Peshawar in September 1986. His family is in Kabul: "My parents do not know about my coming here, but the school knows." Masud was recruited by the party secretary in his school, a man of about thirty. "I was sent to Pakistan to search for the houses of resistance commanders. I was supposed to go back and lead others to them. I was given a little money—five hundred afghanis—and told I would get more here. But I was seized after three days."

Masud spoke easily, engagingly, but his comments revealed his confusion and indiscriminate desire to please. "I was deceived. I was told that when I came back I would be sent to the U.S.S.R. to study spying. Yes, I wanted to be a spy. We were told it was a very good job. The salary was high. No, now I understand that it is not a good job. Because I could not do it. I want to study here in Pakistan. I want to study Islamic studies. I will not tell my parents that I am here. Yes, I will write them a letter. Yes, I am happy here. No, I do not have any friends. Yes, I will make friends. No, I do not need anything."

In September 1986 we interviewed an orphan named Nuryalay, then fifteen, who had been sent to the Soviet Union at the age of eleven and trained to be a spy. "I was eager to go," he reported. "It was a very luxurious life. We had dancing and films on alternate nights. After a month and a half, I was sent back to Kabul and told to spy on the mujahedin." Nuryalay was captured and held in a mujahedin camp for a year before being sent to an orphanage in Pakistan. He is now kept under strict surveillance.

Sayed Asar, a fourteen-year-old spy from Kabul, had been held by the resistance for three months when we interviewed him in September 1986. His fear was painful to witness: his hands were shaking and there was a noticeable tremor in his neck. He is fatherless, a street child from Kabul, recruited by a neighbor who worked for the secret police and sent to spy, first in Kabul and then in Peshawar. He was captured by mujahedin the very night he arrived in Peshawar, a suspicious-looking youth, obviously nervous, wearing conspicuous Kabuli clothes. "Yes, I wanted to go to Russia, but now I don't want to. I have become a Muslim."

A resistance commander who claimed to have re-educated more than sixty-five such boys in the previous three years saw it as his "duty to bring them back to Islam." He made it clear that the resistance also used young boys to spy, including some of the captured child spies who had been re-educated.

> "If we don't have spies in Kabul, we would perish. We must know their operations. We use young boys and older boys. We use everyone."

In 1985 some Western journalists filming covertly inside Afghanistan interviewed a nine year old, nicknamed "Cherokee" (Little Guerrilla), who was a hit-and-run assassin for the mujahedin. "There are many more like him," they were told. Showing off for the camera, Cherokee demonstrated with his hands how he threw grenades at Russians in the bazaar or shot them with his machine gun. He looked like any nine year old playing with pretend weapons. Five days after he was filmed Cherokee was captured by the Afghan Army.

Abdul Haq, a well-known resistance commander, said that he had also captured a number of child spies. He was not optimistic about their prospects for rehabilitation.

> "This is the problem. We keep them. We try to teach them. It is not easy for us, you have to be a specialist. They can turn and kill you. There are guns there in the camp. . . . Mostly we get fed up. We send them back to the cities. We tell them: 'Do what you want to do.' "

Abdul Haq said that he did not approve of the mujahedin training young boys as spies and assassins. But he also tried to justify the practice:

"A kid every day sees guns and bombs. He grows up with such things. He sees Soviet jets come bombing, he sees Soviet tanks come killing. He's an Afghan boy. He wants to protect his country. Of course, we want to live in peace. We want our children to be engineers and doctors. But we don't have tanks or helicopters. We have to use what we have. What you have in your hands, you use it to protect yourself."

NOTES ON METHODS AND SOURCES

"When an Afghan woman tells you she left home because Russian soldiers killed almost everyone in her village, including her children, you wonder. But over the months, when two dozen more Afghan women from various parts of the country come in with exactly the same story, it begins to seem inescapably true."
—A European physician working with refugees in Pakistan

The atrocities described in this book are so brutal, so sadistic, that the reader may very well be inclined to question their veracity. Moreover, the information upon which we base our conclusions comes not through on-site inspections within Afghanistan but from the testimonies of others, and many of those testimonies come from refugees who are neither objective nor skilled in giving unembroidered facts. For all these reasons, it seems necessary to explain how we assembled the information for this book and the various sources that we used.

Our findings are based on research and on interviews that we have been conducting, separately and together, since 1984. In the process we have traveled to many different cities—Paris, London, New York, Washington, Chicago, Stockholm, Vienna, and New Delhi—and made four trips to Baluchistan and the North-West Frontier Province of Pakistan. In Pakistan we interviewed refugees and others in Peshawar, Quetta, and Islamabad, and in the North Waziristan and Bajaur tribal agencies.

Our findings have been replicated by other human rights investigators, including Felix Ermacora, the Special Rapporteur on Afghanistan of the United Nations Human Rights Commission, and Amnesty International. They are also supported by information that has appeared in articles in the international press.

Because we want our readers to be able to read and judge the evidence for themselves, much of our report contains direct quotations from witnesses. These quotations also serve to give voice to people who might otherwise remain silent victims of an underreported war.

Our written sources of information include books, scholarly and mass-circulation journals, magazine articles, wire service and newspaper reports, private documents, and publications of humanitarian and political organizations. We also follow the Soviet and official Afghan press and radio broadcasts and the specialized newsletters published by exiled Afghan intellectuals. A detailed bibliography follows this chapter.

But the bulk of the information included in this book comes from hundreds of interviews with a wide variety of people who can attest to facts not previously gathered together in such quantity. The individuals interviewed fall into several general categories: foreigners with special knowledge and experience in Afghanistan; former Soviet soldiers who have defected to the resistance; and Afghan refugees, both urban intellectuals from Kabul and rural refugees from the war-torn countryside.

Many of the foreigners we interviewed had been inside Afghanistan, including journalists from France, Sweden, Norway, England, and the United States, and doctors and other relief workers from France, Sweden, Holland, Belgium, and the United States. We also spoke with foreigners working with the refugees in Pakistan, providing medical and other humanitarian services, from Switzerland, France, Germany, England, Pakistan, and Egypt.

We interviewed eight former Soviet soldiers who had defected in Afghanistan; read transcripts of interviews with five others, and met and discussed those transcripts with the reporter who had conducted the interviews. We also utilized information from several other interviews with defectors published in some of the major Western newspapers.

Among the exiled Afghan intellectuals we interviewed, some have devoted themselves to systematically collecting and publishing information about Afghanistan, while others are working daily with the massive refugee population and are familiar with their accounts. These people include former doctors, lawyers, professors, and other professionals from Kabul and other Afghan cities.

Afghan refugees from the countryside were interviewed in refugee camps and elsewhere. We sought out recent arrivals, people who had not previously been interviewed. Wherever possible, we compared one person's testimony with that of another from the same village who had witnessed the same events and could separately verify the reported facts.

It was clear to us that not every detail of the refugee testimonies was accurate. Victims of bombings and massacres are often in a state of shock, especially uneducated people whose previous lives have not prepared them for being witnesses to such events. Estimates of the number of people killed in a massacre often varied, as did other details in the perception of events. But the testimonies we received establish a distinct and unwavering pattern with a strength and consistency that are overwhelming. Moreover, the efforts of the Soviets and the Afghan government to prevent independent observers from entering Afghanistan also give us reason to believe that there is something to hide.

In a similar fashion, when we interviewed refugees from the cities, there was no way for us to verify the particulars of a former prisoner's account of interrogation, torture, and imprisonment. But the accumulation of numerous, independent accounts with similar and often identical details increases the weight of evidence in favor of the existence of specific patterns of abuse.

We were able to converse in English or French with some of the refugees, mainly urban intellectuals from Kabul. With others, although one of us speaks some Persian, we made use of several Afghan interpreters, including an engineer trained at the University of Wyoming, a former diplomat, an economist trained at Columbia University, a research biologist affiliated with an institute in France, and several prominent former members of the faculty of Kabul University. We taped most of our interviews and, in a few cases, had the testimony carefully retranslated after our return. With each testimony, we indicate the background and former profession or situation of the witness, although in some cases it has been necessary to withhold the witness's name.

Only a fraction of the sources we consulted actually made their way into this book. The following analysis illustrates the range of sources on which we rely. Tables 1 and 2 classify by category the sources used in several major portions of this book. Table 1, "Sources Cited on Human Rights Violations in the Afghan Countryside," analyzes material that appears in chapters 2, "Crimes against the Rural Population," and 3, "Destruction of the Rural Economy." Table 2, "Sources Cited on Human Rights Violations in Afghan Cities," analyzes material from chapters 5, "Repression in the Cities," and 6, "Suppression of Civil Liberties and Independent Institutions."

Table 1

Sources Cited on Human Rights Violations in Afghan Countryside

Sources		No. of Citations
AFGHAN REFUGEES		
Our interviews with rural refugees in camps		44
Located with help of camp administration	22	
Met randomly	22	
Our interviews with rural refugees outside camps		26
Others' published interviews with rural refugees		29
Interviews by:		
Afghan intellectuals	19	
Western press	10	
Our interviews with urban/professional refugees		27
Total Afghan refugees		126
SOVIETS		
Our interviews with defectors		3
Press interviews with defectors		6
Soviet press reports		1
Total Soviets		10
OTHER NON-AFGHANS		
Testimonies from inside Afghanistan		38
A. By source:		
Our interviews	19	
Written reports	19	
B. By nationality		
French	22	
American	8	
British	3	
Belgian	2	
Swedish	1	
Norwegian	1	
Pakistani	1	
Expert views		2
Total non-Afghans		40
TOTAL CITATIONS		176

Table 2

Sources Cited on Human Rights Violations in Afghan Cities

Sources		No. of Citations
AFGHAN REFUGEES		
Our interviews in refugee camps		4
Located with help of camp administration	1	
Met randomly	3	
Interviews published by Afghan intellectuals		8
Our interviews with D.R.A. defectors		12
Our interviews outside camps (mostly with urban intellectuals)		92
Contacted:		
Directly	13	
Through other urban refugees	40	
Through relief or support groups	33	
Through resistance parties	6	
Total Afghan refugees		116
SOVIET/D.R.A. OFFICIAL PUBLICATIONS		7
OTHER NON-AFGHANS		
Testimonies from inside Afghanistan		8
Our interviews	1	
Written reports	7	
Expert views		29
Amnesty International	21	
Other	8	
Total non-Afghans		37
TOTAL CITATIONS		160

Notes on the Above Tables

Nearly a fourth of the testimonies about the rural areas of Afghanistan came from Westerners who had visited areas under the control of the resistance, mostly journalists or medical personnel. Over half of these citations were from the French, who have been the most active in setting up relief programs inside Afghanistan. Some of these witnesses had kept diaries or taken photographs or notes, which they consulted.

About three-quarters of the sources cited on conditions in the country-side were rural refugees. Despite the vast gap in culture and education between them and the French doctors, there was no appreciable difference in their description of the situation. We met some of these rural refugees in refugee camps that we visited with the cooperation of Pakistani officials. In the camps we were given the opportunity to speak with anyone we chose, and one of us who is a woman was also able to interview women and children. When we asked to see refugees from a specific area of Afghanistan (where, for example, there had been reports of a massacre), we were directed to them either by other refugees or by camp officials. When camp officials assisted us, no attempt was made to organize a presentation, although the camp administration was occasionally present at the interview. We have classified such interviews as "located with help of camp administration."

During one of our visits to Peshawar, we spotted several groups of new arrivals sitting by the side of the road. We were able to return and speak to these refugees on several occasions in the next few days, witnesses who had not yet been interviewed by anyone. Such sources we classify as "met randomly."

We also met rural refugees outside the camps, people who were introduced to us by Afghan intellectuals in exile who knew them through family ties or other connections; for instance, several former professors from Kabul University brought new arrivals to us at our hotel. These are the sources we call "rural refugees outside camps."

The reports of some Western reporters, as well as testimonies collected by Afghan intellectuals in exile, have been classified as "others' published interviews with rural refugees."

Some Afghan urban professionals—doctors, former government officials, people with relatives still in Afghanistan—have direct knowledge of the situation in the rural areas. These are the sources called "interviews with urban/professional refugees" in table 1.

Tables 1 and 2 count quotations or specific references in the text of the book, not interviews. If we cite one interview five times, in different contexts, it figures five times in the tables. The numbers were compiled from a draft, and final editing may have changed them slightly.

1. HISTORICAL BACKGROUND

1 Jacky Mathonnat, "Une économie impulsée de l'extérieur," in *Afghanistan: La colonisation impossible*, M. Centlivres-Demont et al. (Paris: Editions du Cerf, 1984), pp. 143–78.

2 Some Pashtuns call themselves "Pakhtuns," in the northern dialect of Pashto

(Pakhto). In India and Pakistan they are known as Pathans. The term *Afghan* seems to be of Persian origin. There is an extensive literature on Pashtuns. Two major works are Olaf Caroe, *The Pathans* (Oxford: Oxford University Press, 1958) and Akbar S. Ahmed, *Pukhtun Economy and Society: Traditional Structure and Economic Development in a Tribal Society* (London: Routledge & Kegan Paul, 1980). For surveys of ethnicity in Afghanistan see Louis Dupree, *Afghanistan*, 3rd ed. (Princeton: Princeton University Press, 1980; 1st ed. 1973), pp. 57–65; or Bernard Dupaigne, "Les peuples," in *Afghanistan*, Centlivres-Demont et al., pp. 27–56.

3   The variety of Persian spoken in Afghanistan is known as Dari, meaning "court language," but it is basically the same language as that spoken in Iran.

4   On Islam in Afghanistan see Olivier Roy, *Islam and Resistance in Afghanistan* (Cambridge: Cambridge University Press, 1986), pp. 30–68.

5   On the origins of the Durrani monarchy see Dupree, *Afghanistan*, pp. 319–41; and M. Nazif Shahrani, "State Building and Social Fragmentation in Afghanistan: A Historical Perspective," in *The State, Religion, and Ethnic Politics: Afghanistan, Iran, and Pakistan*, ed. Ali Banuazizi and Myron Weiner (Syracuse: Syracuse University Press, 1986), pp. 23–74.

6   Hasan Kawun Kakar, *Government and Society in Afghanistan: The Reign of Amir 'Abd al-Rahman Khan* (Austin: University of Texas Press, 1979); Vartan Gregorian, *The Emergence of Modern Afghanistan: Politics of Reform and Modernization, 1880–1946* (Stanford: Stanford University Press, 1969), pp. 129–62, 181–205.

7   The major studies of this period are Leon Poullada, *Reform and Rebellion in Afghanistan, 1919–1929* (Ithaca, N.Y.: Cornell University Press, 1973); and Gregorian, *Emergence of Modern Afghanistan*, pp. 227–92. For revisionist interpretations see Roy, *Islam and Resistance*, pp. 62–68; and Shahrani, "State Building and Social Fragmentation," pp. 45–50.

8   Henry S. Bradsher, *Afghanistan and the Soviet Union* (Durham, N.C.: Duke University Press, 1983), pp. 17–32.

9   On Daoud's policies see Dupree, *Afghanistan*, pp. 499–558, for an optimistic, pre-1978 assessment; and Shahrani, "State Building and Social Fragmentation," pp. 58–63, for a later reassessment.

10 On the politics of the New Democracy period see Dupree, *Afghanistan*, pp. 600–623; Anthony Hyman, *Afghanistan under Soviet Domination, 1964–1983* (London: Macmillan, 1984), pp. 51–73; and Hasan Kawun Kakar, "The Fall of the Afghan Monarchy in 1973," *International Journal of Middle East Studies* 9 (1978): 195–214.

11 On the origins and development of the PDPA see Anthony Arnold, *Afghanistan's Two-Party Communism: Parcham and Khalq* (Stanford: Hoover Institution, 1983); Bradsher, *Afghanistan and the Soviet Union*, pp. 32–52; and Etienne Gille, "L'accession au pouvoir des communistes prosoviétiques," in *Afghanistan*, Centlivres-Demont et al., pp. 179–89. Note that "Karmal" is not Babrak Karmal's surname (his father is named Mohammad Hussain) but a nickname meaning "hardworking" or "friend of labor." We therefore refer to him as "Babrak" without intending undue familiarity.

12 Although most writings on the Afghan conflict discuss the origins of these groups, the authoritative work is Roy, *Islam and Resistance*, pp. 69–83.

13 For a minute-by-minute account of the coup, see Louis Dupree, "Red Flag over Hindu Kush, Part II: The Accidental Coup, or Taraki in Blunderland," Hanover, N.H.: *American Universities Field Staff Reports*, Asia, no. 23 (1980). For differing evaluations see Bhabani Sen Gupta, *Afghanistan Politics, Economics and Society: Revolution, Resistance, Intervention* (Boulder, Col.: Lynne Rienner, 1986), pp. 17–31; Bradsher, *Afghanistan and the Soviet Union*, pp. 53–73; and Anthony Arnold, *Afghanistan: The Soviet Invasion in Perspective*, rev. and enl. ed. (Stanford: Hoover Institution, 1985), pp. 67–73.

14 AGSA is an acronym in Pashto for Organization for the Protection of the Interests of Afghanistan. After Amin assassinated Taraki in September 1979 and took full power, he renamed it KAM, the Workers' Intelligence Agency. On the "reforms" see M. Nazif Shahrani, "Introduction: Marxist 'Revolution' and Islamic Resistance in Afghanistan," in *Revolutions and Rebellions in Afghanistan: Anthropological Perspectives*, ed. M. Nazif Shahrani and Robert L. Canfield, Research Series, no. 57 (Berkeley: University of California Institute of International Studies, 1984), pp. 3–56; and Roy, *Islam and Resistance*, pp. 84–97.

15 Amnesty International, *The Disappeared* (London: Amnesty International Publications, 1979), pp. 64–65, lists categories of the population that were arrested in Kabul, as does Roy, *Islam and Resistance*, pp. 95–97. Roy also gives a partial list of religious figures arrested and killed in the provinces. Dupree, "Red Flag over the Hindu Kush, Parts V and VI: Repressions, or Security through Terror," *American University Field Staff Reports,* Asia, nos. 28, 29 (1980), distinguishes six purges in Kabul, but as he notes (Part VI, p. 9), "The arrests and executions never stopped."

16 Michael Barry, "Afghanistan–another Cambodia?" *Commentary* August 1982, pp. 33–34. Some of the testimonies on which this article was based were first published in *Libération*, Paris, 19–20 April 1980, and all were later assembled in Michael Barry, "Repression et guerre soviétiques," *Temps modernes*, July–August 1980, pp. 171–234. A prison testimony from the same period is that of American anthropologist Louis Dupree, arrested in Kabul in November 1978 during a purge of the universities. See his "Red Flag over the Hindu Kush, Parts V and VI."

17 Quoted in Barry, "Repression et guerre soviétiques," p. 227, our translation. This well-documented incident was first reported in Edward Girardet, "A Grim Chapter in Afghanistan War," *Christian Science Monitor*, 4 February 1980. According to Girardet's witnesses, as well as an Afghan soldier who witnessed the killings and testified in Oslo in March 1983, a group of Soviet advisers accompanied the Afghan unit and approved the order to shoot.

18 Barry, "Repression et guerre soviétiques," pp. 211–13, gives several independent accounts.

19 Testimonies in ibid., p. 204; also reported in *Le Monde*, 17 August 1979.

20 After Hafizullah Amin took power in September 1979, the Ministry of the Interior announced that it would publish the names of twelve thousand people who had died in Kabul jails since April 1978. The list was never published, however. *Amnesty International Report 1980*, p. 177. Barry, "Afghanistan—another Cambodia?" p. 30, gives the number on the list as fifteen thousand and claims that it was in fact published. According to Dupree ("Red Flag over the Hindu Kush, Part VI," p. 9), "The Amin regime attempted to place blame for the repressions on Taraki by announcing a list of 12,000 persons executed prior to September 15. . . . The announcements stopped abruptly after about half the names had been released,

because 10,000 demonstrators in front of the Ministry of the Interior demanded more details, and the government feared an outbreak of violence."

After the Soviet invasion the new government and other sources gave various numbers for those killed by "Amin" in Pol-e Charkhi, ranging from 4,854 (given by the Kabul government to Amnesty International) to 17,000 (reported by Michael Barry). *Amnesty International Report 1980*, p. 179, states that during a February 1980 visit to Kabul by an AI delegation, "The Ministry of the Interior revealed that it possessed a list of 4,854 people killed whose names it had not published; the list was far from complete. Many inquiries had been received about the fate of 9,000 individuals who had 'disappeared' after arrest in the Kabul area."

21 Roy, *Islam and Resistance*, pp. 95, 97.

22 On the processes of revolt, including the examples given, see ibid., pp. 98–109.

23 Bradsher, *Afghanistan and the Soviet Union*, pp. 96–98.

24 Sen Gupta, *Afghanistan Politics, Economics and Society*, pp. 83–84; Bradsher, *Afghanistan and the Soviet Union*, pp. 126–88; Joseph J. Collins, *The Soviet Invasion of Afghanistan: A Study of the Use of Force in Soviet Foreign Policy* (Lexington, Mass.: Lexington Books, 1985).

25 For the U.S. government's assessment of the withdrawal, see "Afghanistan: Seven Years of Soviet Occupation," Special Report no. 155 (Washington, D.C.: Department of State, December 1986), p. 10.

26 On prospects for a negotiated solution, see the Epilogue.

2. CRIMES AGAINST THE RURAL POPULATION

1 Although we received some reports of killings of civilians by Afghan soldiers, most of the killings we documented involved Soviet soldiers, sometimes assisted by a few Afghans acting as guides or interpreters. This is consistent with subsequent reports by Amnesty International, which "received reports of extrajudicial executions in a number of provinces during 1985 by Soviet troops supported by Afghan military personnel" (*Annual Report 1986*, p. 205). In each interview distinctions were made among Soviet troops (*shurawi*) or Russian troops (*rus*); government forces, sometimes called *askar-e dawlat* or *askar-e Babrak*; and PDPA members, who were identified as Khalqi or Parchami. There is reason to believe that Soviet officers are distrustful of the Afghan soldiers, most of whom are reluctant draftees with a high rate of desertion or defection to the resistance.

2 *Les nouvelles d'Afghanistan* no. 15 (December 1983), p. 5.

3 On the Kandahar massacre, see *The New York Times*, 20 October 1983; *Les nouvelles d'Afghanistan*, no. 17, March–April 1984; *Chicago Tribune*, 15 July 1984; *Afghan Information Centre Monthly Bulletin*, no. 34, January 1984, p. 5.

4 *Le Monde*, 3–4 June 1984.

5 *The Times*, London, 28 June 1984.

6 *Radio Liberty Research Bulletin*, 19 March 1984, pp. 324.

7 Mohammad Taher, a forty-year-old graduate of the Kabul University Engineering Faculty and son of the village headman (*arbab*), also attributed the massacre to the villagers' past activities: "The mujahedin of this village had attacked the Soviets many times. They even captured a Russian general and executed him six months before, so they came to take their revenge" (interview in Panyian refugee camp, Haripur, NWFP, Pakistan, 23 August 1985).

8 Five hundred is the low estimate of civilian deaths during this offensive. Some estimates place the total closer to one thousand. We used the following sources in reconstructing events in Laghman: *Afghan Information Centre Monthly Bulletin*, nos. 49 and 51, April and June 1985; "The April Massacres of Laghman," testimony of Jalad Khan, functionary of the cultural department of the (now defunct) alliance of traditionalist or moderate resistance parties, edited and translated by Abdul Karim Muheb, Peshawar University; "Transcript of Interviews with Refugees from Laghman Province, Afghanistan, Munda Camp, North-West Frontier Province, Pakistan, 5/16/85," interviews by Syeed Farhad, translation by Sher M. Etibari; Rob Schultheis, video and audio tape furnished to us by Rosanne Klass of Freedom House and by the Congressional Task Force on Afghanistan; and interviews we conducted with refugees from various villages of Laghman in Munda camp on 21 August, and in Panyian camp on 23 August 1985.

9 *Afghan Information Centre Monthly Bulletin*, no. 51, June 1985, pp. 5–6.

10 This village is actually in a portion of Nangarhar Province adjoining the area of Laghman where the main offensive took place. According to Shir Dal of Kats, quoted earlier in this chapter, after the main offensive in Laghman, the Soviets "came back to Surkhrud [Nangarhar], and they did more things there."

11 Testimonies of Jamruz, son of Abdul Hafez, of Qarghai, Laghman, member of Jamiat-e Islami, *Afghan Information Centre Monthly Bulletin*, no. 51, June 1985, p. 6; Mohammad Yossof, former Afghan Army officer, of Kanda, near Laghman provincial center, ibid., p. 5; Jalad Khan, "The April Massacres of Laghman," pp. 2–3.

12 "Afghanistan People's Tribunal, Stockholm: 1981—Paris: 1982; Selected Minutes from the Tribunal's Meetings," special issue of the *The Letter from the B.I.A.* (Paris: Bureau International Afghanistan, 1983), p. 15.

13 *The Times*, London, 28 June 1984. *The Times* added that Rykov said he had seen five villages of one hundred to two hundred people destroyed in this way.

14 Numerous reports tell of Soviet soldiers burning the bodies of the slain. This is an affront to Muslim religious practice, which places great emphasis on decent burial and respect for the dead.

15 A note in the *Bulletin* added: "At first the editor was suspicious about the sickle and thought the reporter, by using the famous symbol, was perhaps looking for effect. But the eyewitness is a simple villager and does not seem to have any idea about the symbolism. The report was re-checked, and it appears that the deadly sickle does actually exist" (p. 8).

16 The written testimony was taken inside Afghanistan by Engineer Mohammad Yousof Ayubi, public relations officer of Jamiat-al-Ulama of Afghanistan, and given to us in Quetta on 2 October 1984.

17 His account, entitled "Les 'vacances': Jalrez," is available from Médécins sans Frontières in Paris.

18 *Afghan Information Centre Monthly Bulletin*, no. 25, April 1983, p. 13; Agence

France Presse, Peshawar, 18 April 1983; *Afghan Information Centre Monthly Bulletin*, no. 41, August 1984, p. 9; Associated Press, Islamabad, 21 August 1984.

19   *The Christian Science Monitor*, 10 October 1984.

20   Dr. Claude Malhuret, "Report from Afghanistan," *Foreign Affairs* 62 (Winter 1983/1984): 430.

21   Médécins sans Frontières has a photograph of an unexploded canister, which holds about sixty mines.

22   *Les nouvelles d'Afghanistan*, no. 15, October-November 1983, p. 16.

23   Nasser Ahmad Faruqi, in "International Afghanistan Hearing: Final Report, Oslo, 13–16 March 1983," published February 1984. The original tape recordings have been deposited with the Norwegian Ministry of Foreign Affairs.

24   Dr. Mahmoud K.A.Y. Booz, director, Kuwait Red Crescent Hospital for Afghan Refugees, Peshawar, Pakistan; interviewed in Peshawar, October 1986.

25   Lt. Col. V. Skrizhalin, "Who Are Their Targets: Press Conference in Kabul," *Krasnaya Zvezda*, Moscow, 12 June 1985. Quoted in *Foreign Broadcast Information Service* (FBIS) 3 (13 June 1985): D-3. The press conference was also reported on Kabul radio's domestic service, 1600 GMT, 9 June 1985, quoted in FBIS 8 (11 June 1985): C-2.

26   Rob Schultheis, "Among the Believers: Face-to-Face with the MIGs in Afghanistan's Valley of Death," *Mother Jones*, November–December 1985, p. 46.

27   "International Afghanistan Hearing," p. 19.

28   Engineer Ayoubi, who interviewed Feda Mohammad, reported: "He showed the signs of blue scars and some bloodstained areas, and his ankles and wrists, which had scars like stripes due to electrification effects. He showed wounds on the head." Amnesty International cites a former prisoner from Kandahar who was tortured with a "small device which looked like a microphone" hooked up to "a machine that looked like a computer screen." A Soviet officer supervised the torture. See Amnesty International, "Afghanistan: Torture of Political Prisoners," November 1986, p. 39.

29   "International Afghanistan Hearing," p. 17.

30   *Afghan Information Centre Monthly Bulletin* no. 51, June 1985, p. 6.

31   There is a Soviet military base in Khairkhana, which may explain why there are reports of two similar incidents in this particular neighborhood.

32   James Rupert, "Depopulation Campaign Brutally Changes Villages," *The Washington Post*, 15 January 1986, p. A26.

3. DESTRUCTION OF THE RURAL ECONOMY

1   Aleksandr Prokhanov, "A Tree in the Center of Kabul," *Soviet Literature*, 1983.

2   The name and precise former position of the witness are withheld at his request.

3   *Libération*, 19–20 April 1980, p. 12.

4   This witness requested anonymity to protect family members still in Afghanistan.

5   Several villagers told us with ridicule and amusement how Soviet soldiers had gunned down chickens with automatic rifles.

6   Dupree, *Afghanistan*, p. 40.

7   "International Afghanistan Hearing," p. 174.

8   *Les nouvelles d'Afghanistan*, no. 11, December 1982, cover and p. 16.

9   "International Afghanistan Hearing," p. 195.

10 There are other accounts of the deliberate profanation of Muslim symbols. Edward Girardet reported seeing a mosque in Dasht-e Rawat, Panjsher, that Soviet soldiers had used as a latrine. *U.S. News and World Report,* 15 October 1984, p. 44.

11 Dupree, *Afghanistan*, p. 316.

4. TORTURE AND KILLING OF PRISONERS OF WAR

1   Public meeting in New Haven, Connecticut, 27 February 1984.

2   There are other reports of captured fighters being crushed under combat vehicles. For instance, Agence France Presse reported from Islamabad on 18 February 1981 that twenty suspected insurgents had been crushed under tanks in the Tangi Valley.

3   *Le Monde*, 3–4 June 1984, our translation.

4   Ibid.

5   ICRC press release of 20 May 1984, published in ICRC *Bulletin*, June 1984.

6   See Steven R. Weisman, "Blast in Pakistan Has Officials Jittery," *The New York Times*, 16 May 1985.

7   Agence France Presse, Islamabad, 22 August 1985.

8   BAKHTAR (Afghan government news agency), Kabul, 5 September 1985. Quoted in *FBIS* 8 (5 September 1985): C-1.

9   Reuters, Islamabad, 10 April 1987.

10 Jeff B. Harmon, "Toe to Toe with Russians in Kandahar's Holy War," *Sunday Times*, London, 11 August 1985.

11 Agence France Presse, Barri Fort, East Afghanistan, 1 May 1983, our translation.

12 Agence France Presse, Islamabad, 22 July 1981.

13 Harmon, "Toe to Toe with Russians."

14 According to the tribal code of Pashtunwali, the family of a murder victim has the right to take vengeance, *badal*. The Islamic fundamentalist parties are opposed to the tribal code, in place of which they favor the Islamic law or *shari'a*, to whose requirements Théollier referred. Apparently they lacked either the means or the will to enforce it, however, so the case remained unresolved in either code.

15 *Afghan Information Centre Monthly Bulletin*, no. 21, June 1983, p. 3.

16 Agence France Presse, Islamabad, 17 April 1984, our translation.

5. REPRESSION IN THE CITIES

1 KHAD is an acronym for Khedamat-e Etela'at-e Dawlati, Persian for State Information Services. In January 1986 KHAD was upgraded to a ministry, the Ministry of State Security, known as WAD (Wazarat-e Amaniyat-e Dawlati). KGB, of course, stands for Committee of State Security.

2 French ethnologist Bernard Dupaigne learned this from high-level contacts in Kabul during 1980, as he told us in an 19 October 1984 letter.

3 During a May 1983 visit to Kabul, Agence France Presse correspondent Yves Heller was told by a PDPA official that the KHAD had ten thousand employees in Kabul. Taking the maximum population figures for Kabul, including close to a million new internal refugees, this would mean that 1 out of every 150 residents of Kabul (including children) was an employee of the KHAD. Agence France Presse, Kabul, 9 May 1983.

4 Amnesty International, *Torture in the Eighties*, p. 182.

5 Letter reprinted in *Les nouvelles d'Afghanistan*, no. 14, June–August 1983, p. 6.

6 "Night letter" (*shab nameh*) means an underground leaflet. It is a play on the Persian word for newspaper, *ruz nameh*, literally "day letter."

7 Amnesty International, "Background Briefing: Afghanistan (London: Amnesty International Publications, 1983)," pp. 7–8.

8 Yves Heller, Agence France Presse, Kabul, 10 May 1983.

9 Amnesty International, "File on Torture," 12 December 1984.

10 Ibid.

11 "Sedarat" means "Prime Ministry." KHAD, before becoming a ministry in 1986, was formally part of the prime minister's office. Hence, whenever the KHAD took over a new house or apartment for use as a detention center, the site was "somewhat prudishly called a 'dependency of the Prime Ministry'" (Yves Heller, Agence France Presse, Kabul, 9 May 1983.

12. "Afghanistan: Torture of Political Prisoners," pp. 6–7.

13 Interview in Peshawar, 30 September 1984. Name withheld on request.

14 "Afghanistan: Torture of Political Prisoners," p. 7.

15 Women and some other prisoners go immediately to Sedarat, while a few prisoners apparently stay for long periods of time in other detention centers. "Amnesty International was told of a man who was arrested by the KHAD in June 1981 and held in Sheshdarak detention centre incommunicado until 1983" ("File on Torture").

16 Said Noor Ahmad Hashimi, a resistance leader from Badakhshan Province, told the *Chicago Sun-Times*, 23 September 1984, a similar story. He was tortured in the regional KHAD center in Badakhshan, then taken to Pol-e Charkhi Prison,

where he was "confined in a cell barely 4 feet high by 4 feet long . . . a special cell, for those they would like to see suffer most." The reporter observed that thirty-two-year-old Hashimi stoops like an old man: "His memories are of beatings and electric shock tortures at the hands of Soviet KGB agents and the Afghanistan State Information Police, the KHAD." A former official of Pol-e Charkhi Prison described a "special block of cells for dangerous prisoners. In these cells there is no room to stand up" (interview in Peshawar, 25 August 1985).

17 This is consistent with a pattern reported by Amnesty International: "Women prisoners reported being directly subjected to physical torture. . . . But there are also consistent accounts from women of being forced to witness the torture of male prisoners and, in three separate cases, of being incarcerated in the presence of a dead body" ("Afghanistan: Torture of Political Prisoners," p. 15).

18 See Pierre Blanchet, "Le récit de Farida," *Nouvel observateur*, 25 December 1982, p. 41. Farida Ahmadi's case was also cited in the entry on Afghanistan of Amnesty International's *Annual Report 1983*.

19 Farida Ahmadi was apparently taken to the same room: "The first thing they showed me in KHAD were corpses and pieces of corpses" (Blanchet, "Le récit de Farida," p. 41).

20 "Afghanistan: Torture of Political Prisoners," p. 17.

21 Ibid., pp. 18–19.

22 Interviews in Peshawar on 25 and 30 September 1984.

23 See interview with Abdul Majid Mangal, chargé d'affaires at the Afghan Embassy in Moscow until his defection in March 1984, *Afghan Realities*, 15–31 May 1984. See also Roy, "La politique de pacification soviétique en Afghanistan," in *La guerre d'Afghanistan*, ed. Andre Brigot (Paris: Documentation Française, 1985); and Edward Girardet, *Afghanistan: The Soviet War* (New York: St. Martin's Press, 1985).

24 Not only is the lack of water unsanitary, but it also effectively makes it impossible to observe the commandments of Islam, which include washing after going to the toilet and before obligatory prayer, five times daily.

25 Testimony of a shepherd from Faryab Province. Quoted in Amnesty International, *Amnesty International Newsletter*, p. 5, "File on Torture."

26 Hyman, *Afghanistan under Soviet Domination*, p. 109.

27 "Afghanistan: Torture of Political Prisoners," p. 22.

28 John Fullerton, *The Soviet Occupation of Afghanistan* (Hong Kong: Far Eastern Economic Review, 1983), p. 142.

29 Ibid., p. 141.

30 Many former prisoners report that signing such a statement was a condition for release.

31 A number of people we interviewed referred to it as "the KHAD court."

32 Amnesty International, "Afghanistan: Torture of Political Prisoners," p. 21.

33 *Afghan Realities*, 1–15 May 1984, p. 5.

34 Kabul Radio frequently carries such accounts; according to these accounts all trials are open to the public.

35   *Kabul New Times*, 1 January 1980.

36   *Amnesty International Report 1980*, p. 179.

37   Based on Amnesty International's "Background Briefing," Appendix 2, October 1983, and wire service reports.

38   *Amnesty International Report 1985* (London: Amnesty International, 1985), p. 197; *Amnesty International Report 1986* (London: Amnesty International, 1986), p. 207; "Afghanistan: Torture of Political Prisoners," p. 3.

39   Unpublished interview with Borje Almquist, Swedish journalist.

40   *Afghan Information Centre Monthly Bulletin*, no. 35, February 1984, pp. 2–4.

41   Assadullah, a former student of the Polytechnic Institute who was released from Pol-e Charkhi in July 1985, told the Afghan Information and Documentation Centre in Peshawar that he could confirm that condemned prisoners are drained of blood before execution. He claimed that the blood was used for "wounded Communist soldiers." See *Afghan Realities*, 1–15 November 1985, p. 1.

42   Karachi home service, 15 May 1984, summarized in *FBIS*, Afghanistan, FE/7645/C/3, 17 May 1984.

6. SUPPRESSION OF CIVIL LIBERTIES AND INDEPENDENT INSTITUTIONS

1   Microraion is a neighborhood of modern Soviet-built apartment houses in Kabul where government officials and Soviet advisers live. By KGB the witness meant KHAD. Afghans often refer to KHAD as KGB, since they consider KHAD the Afghan branch of the KGB.

2   Anthony Hyman, "Afghan 'Justice': Professor Hasan Kakar," *The Letter from the Bureau International Afghanistan*, no. 7, October 1983, p. 20.

3   The student's name is withheld on request.

4   Testimony by someone close to the Kakar family, interviewed in Peshawar, 20 August 1985.

5   *Amnesty International Report 1984* (London: Amnesty International, 1984), p. 207. We also heard of his death from his former teacher, Sayed M. Yusuf Elmi, in an interview in Peshawar on 21 September 1984.

6   *Les nouvelles d'Afghanistan*, no. 9, May 1982, p. 10.

7   We were able to confirm this report in Peshawar.

8   *Le Monde*, 23, 24, 26, 27, 28, 29 February and 1 March 1980.

9   Hyman, *Afghanistan under Soviet Domination*, p. 81; Girardet, "Afghanistan"; Nancy Hatch Dupree, "Revolutionary Rhetoric and Afghan Women," in *Revolutions and Rebellions in Afghanistan: Anthropological Perspectives*, ed. M. Nazif Shahrani and Robert L. Canfield, Research Series, no. 57 (Berkeley: University of California, Institute of International Studies, 1984).

10   *Afghan Information Centre Monthly Bulletin*, September–October 1984.

11 See also the next chapter, "Creation of a New, Soviet-trained Generation."

12 Rasul Amin, "The Sovietization of Afghanistan," in *Afghanistan: The Great Game Revisited*, ed. Rosanne Klass (New York: Freedom House, 1987). See also the interview with Abdul Majid Mangal, former chargé d'affaires in the Afghan government's Moscow embassy, *Afghan Realities*, 15–31 May 1984; and two articles by Olivier Roy, "L'Afghanistan un an après," *Esprit*, January 1981, pp. 134–35, and "La politique de pacification soviétique en Afghanistan."

13 *Komsomoli Tadzhikistan*, U.S.S.R., 28 September 1984.

14 See, e.g., "Afghanistan: Hassan Kakar," *Index on Censorship*, February 1984, p. 43.

15 Roy, "La politique de pacification soviétique en Afghanistan." More Afghans are now undertaking higher studies in the U.S.S.R. than in Afghanistan.

16 Interview in Peshawar, 21 September 1984.

17 Information given by a former colleague in an interview in Alexandria, Virginia, 25 March 1984.

18 Testimony of a former rector of Kabul University interviewed in Peshawar, 24 September 1984.

19 Edition of 22 May 1983; cited by Roy, "La politique de pacification soviétique en Afghanistan."

20 Yves Heller, Agence France Presse, Kabul, 10 May 1983.

21 Affidavit submitted by a young woman from Kabul in support of her application for political asylum in the United States. Her father was a government official later forced to resign because of differences with Soviet advisers. Agence France Presse, Peshawar, 8 June 1980, reported that four hundred women students who had participated in demonstrations had been forced to go to the Soviet Union.

22 Roy, "La politique de pacification soviétique en Afghanistan."

23 *Afghan Information Centre Monthly Bulletin*, no. 40, July 1984.

24 See chapter 1, "Historical Background."

25 Many Afghans carry membership cards in the resistance parties, even in Kabul. A former high school biology and chemistry teacher, Dad Mohammad, who was carrying a party card when he was arrested in 1980, explained to us in Peshawar on 26 September 1984 that the resistance also runs checks on people's identities, so that it is sometimes worth the risk to carry such a card.

26 SAMA is an acronym for Sazman-e Azadbakhsh-e Mardom-e Afghanistan (Liberation Organization of the People of Afghanistan). It is often described as Maoist. There are other, more orthodox anti-Soviet Marxist-Leninist parties, such as Shola-e Javed and Rahai. Kalakani's native village of Kalakan was also the home of the rebel Bacha-e Saqao, who toppled King Amanullah in 1929.

27 Amnesty International, "Democratic Republic of Afghanistan: Background Briefing on Amnesty International's Concerns," October 1983.

28 See also *Afghan Information Centre Monthy Bulletin*, no. 41, August 1984.

29 Amnesty International, "Background Briefing," p. 10.

30 See "Historical Background" chapter in this book.

31 Fullerton, *Soviet Occupation of Afghanistan*, p. 121.

32 Agence France Presse, Peshawar, 18 January 1983.

33 *The Muslim*, Islamabad, 26 September 1984.

34 See Dupree, *Afghanistan*; and, for the Daoud period, Louis Dupree, "Toward Representative Government in Afghanistan: Part I: The First Five Steps" and "Part II: Steps Six through Nine—and Beyond," Hanover, N.H.: American Universities Field Staff Reports, Asia, nos., 1, 14, (1978).

35 International Afghanistan Hearings, pp. 109–10.

36 *USSR and the Third World*, 7 November 1982–6 March 1983.

37 United Press International, 15 May, 1984.

7. CREATION OF A NEW, SOVIET-TRAINED GENERATION

1 Dr. Safi lived for seven years in the Soviet Union (the Crimea), where she received her medical education.

2 Reuters, London, 12 June 1984.

BIBLIOGRAPHY

Ahmad, Aziz. *Studies in Islamic Culture in the Indian Environment*. Oxford: Oxford University Press, 1964.

Ahmed, Akbar S. *Pukhtun Economy and Society: Traditional Structure and Economic Development in a Tribal Society*. London: Routledge & Kegan Paul, 1980.

Anderson, Jon W. "How Afghans Define Themselves in Relation to Islam." In *Revolutions and Rebellions in Afghanistan*, edited by Shahrani and Canfield, pp. 266–87.

_____. "Khan and Khel: Dialectics of Pashtun Tribalism." In *The Conflict of Tribe and State in Iran and Afghanistan*, edited by Tapper, pp. 119–49.

Arnold, Anthony. *Afghanistan's Two-Party Communism: Parcham and Khalq*. Stanford: Hoover Institution, 1983.

_____. *Afghanistan: The Soviet Invasion in Perspective*. Rev. and enl. ed. Stanford: Hoover Institution, 1985.

Banuazizi, Ali, and Myron Weiner, eds. *The State, Religion, and Ethnic Politics: Afghanistan, Iran, and Pakistan*. Syracuse: Syracuse University Press, 1986.

Barfield, Thomas J. "Links on a Rusty Chain: Structural Weaknesses in Afghanistan's Provincial Government Administration." In *Revolutions and Rebellions in Afghanistan*, edited by Shahrani and Canfield, pp. 170–83.

Barry, Michael. "Afghanistan—another Cambodia?" *Commentary*, August 1982, pp. 33–34.

_____. "Repression et guerre soviétiques." *Temps modernes*, July–August 1980, pp. 171–234.

_____. *Le royaume de l'insolence: La résistance afghane du Grand Moghol à l'invasion soviétique*. Paris: Flammarion, 1984.

Bradsher, Henry S. *Afghanistan and the Soviet Union*. Durham, N.C.: Duke University Press, 1983.

Canfield, Robert L. "Ethnic, Regional, and Sectarian Alignments in Afghanistan." In *The State, Religion, and Ethnic Politics*, edited by Banuazizi and Weiner, pp. 75–103.

_____. "Islamic Coalitions in Bamyan: A Problem in Translating Afghan Political Culture." In *Revolutions and Rebellions in Afghanistan*, edited by Shahrani and Canfield, pp. 211–29.

Caroe, Olaf. *The Pathans*. Oxford: Oxford University Press, 1958.

Centlivres, Pierre, and Micheline Centlivres. "La société afghane, structures et valeurs." In *Afghanistan: La colonisation impossible*, Centlivres-Demont et al., pp. 57–80.

Centlivres-Demont, M., et al. *Afghanistan: La colonisation impossible*. Paris: Editions du Cerf, 1984.

Collins, Joseph J. *The Soviet Invasion of Afghanistan: A Study of the Use of Force in Soviet Foreign Policy*. Lexington, Mass.: Lexington Books, 1985.

Dupaigne, Bernard. "Les peuples." In *Afghanistan: La colonisation impossible*, Centlivres-Demont et al., pp. 27–56.

Dupree, Louis. *Afghanistan*. 3rd ed. Princeton: Princeton University Press, 1980.

———. "Islam in Politics: Afghanistan." *Muslim World* 16 (1966): 269–76.

———. "Red Flag over Hindu Kush, Part II: The Accidental Coup, or Taraki in Blunderland." Hanover, N.H.: *American Universities Field Staff Reports, Asia*, no. 23 (1980).

———. "Red Flag over the Hindu Kush, Parts V and VI: Repressions, or Security through Terror." Hanover, N.H.: *American University Field Staff Reports, Asia*, nos. 28, 29 (1980).

Franck, Peter G. *Afghanistan between East and West*. Washington, D.C.: National Planning Association, 1960.

Fry, Maxwell. *The Afghan Economy: Money, Finance, and the Critical Constraints to Economic Development*. Leiden: E. J. Brill, 1974.

Fullerton, John. *The Soviet Occupation of Afghanistan*. Hong Kong: Far Eastern Economic Review, 1983.

Gille, Etienne. "L'accession au pouvoir des communistes prosoviétiques." In *Afghanistan: La colonisation impossible*, Centlivres-Demont et al., pp. 195–96.

Girardet, Edward. *Afghanistan: The Soviet War*. New York: St. Martin's Press, 1985.

Gregorian, Vartan. *The Emergence of Modern Afghanistan: Politics of Reform and Modernization, 1880–1946*. Stanford: Stanford University Press, 1969.

Halliday, Fred. "Revolution in Afghanistan." *New Left Review* 112 (Nov.–Dec. 1978): 3–44.

Hammond, Thomas T. *Red Flag over Afghanistan: The Communist Coup, the Soviet Invasion, and the Consequences*. Boulder, Col.: Westview Press, 1984.

Harrison, Selig. "A Breakthrough in Afghanistan?" *Foreign Policy* 51 (1983): 3–26.

Hyman, Anthony. *Afghanistan under Soviet Domination, 1964–1983*. London: Macmillan, 1984.

Kakar, Hasan Kawun. "The Fall of the Afghan Monarchy in 1973." *International Journal of Middle East Studies* 9 (1978): 195–214.

———. *Government and Society in Afghanistan: The Reign of Amir 'Abd al-Rahman Khan*. Austin: University of Texas Press, 1979.

Katz, David J. "Responses to Central Authority in Nuristan: The Case of the Vaygal Valley Kalasha." In *Revolutions and Rebellions in Afghanistan*, edited by Shahrani and Canfield, pp. 94–118.

Mathonnat, Jacky. "Une économie impulsée de l'extérieur." In *Afghanistan: La colonisation impossible*, Centlivres-Demont et al., pp. 143–78.

Metge, Pierre. *L'URSS en Afghanistan: De la coopération à l'occupation: 1947–1984*. Cahiers d'Etudes Stratégiques, 7. Paris: Centre Interdisciplinaire de Recherches sur la Paix et d'Etudes Stratégiques, 1984.

Novosti Press Agency. *The Truth about Afghanistan: Documents, Facts, Eyewitness Reports*. Moscow: Novosti Press Agency, 1980.

Poullada, Leon. *Reform and Rebellion in Afghanistan, 1919–1929.* Ithaca, N.Y.: Cornell University Press, 1973.

Roy, Olivier. "Afghanistan: La 'révolution' par le vide." *Esprit*, March 1980, pp. 78–88.

———. "L'Afghanistan un an après." *Esprit*, January 1981, pp. 134–35.

———. *Islam and Resistance in Afghanistan.* Cambridge: Cambridge University Press, 1986.

———. "La politique de pacification soviétique en Afghanistan." In *La guerre d'Afghanistan*, edited by Andre Brigot. Paris: Documentation Francaise, 1985.

Schneiter, Vincent. "La guerre de libération nationale au Nouristan." *Temps modernes*, July–August 1980, pp. 237–44.

Sen Gupta, Bhabani. *Afghanistan Politics, Economics and Society: Revolution, Resistance, Intervention.* Boulder, Col.: Lynne Rienner, 1986.

Shahrani, M. Nazif. "Introduction: Marxist 'Revolution' and Islamic Resistance in Afghanistan." In *Revolutions and Rebellions in Afghanistan*, edited by Shahrani and Canfield, pp. 3–57.

———. "Causes and Context of Responses to the Saur Revolution in Badakhshan." In *Revolutions and Rebellions in Afghanistan*, edited by Shahrani and Canfield, pp. 139–69.

———. "State Building and Social Fragmentation in Afghanistan: A Historical Perspective." In *The State, Religion, and Ethnic Politics*, edited by Banuazizi and Weiner, pp. 23–74.

Shahrani, M. Nazif, and Robert L. Canfield, eds. *Revolutions and Rebellions in Afghanistan: Anthropological Perspectives.* Research Series, no. 57. Berkeley: University of California Institute of International Studies, 1984.

Strand, Richard F. "The Evolution of Anti-Communist Resistance in Eastern Nuristan." In *Revolutions and Rebellions in Afghanistan*, edited by Shahrani and Canfield, pp. 77–93.

Tapper, Richard. "Ethnicity and Class: Dimensions of Intergroup Conflict in North-Central Afghanistan," in *Revolutions and Rebellions in Afghanistan*, edited by Shahrani and Canfield, pp. 230–46.

———, ed. *The Conflict of Tribe and State in Iran and Afghanistan.* London: Croom Helm, 1983.

Tavakolian, Bahram. "Sheikhanzai Nomads and the Afghan State: A Study of Indigenous Authority and Foreign Rule." In *Revolutions and Rebellions in Afghanistan*, edited by Shahrani and Canfield, pp. 249–65.

Engineer Mohammad Eshaq, Foreign Affairs Representative of Panjsher.

Professor Sayd Bahauddin Majrooh, former Director of the Afghan Information Centre, Peshawar.

Professor Sayed Mohammed Yosuf Elmi.

Commander Abdul Haq.

Jeri Laber with Pakistani refugee officials.

Former Soviet soldiers, deserters: Dzhamalbekov (left) and Balabanov.

Young Russian soldier with his arms raised, still holding an AK-47, as an Afghan guerilla points his weapon at him.

Man from Bela with schrapnel.

Refugee, Peshawar.

Refugees in Pakistan.

Refugee, Peshawar. October 1984.

Tajwar Kakar, schoolteacher from Kabul.

Fahima Naseri.

Refugees, North Waziristan.

Mujahedin of Abdul Haq demonstrates how he was tortured.

Refugees.

Children in refugee camp: North Waziristan Tribal Agency, 1986.

Unexploded butterfly mine.

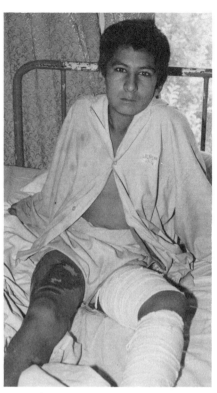

Wounded refugee in hospital in Peshawar.

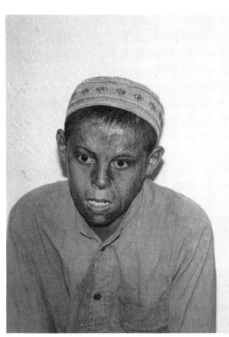

Burn victims, Peshawar.

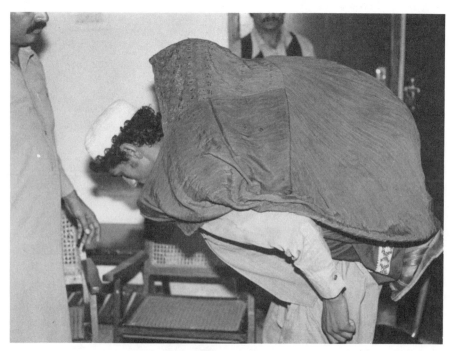

Thirteen-year-old paraplegic burn victim and her brother, Peshawar.

School for refugee children in Pakistan refugee camp.

Refugees, Peshawar, October 1984.

Refugee camp north of Peshawar.

Refugee child in Pakistan.

Children in refugee camp near Peshawar, 1986.

Refugee child, 1986.

Habibullah Ghaleb, orphanage director, Madina Munawwarah Charity Trust, Peshawar, with orphan.

Refugee children.

Refugee child in Peshawar.

Atiqullah, refugee in Peshawar from Laghman Province.

Sakhidad, schoolboy, leading rally in Peshawar classroom.

School for Afghan refugee boys in Peshawar.

Refugee child in Peshawar.

EPILOGUE

There are growing signs that 1988 may be the year in which Soviet troops leave Afghanistan. Soviet Foreign Minister Eduard Shevardnadze said as much in an interview in Kabul on 6 January. Representatives of Pakistan and the government of Afghanistan (which recently changed its name back to the Republic of Afghanistan, as it was before the coup in 1978) will meet again in Geneva in February and, before this book reaches the public, may sign an agreement aimed at ending the war.

This agreement, which was drafted during more than five years of negotiations mediated by United Nations Under Secretary General Diego Cordovez, would provide for an end to outside aid to the Afghan resistance, the complete withdrawal of all Soviet troops in a fixed timetable, and the voluntary repatriation, under U.N. protection, of all Afghan refugees who wish to return. The United States and the Soviet Union would formally guarantee observance of the agreement by the signatories, Pakistan and Afghanistan, and would also agree to respect Afghanistan's neutrality. The cutoff of aid to the resistance would take effect as the withdrawl begins, sixty days after the signing of the agreement.

Such an agreement would remove one major cause of human rights violations in Afghanistan: the Soviet occupation. It would not deal with another source of abuses—the repressive apparatus and monopoly of power of the PDPA-controlled government in Kabul. Ending the pattern of abuses we have described would require changing these as well. Furthermore, formation of a new government, one acceptable to the people of Afghanistan, is necessary for any peace agreement. Therefore the U.N., with the agreement of the Soviets, the U.S., and Pakistan, is trying to encourage the Afghan resistance, the exiled former king, Zaher Shah, and elements of the PDPA to meet to choose a broadly representative transitional government.

It is too soon to know whether these efforts will succeed, but even if they do, Afghanistan faces the possibility of power struggles and continued, if less pervasive, violence. Already, as rumors of an impending Soviet pullout spread, the Hezb-e Islami of Gulbuddin Hekmatyar has stepped up attacks on resistance groups it accuses of willingness to compromise with the Soviets.

In the more than eight years since the Soviet invasion, a third of the population of Afghanistan has fled, perhaps as many as a million have died, and even leaders of the resistance have feared that "a whole nation is dying." But Afghanistan is still fighting for its life, and it may yet prevail.

The Authors
January 1988

INDEX

Prison conditions, xv, 74–75, 94–99
Prisoners, 99, 100, 107; execution of, 7, 69–76; torture of, xv, 6, 69–76

Radio-Television, Afghan, 108
Rape, 25, 31, 52–55
Reeves, Richard, 122
Refugees, xii, 10, 37, 53; caravans of, attacked, xiv, 35, 41; numbers of, 8; testimony of: on arrests and trials, 73, 78, 99, 100–102, 107–8; of atrocities against children, 10, 13, 19, 21, 25, 28, 53, 55–57, 126–37; on atrocities against women, 25, 52–55, 85–86, 90–92, 96; on bombardments, 12–17, 24; on burning alive, 21, 23, 32; on destruction of food, 53, 61; on destruction of harvest, 58–61; on destruction of livestock, 53, 63; on destruction of villages and countryside, 9, 11, 15, 23–24, 53, 63–64; on massacres, 6, 10, 20, 21, 22, 23, 25–26, 27, 28, 29, 31–32, 34, 53, 68; on mines, 43, 46, 47; on political pressure, 113–14; on prison conditions, 6, 7, 96, 97, 98; on religious repression, 122; on reprisal killings, 7, 17–18, 19, 22; on Soviet presence in prisons, 94–98; on summary executions, 24, 36, 102–4; on theft, 65; on torture, 6, 49, 50, 52, 66–76, 80, 81–94, 96, 97; on weapons, 33–34
Religious Affairs Directorate, 121
Reprisals, 19, 20, 25, 60; killings, 6, 10, 18–20, 22
Revolutionary Court, 99, 100, 104
Roy, Olivier, 7, 63, 118

SAMA, 119
Sarshar-e Shomali, Ghulam Shah, 108
Salim, Mohammad Amin, 15, 36
Sawr Revolution, 5, 7
Sazman, 127
Schultheis, Rob, 32, 52, 57
Seynaeve, Rudy, 12–14, 47–48
Shola-e Javed (Eternal Flame), 119, 120
Simon, Robert, 50
Society of Islamic Scholars, 121
Soviet defectors and deserters: testimony of, 17–18, 66–67; on arrests, 49; on legal sys-

Soviet defectors and deserters (*continued*)
tem, 124; on mines, 43; on murder of children, 38; on summary executions, 35–36; on torture, 88; on treatment of prisoners, 51, 66; on use of grenades, 20
Sovietization, of youth, 128–31; of cultural life and policy, xiii, 118–19
Southeast Asia Treaty Organization (SEATO), 4
Soviet Union, 4, 7, 8, 10, 126, 127, 130
Special Rapporteur on Afghanistan, xvi
Swedish Committee for Afghanistan, 52

Taraki, Nur Mohammad, 4, 5, 6, 7, 8, 15, 124
Theft, 64–65
Théollier, Stephane, 74, 75
Torture, 6, 7, 49, 66–76, 81–94; administered by KHAD agents, xiii, 51, 80, 82, 85, 87, 88, 90, 91; electric, 6, 50, 80, 84–85, 87, 88, 89–90, 91, 94; methods of, 85, 89; of prisoners, 6, 69–76; Soviet participation in, xiii, 50, 85, 86, 92–94
Trials, 99, 101

Union of Soviet Socialist Republics (U.S.S.R.). *See* Soviet Union
United Nations Human Rights Commission, 138
United States, 4, 8
Universities, xv, 115, 116

Valls, Eric

Washington Post, 56
Weapons: bayonets, 20–21, 25, 26, 29, 30–31, 36; bombs, 12, 14, 30, 61; burning light, 28, 33–34; dynamite, 38; exploding gas, 38; grenades thrown through windows, 20, 25, 26, 29, 30, 31, 37, 40
Women, atrocities against, cultural repercussions of, xvi, 20

Yunos, Khales, 5

Zabibullah, Maulana, 111
Zaher Shah, 3, 4
Zalmy, M.N., 124